PRISON WITHOUT BARS

Cover illustration by Jackie George

Frank Keiller, pictured three years after Liberation, wearing an RAF Association pin.

PRISON WITHOUT BARS

*Living in Jersey
under the German
Occupation, 1940-45*

Frank Keiller

Seaflower Books

Published in 2000
Reprinted in 2004 by
SEAFLOWER BOOKS
1 The Shambles
Bradford on Avon
Wiltshire BA15 1JS

Design and typesetting by
Ex Libris Press

Printed by Cromwell Press
Trowbridge, Wiltshire

ISBN 1 903341 00 0

*For my mother, and for all the other women
of the islands, who gave from their own
meagre rations, so that their children
could have a little more to eat.*

CONTENTS

Acknowledgements

This book is a distillate of my own memories and the recorded experiences of many others. I could not have written about growing up during the war in the Channel Islands without great help from several books, particularly Leslie Sinel's *Occupation Diary*, Alan and Mary Wood's *Islands in Danger* and Dr Charles Cruickshank's official history, *The German Occupation of the Channel Islands*. I also delved into *A Doctor's Occupation* by John Lewis, *Lord Coutanche* by H.R.S.Pocock and *Lest We Forget* by Roy Thomas. I read Peter King's *The Channel Islands War 1940-1945* and Madeleine Bunting's *A Model Occupation* and listened to tape recordings, to many personal accounts by Islanders who recalled their experiences in a series of BBC programmes in 1985.

More recently, I am pleased to acknowledge the research done by Freddie Cohen, President of the Jewish Congregation in Jersey, and the haunting account of those who died in the camps, by Paul Sanders, in *The Ultimate Sacrifice*. All these sources provided a background and an aid to my own memories. To all of them I owe my thanks and acknowledgement of their valuable contributions to the history of the German Occupation of the Channel Islands.

Finally, I must thank Brigadier Peter Evans and John Trotter in Australia for their encouragement and advice; John Trotter particularly for his time-consuming correction of the draft and final manuscripts. I owe a tremendous debt to Michael Ginns MBE, in Jersey; as an historian, and in his capacity as Secretary of the Channel Islands Occupation Society, he provided much extra information, made many wise suggestions, and ensured both my historical accuracy and impartiality.

Frank Keiller
Australia, 1999

Chapter One

PROLOGUE TO AN OCCUPATION

At the outbreak of war in September 1939 I was twelve. To my boyish self it was exciting. But it wasn't exciting to my parents' generation. For several years I had observed their concern as first Abyssinia, then Spain, erupted into violence. Hitler marched into Austria and, soon after, into Czechoslovakia. As crisis followed crisis, the newspaper headlines appeared in bigger, bolder print, and were full of dark forebodings, but amongst ourselves we youngsters talked of adventure and read about the courage of our fighting men in earlier wars, not about risks, not about death or defeat.

We sang silly little ditties.

> *Whistle while you work.*
> *Hitler is a twerp,*
> *Goering's barmy, so's his army,*
> *Whistle while you work.*

Our elders and betters saw things differently. They remembered only too well the long casualty lists of the First World War. The 'Great War' they called it. Many served in the trenches. Those who fought had one thing in common. They never talked about it. Most families lost at least one relative. It was only twenty years before.

At school we were encouraged to read *The First Hundred Thousand*, by Ian Hay, and similar books by Sassoon and others; and we saw 'All Quiet on the Western Front' at the pictures. We learned the poems of the soldier poets:

> *If I should die, think only this of me;*
> *That there's some corner of a foreign field,*
> *That is forever England.*

But England is far to the north, nearly a hundred miles away. France is less than fifteen and on a clear day we can see cars travelling up and down the French coast road; sometimes we can see the spires of Coutances Cathedral.

Jersey is in the great bay of northern France, in the Gulf of St. Malo, between

Normandy and Brittany, the largest of the Channel Islands and the farthest south. The Islands are the sole remaining part of Normandy loyal to the English Crown. William of Normandy conquered England in 1066, and with some truth Jerseymen claim that England is their oldest colony.

Soon after 11am on Sunday, 3 September 1939, my father told us from his pulpit that we were at war with Germany. Chamberlain had broadcast to the Nation on the wireless, and someone had brought in the news. We prayed for victory. "God is on our side," the self-righteous said, "It will all be over by Christmas."

The air raid siren sounded soon after, but it was only a practice alert and I felt disappointed. The wailing cadence of the warning and the single note of the all clear became familiar sounds in the years ahead.

The 'phoney war' introduced us gently to our first restrictions and to wartime regulations. Hints of shortages and tyrannies to come.

We learnt how to find our way about in the blackout. We walked and stumbled through the pitch-black streets, our torches dimmed with transparent coloured paper between the glass and bulb. 'They' told us not to shine the torches upwards because 'bombers could see them miles away.' Mechanics fitted black metal hoods to dim the headlamps of the cars. The downward-sloping slits directed the beam of light towards the surface of the road and made the drivers slow down, but accidents increased. A carpenter came to the vicarage and fitted plywood shutters to the insides of all the windows. They were easy to put up and easy to take down. I think they survived until VE-Day, but they may have gone for firewood in the final months of 1944 when I wasn't there. There wouldn't have been much point keeping them when there was no electric light.

One night, we forgot our torches, and when we came out of the Forum Cinema into the dark streets, the only lights we could see were the will-o'-the wisps of other people's torches, and as we walked across town and up Val Plaisant, to our home in Springfield Road, we laughed all the way, bumping into each other, bumping into other people. I can't remember what we saw, but it was a comedy. Will Hay, or Laurel and Hardy.

The air raid precaution authorities, the ARP, gave out gas masks in square, cardboard boxes with a length of string, so that we could hang them from our shoulders. We tried them on in Father's study. The rubber smelt like an anaesthetic mask and reminded me of going to the dentist to have a tooth out under nitrous oxide – 'laughing gas'. My sister, Margaret, kicked and screamed, and tried to tear hers off; they told us to 'carry them at all times.' Like other tiny children, Margaret finished the Occupation without knowing what an orange looked like.

Soon, neat piles of sandbags appeared in front of doors and round the walls of many public buildings. Impressive piles guarded the steps and entrance to

Springfield Stadium, the sports ground and pavilion opposite the vicarage. Large painted wooden noticeboards said AIR RAID SHELTER or DECONTAMINATION CENTRE. They appeared overnight on doors and walls, and big, black arrows showed the way.

At Christmas, we went to the last children's party at West Park Pavilion. It soon housed slave labourers, but in 1939 there were sandbags there too, and above an advertisement for Vat 69 Whisky another sign said MEN AND WOMEN. THIS WAY FOR WOUNDED AND GASSED CASES. More arrows pointed out which way to go.

I wondered what it would be like to be bombed, gassed or wounded. There were still men around whose lungs were ruined in the Great War. They coughed and spat and left globs of yellow sputum on the pavement. My Maths tutor, 'Peg Leg' Le Breton, had lost a leg on the Somme. He didn't talk about it either, but he had a discharging sinus on his amputation stump and it leaked pus from time to time. He tried to disguise the odour of corruption with verbena, or citronella, and by chain-smoking his pipe.

New notices appeared almost daily in the *Evening Post*. We were told what to do, where to go if there was an air raid, what to do if we were caught in the open. "Lie down," they said, "Lie in the gutter if there's nowhere lower, and don't forget to open your mouth, so the blast doesn't damage your lungs or burst your eardrums."

Buckets of sand and red-painted water buckets appeared in corridors and halls. Stirrup pumps and hosepipes hung from the walls of schools, in offices and in public buildings. Strips of adhesive paper crisscrossed windowpanes. I read in a textbook of surgery that a man walked into a London hospital during the Blitz and dropped down dead. He appeared unmarked, until they found a sliver of glass from a blasted window sticking in his heart.

They told us that enemy bombers could see even the smallest chink of light miles away. We imagined direct hits. Air Raid Wardens yelled, 'Put out that light.' I was told recently that such extreme precautions were unnecessary. If we had known then, it might have saved a few windowpanes. Once the Germans arrived and we were occupied, it was considered patriotic to show a light if you heard aircraft overhead. A few rounds from passing patrols soon put an end to that. They were probably German planes anyway, patrolling the islands, or bringing in the soldier's mail from Germany.

In May 1940, there was still plenty of food. Weekly rations before the Occupation were generous, more than adequate. In those days, we still had milk delivered to the vicarage by a milkman who drove a horse-drawn cart. When we heard him at the back door, we went to meet him with a jug and he ladled it out from a large traditional Channel Island milk can. The cream was thick and almost orange. When we poured it into a tumbler and gave it time to settle, the cream came more than halfway up the glass, not like the pasteurised milk they sell in supermarkets today. When I first took my wife to Jersey, she couldn't drink the Island milk. It was much too rich, even in tea.

The Island authorities and the British Government encouraged 'National Savings' and each week we gave a little of our pocket money. It was the patriotic thing to do. But the school Tuck Shop beckoned the appetites of healthy, growing boys and there was a serious conflict of interests.

We didn't save much, as far as I remember. A 'Bar and Bun' was my favourite mid-morning snack, a penny bar of milk chocolate in a buttered currant bun. How I dreamed about them later.

There were constant appeals for money to 'Help to buy a Spitfire.' The authorities collected unwanted metal to melt down, to make shells and ships and tanks. We gave all our old kettles and saucepans and Father collected various bits and pieces from his parishioners. When the Occupation began, he was left with a box full of things he didn't want and which he didn't know how to get rid of.

I remember a blue metal sheet that advertised Mazawattee Tea. It was on the outside wall of a shop at Léoville. It survived the collection because it was still there in 1941 when we passed the store on our way to swim at Grève de Lecq. Maybe the Germans got it later. In 1943, they took the old cannon from Elizabeth Castle and Fort Regent, but their strict code of military honour prevented them from taking the cannon from around General Don's statue in the Parade. They considered taking the church bells and the iron railings around the Town Church, but the Bailiff managed to put a stop to that.

Posters pleaded with us to help the war effort. Women knitted socks, mittens and other woollen garments for soldiers, sailors and airmen. No one ever seemed to mention Royal Marines. Young ladies were encouraged to write to lonely soldiers, and a picture of an RAF airman appeared on an advert for a well-known hair cream. It was the start of that pejorative term for Air Force personnel – 'The Brylcreem Boys'.

In the summer holiday from school we worked on the land. It was hot, but we worked hard to DIG FOR VICTORY. When conscientious objectors arrived from England to help with the potato harvest, we greeted them with all the contempt our adolescent minds could muster. 'Bloody Conchie' was about as insulting as you could get. Later, the insult was overshadowed by Quisling, Collaborator, or Jerrybag. With the arrogance of youth we poured scorn on men who didn't volunteer at once, men who were 'dodging the column.' We didn't hand out white feathers but would probably have needed little encouragement if it had been suggested.

Those boys still at school who were old enough joined the OTC, the Officers Training Corps, and played soldiers seriously. Others did something patriotic with the Boy Scouts. Mainly chasing Girl Guides, if I remember correctly. We admired those Old Boys who proudly turned up at school to show off their brand new uniforms – the prefects of a year ago – and we looked forward to being old enough to join. We had been well indoctrinated, and espoused all the tenets of the English Public Schoolboy. The same ideals which twenty years before took so many subalterns to an early death in Flanders. *Dulce et decorum est, pro patria mori* – It is a sweet and fitting thing to die for one's country. We believed. We would follow.

I wanted to be a Naval officer but if that was unattainable – and the fees for the Royal Naval College at Dartmouth were a serious consideration in a vicarage – then a cadet in the Merchant Navy would do. I read sea stories avidly, couldn't get enough of them. *Mr Midshipman Easy* and books by Percy F. Westerman were great favourites. Some I read several times. And then read them again during the Occupation when there was nothing much else to do but read. I had an application form for Dartmouth and a slick prospectus, and another for the Merchant Navy Training Ship, *HMS Worcester.* I worried that I might be colour blind, or that I might not pass the entrance exam. I was hopeless at mathematics, but 'Peg Leg' Le Breton did his best with poor material. The Germans put an end to those ambitions. Perhaps they saved me from a watery grave. Midshipmen and Merchant Navy cadets go to war younger than most.

At school, our worries were more mundane. Would we make it into the House cricket team? In term, we had to wear school uniform in public all the time and woe betide the youth caught in Town without his College cap. At night, we needed a signed authority from our parents to be out, to go to the pictures. Serious misdemeanours were punished with the cane; the little queue of anxious miscreants outside the Headmaster's study, waiting for six of the best, was graced more than once by my presence. For lesser offences our names were 'put in the book'. Then we had to spend all Saturday morning in detention, instead of on the playing field, or at some other form of recreation.

Most masters at Victoria College had nicknames: 'Punch' Kennett, 'Dad' Rowley, 'Chick' Fowler, 'Rufus' Robinson, 'Boozy' Bonne, 'Dolly' Vardon. 'Boozy' was never without a hip flask in his pocket, and smelt of alcohol and garlic. After school his bike was always parked outside the Stag Hotel in La Motte Street. 'Punch' Kennett and 'Dolly' Vardon were taken as hostages in 1941. We were still at school and wrote a cruel poem:

> *The Jerries have taken old Punch to Jail*
> *And he can't get out 'cause there ain't no bail*
> *We'll go and see him every day*
> *And watch the bastard rot away.*

Why were we so insensitive? He was strict, but fair. Later, in a camp in Germany, he trained himself to drink almost boiling soup. If there was any over, he was first in the queue for seconds. If you are still alive Punch, forgive what passed for schoolboy humour. Thanks to you I can still chant a few irregular Latin verbs: *fero, fere, tuli, latum* and *cano, caneri, cecini, cantum.*

It wasn't only the masters who had nicknames. There was a zoo full: 'Toad' Pallot, 'Pig' Boomer, 'Cow' Touzel, and my *copain*, 'Mouse' Le Brun. No one remembers now how the vogue started, nor the origin of those names, but one or two still stick from force of habit.

Every night we listened to the BBC News, 6pm and 9pm, on the dot. The older members of the family followed the war on a big map of Europe pinned to the kitchen wall. It lasted the Occupation, full of new names to learn: Benghazi, Tobruk, Smolensk and Nzhniy Novgorad. Father loved to roll those foreign place-names off his tongue; and the names of the Russian Generals: Zhukov, Timoshenko, Voroshilov. Later, we had to be careful. If you were overheard using those names or humming the wrong tune, you had been listening to the BBC.

At the end of the 9 o'clock news each evening, they played the national anthems of all the Allied Nations. Later, when we were only supposed to listen to German or German-controlled stations, or we were forbidden to have radios at all, we didn't switch off until the last note faded. It increased the risk, but the anthems gave us hope. We felt less alone, less isolated. In public, we hummed 'J'attendrai' or 'Je suis seul ce soir'.

In 1942 we searched the map again, for other names, looking for Wurzach, Biberach and Laufen, the camps to which our relatives and friends had been deported at the whim of Adolf Hitler.

✳

The months of the Phoney War passed slowly, with only sporadic military activity on land. There was more action at sea and we were suitably outraged when the passenger liner *Athenia* was torpedoed, and we mourned the loss of the aircraft carrier *HMS Courageous*. At the pictures we saw newsreels of the fall of Poland: smoke and flames, bodies, a boy's anxious eyes quartering the sky, eyes that expressed more than words ever could.

Over the year we saw more photographs, more newsreels. We saw strange people around us, and looked into their eyes. Soldiers after combat. Refugees. Slave labourers. The living dead. Eyes that advertised despair, mirrored destruction of the soul.

We mourned again when a submarine sank the *Royal Oak* in Scapa Flow and, though we acknowledged the bravery of the U-Boat commander and his crew, it was only grudgingly. We became impatient at the lack of fighting on the

Western Front, craved by proxy the excitement of reported action; little did we think that it would soon erupt, and to our disadvantage.

We listened to Lord Haw Haw and laughed in scorn. He was funny then.

'The Maginot line is impregnable,' the newspapers reassured us. 'The Germans can't break through into France, never mind reach as far as Jersey.' It was unthinkable, and our illusion of safety was reinforced when new boys arrived at Victoria College, sent by anxious parents who thought they would be safer in Jersey than at school in England. We could see no need to worry when the British Press advertised the Island as 'a good, safe place to have a wartime holiday!' On the Music Hall stage and on the radio they sang, 'We're going to hang out our washing on the Siegfried Line.'

Admiringly, we followed the defence of Finland in *Picture Post* and on the radio. Finland, the little battler, fighting off the Russian bully. We lauded Field Marshal Mannerheim and his men as heroes, and we gloated over photographs of dead Russians, their bodies frozen into bizarre shapes in foxholes or stacked like logs in snow-covered piles. We were thirteen; we had little compassion and even less insight. We didn't see ourselves as victims.

Patriotic enthusiasm spilled over to greet the news that the German pocket battleship, *Graf Spee*, had slunk into a neutral harbour after the Battle of the River Plate. We cheered when the crew scuttled her. 'It proved the Hun was basically a coward. That he couldn't face cold steel.' We were as much the victims of wartime propaganda as the Germans were. But where *was* the *Ark Royal*? Lord Haw Haw wasn't funny later on.

They told us about magnetic mines and a new propaganda line assured us that, 'only the Hun could invent something so cowardly and evil.' We learned about degaussing and other 'marvels' of British science. But now there were new losses, almost every day. *HMS Exmouth. HMS Grenville. HMS Daring.* Slowly, our boyish minds began to understand: death was not just for the other side.

Security was tight by 1940. Posters told us CARELESS TALK COSTS LIVES. Sailors on leave wore cap bands that just said 'HMS'. They no longer sported their ship's name with pride.

We got some revenge though when the Altmark prisoners were freed, and at the pictures, we cheered the crew of *HMS Cossack*, and we cheered again when the crews of *Ajax* and *Exeter*, who helped to dispose of the *Graf Spee*, marched through the streets with bayonets fixed, drums beating and flags flying, to receive the Freedom of the City of London. Later we saw German News-reels, UFA KLANGFILM; there was nothing to cheer about then.

8 April 1940 was a Monday. We still weren't concerned when we heard that German troops were in Denmark and Norway. But we learnt another insult for the years to come: 'Bloody Quisling.'

Narvik was a victory for the Royal Navy. Then came defeat and our side was bundled out of Norway. It was the first real rout, the first of many.

I helped out on the land in the school holidays. I remember how dry and dusty the soil was and how it stuck to my skin, and I could smell it in my sweat as I cycled home along Colomberie. I worked on a friend's father's farm. I didn't know then that his sisters would be Jerrybags. It was the start of what the Germans called 'Hitler Weather', in that long, hot, victorious summer.

10 May 1940 was a Friday. My memories are vivid now, carved in stone. We learnt that Hitler's men were in Belgium, in Holland, and then in France. We felt the first pangs of fear, and a new word entered our vocabulary. *Blitzkrieg* – 'Lightning War'. They came by land and air, like a plague of locusts, eating up the map. They came closer every day. Then Belgium surrendered. 'Gallant Belgium' they called her in the first war, the Great War. 'But not so gallant this time,' the propagandists told us to help explain our own defeat. 'They gave up almost without a fight,' they said. But it wasn't true. Many Belgians fought gallantly.

Newsreels showed us what was
 happening. We saw women and children bombed and machine-gunned on the roads of northern France. We saw refugees, carts and prams, bikes and cars – a few cars, soon abandoned as the fuel ran out – mattresses and bits of furniture, pots and pans piled high on anything that would carry them, dead horses, splintered carts. Bodies.

Our hopes soared when we heard that Chamberlain had resigned and that Churchill was Prime Minister. "We'll show them now," we said.

The Luftwaffe bombed Cherbourg, just across the water. Clouds of smoke climbed high into the soft summer air, while the wireless told us the French capital had been declared an 'open city'.

On 14 June, they informed us that the Germans were in Paris, but some French troops fought on; and De Gaulle spoke *à tous les Français* - to all the French. *La France a perdu une bataille. Mais la France n'a pas perdu la guerre* – France has lost a battle. But France has not lost the war.

We saw more photographs, tourists at Napoleon's tomb, and on the steps of the Madeleine, Field-Grey, *Schickelgruber* in the middle.

The Island quaked with every explosion, adding to an anxiety turning to fear. Shock waves reverberated through the rocky strata we share with France and furniture danced across the living room floor.

We still didn't know that seven weeks after Churchill took office, we would be occupied.

Then we had our own Dunkirk, one that few people outside the Islands know about. The 'Miracle of Saint Malo,' they called it later. After Dunkirk, British troops under Alanbrooke returned to France, but the French couldn't hold and our troops were forced to evacuate. Like they did at Dunkirk, the Germans stopped their advance at the last minute. Apparently, they turned aside to protect their flank and to take the airfield at Rennes, and the British soldiers were safely taken off.

The War Cabinet sent troops to Jersey to cover the retreat and evacuation: anti-aircraft guns, a machine-gun battalion, a squadron of Hurricanes; but in the event, they weren't needed. Small boats from the Island Yacht Clubs, local fishing boats and some larger vessels helped to take the men off. Eddie Langlois, with whom I later shared a cell, helped to crew a yacht. Most of the troops went straight to England. Eddie was on the *Callou*, piloted by his brother, Jim, and crewed by Deaffy Marrett and a man called Gallichan. They ducked in fear when aircraft swooped over them at Saint Malo, coming from inland where the Germans were. But they were Blenheims, not Dorniers.

Demolition teams were already busy when they arrived at the port. A massive lock gate flew through the air as if it was a piece of corrugated-iron roofing blown off in a gale. It landed near them in the water. They saw smoke and dust rising above the town, obscuring the old ramparts. The sky was dark. The fear was palpable. A family of Jews pleaded with them for a place on the boat, a woman and two small children, a boy and girl. They had travelled from Holland, just ahead of the advancing Nazis. They were told to see the officer-in-charge because all civilian boats were under Royal Navy command. Eddie spoke to the officer for them. The officer said "No! Certainly not! But I must go into town, to look for stragglers." They were taken on board and packed down below among the troops. They escaped to America and after the war they wrote to Eddie's mother to say thankyou.

All the defences were withdrawn from the Island as quickly as they had arrived. The Island was in shock. Suddenly, everything became quiet, subdued. People spoke in whispers, as if the Germans were already there and could hear them talking.

They looked at each other anxiously. "What's happening?" they asked. "What's going to happen to us?"

A Royal Engineer officer, a demolition expert, saw the Bailiff, Alexander Coutanche, and told him, "I think its about time I started to blow you up, Sir."

Some years later, in a BBC broadcast, Coutanche recalled their conversation. "Very well! What would you like to blow up first?"

When told it included the electricity, gas, water and sewerage, as well as the harbour and airport, Coutanche replied, "Well of course you must blow up what you are ordered to, but how do you think I'm going to keep 40,000 of the King's subjects alive if you are going to blow up all the public utilities?"

"That hadn't occurred to me," was the answer, "and probably it hasn't occurred to my superiors either. Perhaps we should leave things as they are." They did.

We rode our bikes to Gorey. The guns were closer now, tearing into the shattered remnants of the French Army. The sky was a long black cloud above the coast of France as retreating troops burnt oil-storage tanks in Cherbourg. The day darkened, like an eclipse of the sun, and the flashes of exploding shells were mirrored in the under surface of the pall that covered the sky.

Rumours spread rapidly – 'mephitic' – like a plague. One I heard several times was: 'In France, they're cutting off the index fingers of all males over sixteen. So they can't pull a trigger!' And: 'They are bayonetting babies in France.' People tried to give credence to the tales they told, 'Somebody told me who got it from somebody who knows somebody who knows one of the sailors on a tug which has been to France.'

French sailors and soldiers from Cherbourg landed in Alderney, and more in Jersey. Others arrived from Carteret and Granville. 'A fishing boat came into Gorey, full of refugees, a crucifix nailed to the mast.' Or did it? Was it just another rumour?

It all happened quickly and yet, paradoxically, we seemed to see things in slow motion, as if we were watching ourselves from outside ourselves. Underneath everything else there was a solid core of fear. I remember Father saying later: "It was like waiting for a key to turn in a lock."

Why did we stay? Some people had to. The King ordered the Bailiff and Crown Officers to remain at their posts. Those with responsibilities stayed: doctors, dentists, vets, farmers with animals to feed and milk. Such people stayed.

The States, the Island parliament, offered evacuation to any that wanted to leave, but Father wouldn't abandon his church or his elderly parishioners, and Mother wouldn't go without him. Decision made. We stayed.

A dull, leaden feeling settled in the pit of my stomach as I wondered 'What's it going to be like? What will they do to us?' Our own propaganda had rebounded, made us more fearful than otherwise we might have been.

I watched my parents' faces closely. It wasn't easy for them to decide, not with four children. I saw the same indecision that clouded the faces of those who came to the vicarage for their advice.

The day before they decided to stay, I stood for hours in a long queue that stretched from the Town Hall, all the way up the Parade, past the General Hospital, waiting to register for evacuation, for a place on one of the boats, the boats that were still to come. A Smith's Ice Cream man did a roaring trade. My face got sunburnt.

People changed their minds. Some, two or three times. Now they were going. Now they weren't. There was a constant stream of visitors at the vicarage: parishioners and those we had never seen before; ordinary people, wanting advice from someone they thought would know better than they did themselves about what they should do. Few realised they were asking a man and woman who were as puzzled and anxious as they were.

The diarist, Leslie Sinel, was paying off his house. He had an elderly mother-in-law. He and his family had nowhere to go in England, no relatives there. "It would have been like going to a foreign country," he said later. They stayed, and at great risk he kept a hidden radio and a secret diary throughout the war. It is the living record that helps us remember much of what happened day by day, and which has now helped me to write this book.

A few farmers went, suddenly, in panic. They left cows in agony, waiting to be milked. In Alderney, an abandoned horse, crazed with thirst, tried to jump a fence and broke its neck. Such was the fear, the panic that gripped some people, especially when they told us they weren't going to defend us. The thought of being besieged and bombed and shelled frightened us less than the prospect of living under the jackboot. Some attempted suicide. Of a married couple, one died and one survived. Most people were calm. "We shall see it out," they said, "It won't be for long. Our troops will soon be back. It will be all over by Christmas."

In the town, shops closed, then opened again. For a while the streets were full of people: they stood in small groups on street corners, nodding and shaking their heads, some gesticulating in the French fashion as they engaged in fearful conversation. Queues formed at the banks as people tried to get their money out. The streets emptied, then filled, then emptied again as German aircraft flew above the rooftops. We could still hear the guns in France, but they were further away, like a distant thunderstorm. We no longer saw the flashes. The streets were soon deserted once more, as if the world was in abeyance, waiting for a storm to break.

Families sat patiently on their meagre luggage at the harbour, waiting for the boats. "One suitcase per head," was the order. "No more than 25lbs." A rich couple was said to have asked each other: "What shall we take? The Picasso, or your jewellery?"

The authorities told evacuees to carry enough food for 24 hours. Some families stayed at the harbour for two or three days and slept on the quay, frightened that they would lose their turn in the queue for a place on one of the boats. Shops sold out of suitcases. Families carried their few precious belongings in pillowcases, in brown paper carrier bags, in anything they could find. Pathetic bundles. A small girl clutched a doll.

The boats arrived at last but they were filthy, unfit for passengers. Women and children were crowded into the holds. Sanitation was almost non-existent. Before we were cut off, we heard that the journey across the Channel was terrible. Some who saw the boats changed their minds and stayed. High-flying German planes still circled overhead and we waited for bombs, for the rattle of machine-gun fire.

Families waiting for the boat went home again, then changed their minds, came back, then went home again. Some found their houses ransacked, but we couldn't blame the Germans. They hadn't yet arrived. Abandoned cars, motorbikes, pushbikes, even a couple of prams, cluttered the quay and the roads leading to the harbour.

Pets were put down at the Animal Shelter, six thousand cats and dogs in two days. They took the bodies away by the lorry load. It was said that some of the rich tried to bribe their way on to the few aircraft still flying out, and it was rumoured that a lady leaving in panic had given her Rolls Royce to a young man standing outside the airport.

More refugees arrived from France. They came in small boats, packed with belongings. Packed with rumours.

The King sent a message. It read:

> For strategic reasons it has been found necessary to withdraw the Armed Forces from the Channel Islands.
>
> I deeply regret this necessity and I wish to assure My people in the Islands that in taking this decision My Government has not been unmindful of their position. It is in their interest that this step should be taken in present circumstances.
>
> The long association of the Islands with the Crown and the loyal service the people of the Islands have rendered to My Ancestors and Myself are guarantees that the link between us will remain unbroken and I know that My people in the Islands will look forward with the same confidence as I do to the day when the resolute fortitude with which we face our present difficulties will reap the reward of victory.

It was read out in the States, but they didn't publish it. Nobody told us. We didn't know the King was thinking of us, that he was worried about our welfare. It wouldn't have stopped the Germans if we had been told. But we might have felt less bitter about being abandoned.

With that incomparable ability the British have for making a right royal cock-up in the early stages of a war, the War Office and Home Office didn't tell the Germans we had been demilitarised, that we were an 'open town'. At first, Churchill wanted to defend us, to make us another Malta. He said: "The Royal Navy will keep the Germans out." The Navy had other ideas. With Cherbourg and Brest in enemy hands, the Island within short range of bombers, visible from France and well within artillery range too, they said it was impossible. There was nothing they could do.

The Chiefs of Staff also considered there would be no strategic advantage in holding onto the Islands. They too advised Churchill against defending us as, later, Hitler's generals would advise him. They believed the Islands would be more use undefended. "The Germans will have to keep them supplied with essential goods and services," they told Churchill, "and they will have to maintain a garrison."

They were right. That is what happened. After the war, someone wrote that the Islands did more to help the war effort just by being there; more than they ever could have done by armed resistance. As Cruickshank pointed out, Hitler poured in a reinforced division. He built fortifications of such magnitude that he deprived more important areas of concrete, men and *matériel*. They played no further part in the war. Like the Panzers, they were denied to Rommel after D-Day.

The War Cabinet too failed to tell the Germans that we were an 'open town'. It relied on some hypothetical German Intelligence network to pass on that information to Berlin. Eventually, they did tell them through Joseph Kennedy, the American Ambassador in London. He relayed the news to Berlin. But it was too late. They bombed us.

In comparison with what was to happen later to London, Plymouth, Coventry, and other major British cities, the attack on Jersey and Guernsey was mild. The Germans only dropped 180 bombs. They killed only 44 civilians, fewer than 50 were wounded but, at the time, it was the heaviest raid carried out on British territory.

In the dining room at St. Mark's vicarage we had a heavy wooden dining table. When the siren wailed its warning note, Father made us get under it, together with Ken Preston who was curate of St. Helier Town Church. Then father went outside into the garden – to have a look! The vicarage was a four-storey building. It has since been demolished. The table might have helped if the roof had come in.

They strafed us several times and machine-gun bullets hit roofs and walls; but there were no more bombs. The main damage was at La Rocque and around the harbour in St Helier.

Why do airmen always bomb La Rocque? There's almost nothing there; just a few houses. At least there was a gun emplacement nearby when an American aircraft bombed it later in the war. At the time we were attacked, and for a long time afterwards, we thought the Nazis knew we were unprotected, and had taken advantage of our lack of defence to mount a cowardly attack. It was the impression the British Government gave. *The Times* called it "Murder."

As Father and I walked up Val Plaisant on our way back from Church, a Dornier flew low over our heads, machine-gunning the rooftops. While we sheltered under a stone archway on the side of the road to wait for the all-clear, a drunk staggered out of the pub on the corner, stood unsteadily in the middle of the road, and hurled curses at the departing airmen. Father strode out and poked him in the region of the umbilicus with the tip of his walking stick, and told him, "Get inside, and wash your mouth out."

During the air raid a young girl who took refuge in the cellar of a pub in Seale Street was more worried about what her father would say than she was about the bombs. Her father was a strict teetotaller. People behaved irrationally. A man and his father-in-law saw the spur of the Fort on fire and went by car to have a look. They were machine-gunned for their temerity and had to abandon the vehicle.

❋

Before the Germans arrived and cut off all communications with the other Islands, we heard that Guernsey had been bombed more heavily than Jersey, but that the number of dead and wounded was less than it might have been. Just before the bombers arrived, the main street of St. Peter Port was full of people listening to a speech from the Guernsey Procureur – the Attorney General. They had only just moved off when the bombers came.

Lorries were waiting at the harbour to unload tomatoes for England. Cattle from deserted Alderney were being brought ashore. Several lorries were hit. Their drivers took cover underneath the vehicles and burned to death when spreading petrol burst into flames. The cattle bolted and added to the confusion.

Despite what the War Office might have thought, there were no enemy spies in the Islands no one to tell the German Command that we had been demilitarised. They had no way of finding out except by attacking us. The mailboat, *Isle of Sark*, was in Guernsey harbour and opened up with her anti-aircraft gun.

A Mrs R.J. Stephen was aboard at the time and saw three planes swoop out of the sun. There was a terrific explosion as the first bomb fell. Splinters rattled on the deck. A man standing next to her small son collapsed with blood pouring from a wound in his groin. Some passengers ran below, but others panicked and ran down the gangway towards some sheds and warehouses on the wharf. "They were caught by a raking machine-gun fire from the second and third Nazi planes and went down in rows like ninepins." A policeman who was collecting tickets on the gangway was blown to pieces. The sheds went up in flames.

In fairness to the Germans, their claim that they mistook the transport for ammunition lorries was probably true, much as the local population wanted to believe otherwise. There were potato lorries queueing to unload at the quay in Jersey. The aircrew mistook them too for military transport. More open to condemnation was an attack on the Guernsey lifeboat. It was clearly marked. They killed the coxswain's son.

We heard in Jersey that most Guernsey children had been evacuated, that the staff and boys of Elizabeth College marched to the docks and went to England as a school. Many other children had gone too, leaving only enough to fill two schools. A witness recorded that 'the Island seemed empty with them gone.' Major Sherwill, Guernsey's Attorney General, wrote in his diary: 'No children play in the streets, and mothers mourn their loss and will not be comforted.' Their sorrow lasted five long years.

✳

Families were split. Those who left in the evacuation worried about their friends and family left behind. It was a long time before the first Red Cross letters got through. Even then, we could only write 10 words. There was no room for messages of love and longing.

Those left behind worried about those who had gone. They wondered if they had crossed the Channel safely. German planes still circled overhead, like birds of prey. Later, those left wondered what was happening to their loved ones in England, and how they were being looked after in what was for many a strange country; they were concerned about where they were when German bombs were falling.

German propaganda described the Blitz in detail, and every day during the Battle of Britain the sky above the Island was full of planes marked with swastikas. Endless formations took off in the direction of the English coast.

We learnt that the last evacuation boats went away empty. All those who wanted to leave had gone. The town was almost deserted. Most people stayed at home. Those that did go out to shop, or on important business, watched the sky.

The large number of servicemen on leave who failed to get away in time has always puzzled me. About 150 gave themselves up to be prisoners-of-war in Germany. Did they want to stay with their families in time of danger? Or was it desertion? And why did the military authorities in Britain allow so many to go on leave when they knew that the Island was in the front line and about to be invaded? Apparently, some servicemen had only arrived in the previous 24 hours. Some said they had come to retrieve their families. Others were on special leave after Dunkirk; most of those returned to their units. Michael Ginns also queries the motives of those who did not go back. He told me that after the war, some of them were lucky not to be charged with desertion. In the end, nothing happened and they all got five years back pay.

30 June 1940 dawned as a day of fearful expectation, and more German planes flew low over and around the Island. The sky was a clear, dazzling blue, with not a hint of cloud. The sea was flat calm: 'Hitler Weather'.

My parents didn't think we would be bombed again, or I didn't tell them where I was going. I went for a swim at West Park beach with the Burgess brothers. We were walking towards the sea when a Dornier 'Flying Pencil' came in low. It zoomed out of nowhere, just above our heads, and headed for the harbour wall. I felt a sudden rush of fear as I saw the crew looking down at us, and yelled a warning to the others. We threw ourselves into the water. But they didn't open fire.

Later that day, a plane dropped three bags by parachute. One was found hanging on the railings of the Town Church. Each contained a copy of the German ultimatum. It was almost time.

✳   ✳   ✳

Chapter Two

DRAMATIS PERSONAE

It was not the first invasion, nor the first occupation. Throughout history, the Channel Islands have been attacked time and again: at first by Vikings and many times by the French. When King John lost his French possessions in 1204, the French tried repeatedly to take the Islands. Then, as in 1940, the population lay vulnerable and exposed on the far side of the English Channel.

During the Wars of the Roses, the French invaded and occupied Jersey for seven years. Balleine, the Island historian, has suggested that, like the Germans, the French tried to make it a benign and popular occupation. If so, such a policy may have seen the same cooperation and resistance as in more recent times: a majority who kept their heads down and survived with little danger, with only the discomforts and shortages to mar their daily lives; a few who collaborated and who were rewarded with extra food and other luxuries, a small number who actively defied the enemy and suffered as a consequence. The Bailiff of the day, Nicholas Morin, had to sign Orders from the French, as did Alexander Coutanche under the Germans. Morin signed as 'Bailiff under the High and Mighty Lord, the Count of Maulévrier, Lord of the Isles'. It was probably as distasteful to him as it was to Coutanche nearly five centuries later; though we must remember that the French were not complete strangers, nor culturally and ethnically different like the Germans were; and we cannot know Morin's true feelings with any certainty at a time when cross-Channel loyalties were always suspect. Morin was replaced as Bailiff after the French occupation, but continued to sit as a Jurat. He was not considered a traitor.

Guernsey has always been a separate Bailiwick and includes Alderney and Sark. Each Bailiwick has a Lieutenant Governor. He represents the Crown. In time of war he is also Commander-in-Chief. In the States, the Island parliament, his Chair is a few inches lower than the Bailiff's.

The Bailiff is appointed by the Crown, as are the Attorney General and the Solicitor General. The Bailiff is Chief Judge of the Island, President of the Royal Court, and also President of the States. Island laws go to the Privy Council for Royal Signature, not to the British Parliament. Le Patourel summed up the relationship between the Islands and the Crown as, 'that of a Principality united to another in the person of the Prince only.'

When the Germans got close to the French coast opposite Jersey in May 1940, the Lieutenant Governor, General J.M. Harrison, was recalled to England. The Bailiff was sworn in as Civil Governor for the duration. He was allowed to take an amended oath that absolved him from his historical obligation as a successor of the *Gardiens des Iles*, 'to defend the Island and its castles against all incursions of the enemy.'

What kind of people inhabited Jersey at the outbreak of war? What did we think when we were suddenly faced with the choice of emergency evacuation, just ahead of a rapidly advancing enemy, across a dangerous sea, with hostile aircraft overhead; or of sticking to our homes and confronting the victors, victors we already feared for their ruthless attacks on women and children fleeing down the roads of Northern France, victors who were still caricatured as rapacious, gorilla-like Huns, dripping with the blood of innocents, as portrayed by British and French propaganda posters of the 1914-1918 war?

Most inhabitants of the Island were ordinary Jersey men and women who had inherited a long tradition of resistance to invasion and oppression. They were a small population which in the Great War as well as in the present one had voluntarily given up an ancient right that the young men of the Island could not be called to the Colours to serve overseas 'unless it be to accompany His Majesty in person for the recovery of England, or that the person of His Majesty should be taken prisoner by the enemy.'

The names of Jerseymen who volunteered and died fill the parish war memorials. Among them, without distinction, are the names of those of more recent French origin who were mobilised into the French Army, and the names of British residents called to the Colours who also died on active service.

There were too in the Island the retirees and pensioners who by ancestry or choice, lived where low taxation allowed them to eke out reduced incomes and to live comfortably after long and loyal service to King and Country in foreign parts. There were also rich tax dodgers, like some of those who infest the island today. They didn't hang around long enough to have to make a choice. At the first whiff of powder, they were off.

There were, no doubt, some among the inhabitants who sympathised with Hitler and his policies, and some who couldn't decide which was the greater evil – Hitler or Stalin. Most though were firm in their convictions. Although not part of the United Kingdom, most people were intensely loyal to that country through the Crown.

There were too the people of commerce and banking, and the technicians and the tradesmen: some of whom had been sent to work in Jersey by their firms in England or France: some who had decided for themselves to seek a quiet backwater of Europe – 'fifty years behind the times,' they used to say – free from the frenetic pace of modern life elsewhere, and far from what the

Australian author of 'Waltzing Matilda', Banjo Paterson, called, 'the foetid air and gritty of the dirty dusty city.'

There were doctors, dentists and veterinary surgeons and other professional men and women. There were retired military officers and former colonial officials; there were men like my father who moved us from England to Jersey when he became Vicar of St. Mark's.

There were conscientious objectors sent from England to help with the potato harvest. There were Irish men and women, citizens of neutral Eire. Many were nurses or doctors, most were labourers. And in an island dependent on tourism for much of its wealth, there were Italians and other nationalities, working as chefs, as waiters and as restaurateurs. There were farm workers from Brittany and Normandy. There were even a few Germans. The population was as cosmopolitan then as it is now.

What were the beliefs of those who stayed to face the Occupation? Much the same as those held by people in Britain and throughout the Empire. We were just as patriotic. We believed that Britain and France could never be defeated.

I was thirteen when the Occupation began. I was eighteen when it ended. Not old enough to vote in the 1945 General Election but old enough to join the RAF. I have clear recollections of Hitler's rise to power, of the Italian invasion of Abyssinia – as Ethiopia was then called – and of the Spanish Civil War. Before we moved to Jersey, I was at boarding school in England. From about 1935 boys with strange names appeared, names like Spiegel, Helm, Krott, and Freund-Corvin. They were the lucky ones – like my brother-in-law, Manfred – who escaped the Holocaust.

At that age, I was fuelled with the same beliefs as the rest of my generation, beliefs that stemmed at least in part from a diet of adventure stories in *Boy's Own*, *Skipper*, *Hotspur* and *Rover* magazines, and from Bulldog Drummond novels by Sapper. My parents disapproved. They thought I should read the *Children's Newspaper*, but I was a youngster of my time.

Our family was intensely patriotic. My mother wept when Edward VIII abdicated. Even at home, as many people then did, we stood for the National Anthem. We always listened to the King's speech on Christmas Day. We were a family of our time. It is easy today to mock such attitudes and our strong views about our duty to King and Country, but they were very real, very sincere. They were the ideals and beliefs that in the end won the war.

We believed passionately in the indestructibility of the British Empire, the 'Empire on which the sun would never set.' On Empire Day we had a school holiday. We saw suitable films. We attended ceremonies and listened to speeches that today would be thought hopelessly jingoistic. Unfortunately, some of what we believed included an unpleasant element of racial prejudice. And not just against the Germans. Looking back now, it is difficult to understand how or why we were as awful as we were. With equal prejudice and without any evidence, some of those who had most recently come to live in the Island from Britain would come to consider that those who were collaborating with the enemy during the Occupation were mainly native islanders. The compliment was no doubt returned with equal vigour.

The Occupation lasted five years. It ended on 9 May 1945, the day after VE-Day. Cruickshank wrote: 'For the British the loss of the Islands had little strategic significance, but their demilitarisation was so clumsily handled that had the facts been known to the British people at the time it would have weakened their faith in the government's ability to win the war.'

With so many more important things going on elsewhere, it is a harsh judgment. But it has an element of truth. Things could have been managed better. When it was suddenly announced that we were to be abandoned, to be left undefended, we were devastated, especially as we had only recently seen troops and a squadron of Hurricanes arrive to cover the evacuation from St. Malo. The way the Home Office and the War Office handled matters was sloppy and uncoordinated, but again, in fairness, they did have a lot of other things to worry about at the time.

It was unfortunate too, to begin with at least, that at a time of such obvious danger the British authorities appeared more interested in who should pay for the evacuation ships, than they were about sending them, and that they should have let so many servicemen go on leave to the Islands when the Germans were obviously going to invade at any moment.

From a Jersey population of 50,000, some 23,000 people registered for evacuation. Fewer than 10,000 left. About half of Guernsey's population went. Alderney was virtually abandoned.

On 30 June, the Bailiff, Alexander Coutanche, was sitting at home when the phone rang. It was a call from May Sherwill, wife of Guernsey's Procureur. She told him, 'the Germans have arrived.' Shortly afterwards, he talked to Sir Alexander Maxwell, Permanent Under-Secretary at the Home Office. Maxwell rang to say that he couldn't contact Guernsey. Did Coutanche know what was happening? Coutanche told him.

In his memoirs, Lord Coutanche, as he later became, described their conversation:

> Maxwell began: "It may be a long time before we talk again. There is nothing much that one can say, is there?"
>
> "No. Not very much."
>
> "I repeat that it is the King's personal wish that you and the Bailiff of Guernsey remain at your posts. He will not accept the position of being unrepresented in the Islands in their moment of danger. You are carrying

out the direct wish of the Sovereign. We know that we can rely upon you to face up to the situation, terrible as it may be. There is no advice that one can give to anybody in such conditions. But when we meet again I feel sure I shall be able to say to you that you have worthily followed the example of Burgomaster Max of Brussels."

In the Great War, when threatened by a German officer who crashed the butt of his pistol on the edge of his desk, the Burgomaster did the same thing with his pen, and said, "that is all I have to fight you with."

Despite post-war criticism, I believe Coutanche lived up to that tradition.

Chapter 3

THE KEY TURNS IN THE LOCK

A festering resentment against the bombing of undefended islands continued until well after the war. It was only some years later that we found out the truth. When the Germans attacked us in June 1940, they didn't know that we had been demilitarised and declared an 'open town'. Nobody told them. They didn't know we were undefended.

They began making plans to take the Islands in June, when their headlong advance into France threatened Normandy and Brittany, and they knew they would soon capture the neighbouring coast. What might have happened to us is made clear in captured Nazi documents. Code-named 'Operation *Grüne Pfeile*' – 'Green Arrow' – the Germans planned to land *Kriegsmarine* assault troops, supported by Army units. The *Luftwaffe* would deal with any RAF aircraft that tried to interfere from across the Channel.

The Nazi Command ordered several reconnaissance flights over the Islands. They met no opposition. According to their records, one of their aircraft flew around the Islands at less than 1,000 feet without being fired on, but the Germans were still suspicious. As Cruickshank pointed out, Britain needed a propaganda victory after the forced evacuation from Dunkirk and the German Staff expected their troops to meet stiff resistance. They therefore planned an extensive, preliminary softening-up attack by Stuka dive-bombers.

Fortunately we knew nothing of this, though newsreels of the Nazi advance into Poland, Belgium and France had made us only too well aware of what such attacks could mean for a civilian population. It was not difficult to imagine what would happen if the Islands were defended.

Even more fortunately, such attacks did not take place. Apart from ack-ack fire from the mailboat, *Isle of Sark* during the bombing of Guernsey harbour, the enemy occupied us without a shot being fired at them. The ultimatum dropped by parachute read:

To the Chief of the Military and Civil Authorities, Jersey (St. Helier).
(1) I intend to neutralise military establishments in Jersey by occupation.
(2) As evidence that the Island will surrender military and other establishments without resistance, and without destroying them, a large

White Cross is to be shown from 7am, July 2nd. 1940.

 (a) In the centre of the airport in the East of the Island.

 (b) On the highest point of the fortifications of the port.

 (c) On the square to the north of the Inner Basin of the harbour.

Moreover, all fortifications, buildings, establishments and houses are to show the White Flag.

(3) If these signs of peaceful surrender are not observed by 7am, July 2nd., a heavy bombardment will take place.

 (a) Against all military objectives.

 (b) Against all establishments and objects useful for defence.

(4) The signs of surrender must remain up to the time of the occupation of the Islands by German troops.

(5) Representatives of the Authorities must stay at the airport until the Occupation.

(6) All radio traffic and other communications with the Authorities outside the Island will be considered hostile actions and will be followed by bombardment.

(7) Every hostile action against my representatives will be followed by bombardment.

(8) In the event of peaceful surrender the lives, property and liberty of peaceful inhabitants are solemnly guaranteed.

     The Commander of the German Air forces in Normandy.

       RICHTHOFEN, GENERAL.

It was in German.

The airport is in the west of the Island, but Michael Ginns saw a white cross being painted on one of the fairways of that august body, the Royal Jersey Golf Club, 'just in case.' The indignity, however, was more psychological than physical. It did not scar the course as badly as what followed later in the war, when fortifications and a minefield were a more significant blemish.

A common difficulty in time of war is to find someone at the right time that speaks the enemy's language. None of the Island authorities spoke German. However, Charles Duret Aubin, the Attorney-General, phoned Father Rey at the Jesuit College in St. Helier to get the help of a priest from Alsace. Even so, there was a misunderstanding.

To our chagrin, the Island authorities told us we must fly white flags from every building, including private houses. We found out later it was not what the Germans wanted, but rumour had it that they weren't slow to take advantage of our mistake. Sadly, we removed the Union Jack from a pole which Father used to put out from a small balcony above the front-door of the vicarage on happier occasions and replaced it with a white towel. Stories have circulated since the war that the German propaganda machine superimposed swastikas on our 'white flags' and published pictures in their newspapers with the headline, JERSEY WELCOMES THE VICTORS. Michael Ginns wrote: 'This is one of those old Occupation chestnuts that rears its head from time to time.' He likened it to the story in which a German officer is alleged to have asked a group of children, 'Those who like chocolate raise their right hands.' A photographer then supposedly took a photo of all the Nazi salutes, which was said to have appeared in all the German newspapers with the caption: 'Happy English children welcome German troops to British soil.' A slightly different account had him asking local adults, listening to a military band: 'Those who can't speak German raise their right hands.' These photographs have never been seen by anyone we know.

※

The following somewhat fanciful and pedantically German description of how the Occupation began was written for home consumption by a *Sonderführer* Hans Auerbach, under the heading, HOW A YOUNG LIEUTENANT TOOK THE ISLAND OF JERSEY:

On the 1st. July 1940, the German wireless announced that the Channel Islands had been occupied by a bold stroke of the Air Force. It is of interest to record the true facts of the occupation. This incident of the war will be of value at a later date as it was through this operation that British soil in Europe, for the first time, was occupied by German troops.

From Normandy, from Cape Carteret or Cap de la Hague, the Channel Islands appear grey shadows between the horizon and the sea, shadows which in hazy weather disappear. What do they conceal? The telescopes of coastguards were constantly fixed on them, as this was England; this was the last bastion turned towards Europe after she had been driven from the Continent. Headquarters were, therefore, very much interested in the Islands, as they greatly desired to know what was happening in them. Rumour had it that they had been completely evacuated. Reconnaissance undertook to discover the true state of affairs.

On 30th. June, Lieutenant Kern flew over the Islands for that purpose. He saw Guernsey with its glass-houses, he saw apparently inhospitable Alderney, the small island of Sark, and then he turned to the largest island of Jersey. He flew over beaches and harbours, over small estates and villages until he reached St. Helier. The streets of the town were almost deserted. The Island seemed dead. Finally, after close investigation, people were discernible. They emerged cautiously from the air-raid shelters and gazed curiously upward. There was, therefore, still life in Jersey. The most important fact that could be reported to the General was that there was no sign of defence.

On the second flight, the machine met three 'planes of similar type from the sister squadron. They were flying towards Guernsey and, as was later known, that morning they occupied the Island.

In the meantime the English must have smelt a rat for they sent two Blenheims over the Channel. They met three Dornier fighters near Guernsey, and Lieutenant Forster was able to shoot both down with one reconnaissance 'plane.

As a result of the information obtained the General decided to call upon Jersey to surrender. It was two o'clock in the morning when the summons, signed by the General, reached the Squadron. There were three summons each for Jersey and Guernsey all in the same terms. As it was a letter of parley, the usual coloured pouch could not be used; pouches were, therefore, cut from the bed-linen belonging to the Captain of the French Squadron whose deserted quarters had been taken over by the German Squadron. It was still dark when the machine started for Jersey.

The Island was reached in the early hours. Once more a German 'plane was droning over Jersey. Only a few Islanders were up, but the pouch containing the summons to surrender was soon found and taken to the Authorities. Later, it was recounted in the Island how surprised the dreamy town of St. Helier was to receive such an early visit.

After dropping the summons the 'plane returned, and the General awaited signs of surrender. It can be imagined how tense the German airmen were during the period of waiting. The General had stipulated that, as a sign of surrender, white flags should be flown. There could be no peace of mind until the undertaking had been carried to a successful conclusion.

Wild rumours were running through the services. According to these an English cruiser was supposed to have made its appearance in the vicinity of Jersey. In order to clear up this point, Lieutenant Kern was sent back to the islands. He arrived without being attacked, and could see nothing of any active defence. The Island lay there as peacefully as on the previous day. Then, as the machine flew over the beaches and gardens and town, an idea came to the Lieutenant. He saw life going on peacefully below him; he saw the beautiful Island, and he had been ordered to bring back accurate information. As he flew low towards the Airport and saw the beautifully situated landing ground with its elegant white buildings, he made his decision.

He would take Jersey.

The 'plane banked over the flying field. He gave the order to land.

What were the sensations of the crew? If the field were mined, then it would be all over. If there were means of defence, it would not be much better for them. But if things went smoothly, and no one doubted but that they would, then they would be the first Germans to set foot on British soil. Lonely, the machine rolled over the ground. The Lieutenant strode towards the Administration Building, followed by the 'plane which was to secure the way into the unknown – with its machine-gun ready.

Nothing happened. Finally, from the Airport Building, emerged an excited man who, to the astonishment of the newcomers, spoke German. He took the Lieutenant to the telephone and got in touch with the Bailiff.

Yes, the Bailiff had received the summons to surrender.

Why were the white flags not flying?

Because the Bailiff had to wait for the decision of the States, and the States had in the meantime agreed to unconditional surrender.

The Bailiff requested that the General be informed to that effect. Lieutenant Kern informed the Bailiff that the Island was under German occupation.

Shortly afterwards, the 'planes which had been sent from the Squadron appeared. They were packed with men. While these machines were appearing over the Island, the white flags were beginning to be flown.

It was a strange sight that met the gaze of the Germans flying under the blue sky of that summer's day. That of a pleasant town from which every kind of white, from sheets to pocket handkerchiefs, was flying.

When the Captain of the Squadron landed, the Bailiff, the Government Secretary, and the Chief of Police were waiting to receive him at the Airport. The surrender was concluded in short time, the British officials maintaining a correct attitude. Here also the relations between the Troops of Occupation and the local Authorities have not deteriorated. The first orders were given by the Captain. The men who came over in the first machines took over the apparatus used for communication, the rate of exchange was fixed, and a curfew ordered for the Island. The Germans then drove in waiting cars to St. Helier, being stared at on the way by the policemen and the population. It all happened so naturally that it seemed the Squadron had nothing else to do but to occupy the Channel Islands.

The strokes of the Air Force are audacious and swift. The English have felt them continually, ever since they refused the hand of peace held out to them by the Führer. Swift action brought the Island of Jersey into German hands with a speed not held to be possible by the experience of history.

The next morning, to the pride of the Air Force, a swastika flag, sewn by the inhabitants of the Island, was hoisted into the blue ether.

This last sentence implies that the Islanders welcomed the invaders with open arms. Nothing could be further from the truth. What really happened was that a German Air Force officer went to De Gruchy's store in St. Helier and asked them to make a flag, as they hadn't brought one with them. The first one was a failure, and they had to make another.

For historical correctness, it was the Attorney-General who accompanied the Bailiff to the Airport. Though he was titular head of the Island's Honorary Police, Duret Aubin was hardly the 'Chief of Police' in its usual sense.

This flamboyant German account probably suffers in translation but, in fairness, it must have taken considerable courage for Lieutenant Kern and his crew to land as they did, not knowing if the Airport was mined, or if they would get a hostile reception.

Some years later, John Herbert described the event in a BBC broadcast. He told how he and Charles Roche, the Airport Controller, expected the Germans to land at 3 o'clock. It was Roche who had earlier collected the parachute ultimatum and telephoned the Bailiff. However, at 11 o'clock, the Dornier suddenly appeared and, after circling the airfield, landed. Roche, who had been a fighter pilot in the Great War said, "I suppose we'd better go and see what this gentleman wants."

With some trepidation they walked towards the aircraft, which kept its engine running and covered them with its guns. Lieutenant Kern jumped out, drew his revolver, and said, "I don't want any trouble." He then reholstered his weapon and added, "I want to speak to the Bailiff."

The Bailiff was in his Chambers at the time and was told the news of Kern's landing by telephone. He decided it was time to go up to Fort Regent to lower the Union Flag. While he was there, a second call came to the signalman's hut at the base of the Flagstaff to tell him that the Germans were waiting for him at the Airport.

That evening, the BBC broadcast the following announcement: 'The Ministry of Information issued this statement tonight. As has already been announced, the Channel Islands have been demilitarised. It is now learned that enemy landings have since been made in Jersey and Guernsey. Telegraphic and telephonic communications have been cut, and no further information is at present available.'

The Occupation had begun. The Union Flag did not fly again over Fort Regent for five long years.

✳

The criminal condemned to a term of imprisonment knows the length of his sentence. With remission for good behaviour, he can calculate roughly how long it will be before he regains his liberty. Prisoners-of-war, political prisoners, and the populations of occupied countries do not have that luxury. Nor do they have any guarantee that they will ever be free again. It is one of the more unpleasant aspects of their captivity.

They are also cut off from family and friends and frequently deprived of all news of them for long periods. They are anxious about how their relatives and friends are getting on during enemy attacks. It is even worse when they are denied media information from their own country, and at the same time are subjected to a barrage of enemy propaganda.

Though frequently heavy-handed, German propaganda could be effective, much as we tended to mock it at the time. But the reality for those under occupation in 1940 was that the Germans had no great need of it. They were clearly winning the war. It was superfluous. Accounts of continuing British defeats were true, and we knew it. They just added to our misery and despair.

For the next two years or so, the news was almost always bad. Day after day during the Battle of Britain, we saw hoards of German aircraft forming up over the Island and heading for the English coast. At the cinema we could still see American films, but we saw them at the price of having to watch German news-reels which showed graphic aerial photography of the Battle of Britain and the Blitz from the Nazi point of view. For some time after Dunkirk, we saw endless footage of British prisoners, long columns of them marching into captivity in Germany. There were so many I remember wondering if there were any men of military age left in Britain. Such scenes were repeated after Dieppe, and again when Rommel and the *Afrika Korps* were temporarily victorious in Libya. We booed or cheered appropriately, but it was defiance with a heavy heart, and the Germans threatened to close the cinemas if we didn't behave.

The BBC was some comfort when we were allowed to listen to it. But even the British News was depressing at that time. Perhaps it was because it was so distressing that the Occupying Authority let us keep our radios for as long as they did. They obviously knew we listened to the BBC, even though they made unexpected swoops from time to time. Fortunately, we didn't know then that RAF claims of large numbers of enemy aircraft shot down during the Battle of Britain were grossly exaggerated.

We counted the Luftwaffe going out. We counted them coming back. They were always short, but we never stopped to consider that many had returned safely to base by other routes.

The blackest day was when we heard that *HMS Hood* had been sunk. I had pored over pictures of her in magazines and in my ancient copy of *Jane's Fighting Ships*. Like everyone else, I believed her unsinkable, indestructible. It was a terrible shock. Britain's largest capital ship, the pride of her fleet, had gone to the bottom, and there were almost no survivors. I can still recall the bleak despair that sent my stomach tumbling into my boots when I heard about it. I can still remember the sudden fear I felt that Britain might not after all win the war.

Apart from what happened later, it was easy under such circumstances to work up a consuming hatred of Germans and all things German. A few books written by Islanders soon after the Occupation show the emotions and prejudices we carried long into the post-war years. Some descriptions were tainted by continuing hostility that reflected that understandable hatred, but I shall try to avoid such flaws and to look back on events rationally and fairly. It should be easier from the perspective of more than fifty years, but I have to confess that it was a very long time before I could even consider buying a Mercedes car, or visit Germany.

I have often been asked if I still hate Germans. My answer is: "No! Not now." I think it is true. My wife has reservations. Certainly, I still fear what they have shown themselves capable of, but that too is passing because it is unfair to new generations and to those Germans whom we know resisted Hitler at the cost of their lives, and no nation lacks unpleasant corners in its history. And we should not forget, however we may rationalise and defend it, that it was deliberate British policy to blanket-bomb civilian targets in Germany; and that American and British aircraft destroyed Dresden, Hiroshima and Nagasaki, killing unknown thousands of innocent civilians.

Though many Germans were Nazis, it is no longer fashionable or fair to think they all were. Some showed me personal kindness when least expected. But the hatred we felt was not the simple hatred of the bombed civilian, or the grieving widow; nor was it simply due to loss of freedom. It was more complicated. It was magnified by revulsion, by disgust and loathing at the obvious approval of seemingly ordinary German soldiers for the treatment meted out to slave labourers; by Germans seen to laugh at starved, whipped, beaten, bleeding human skeletons as they shuffled to work; and anger and fear too at threats to shoot innocent hostages from among us for the activities of others.

Forgiveness is still impossible for some Islanders. During the fortieth anniversary of Liberation, I was at a party in the house of friends, Charles and Estelle Gruchy; when talking to another old friend, John Painter, I rather untact-fully suggested that it might be time to forgive and forget. He did not agree. His father and elder brother, Peter, died in the Nazi concentration camp system.

During the early months of the Occupation, German behaviour, though arrogant, was disciplined and not repressive. Our immediate fears faded, but slowly the invaders interfered with more and more of our personal freedoms.

Initially, for children and adolescents, life went on much as usual. We went to school. We played cricket and football. On the beach, German soldiers seeing us kicking a football around, tried to join in and make friends. They were, no doubt, missing their own children. The Island didn't change overnight, but the deterioration was inexorable as shortages occurred.

✳

From the beginning, Orders appeared in the *Evening Post* and were posted up on walls. Red and black printed BEKANNTMACHUNG warned us that some unfortunate person had been shot for an offence against the occupying force. Newspaper advertisements for theatre shows and dances and similar events were no longer introduced with the heading 'By kind permission of the Bailiff,' but 'By order of the *Kommandant*.'

The first *Inselkommandant* – commander of the island – was a Hauptmann Gussek, incorrectly described in several accounts as a paratrooper who was later killed in North Africa or Russia. In fact, he was a career soldier, an infantryman. He had been a POW in Jersey during the Great War, though to his credit he never mentioned it in 1940. Research by Michael Ginns shows that he died in his bed in 1968. He made St. Helier Town Hall his Headquarters and like the Sword of Damocles a large Swastika hung from a Flagstaff over the main entrance. To our sad amusement, a notice informed us that the building was now officially *Das Rathaus*. We could not have agreed more.

Gussek issued his first proclamation on July 1st. 1940. It read:

Orders of the Commandant of the German Forces in Occupation of the Island of Jersey.

(1) All inhabitants must be indoors by 11pm. and not leave their homes before 5am.

(2) We will respect the population in Jersey, but should anyone attempt to cause the least trouble, serious measures will be taken.

(3) All orders given by the Military Authority are to be strictly obeyed.

(4) All spirits must be locked up immediately and no spirits may be supplied, obtained or consumed henceforth. This prohibition does not apply to stocks in private houses.

(5) No person shall enter the Aerodrome at St. Peter.

(6) All Rifles, Airguns, Revolvers, Daggers, Sporting Guns, and all other weapons whatsoever, except souvenirs, together with all ammunition,must be delivered to the Town Arsenal by 12 noon tomorrow, July 3rd.

(7) All British Sailors, Airmen and Soldiers on leave, including Officers in the Island must report to the Commandant's Office, Town Hall, at 10 am tomorrow, July 3rd.

(8) No boat or vessel of any description, including any Fishing Boat, shall leave the harbour, or any other place where the same is moored, without an Order from the Military Authority, to be obtained at the Commandant's Office, Town Hall. All boats arriving in Jersey must remain in Harbour until

permitted by the Military to leave. The crews will remain on board. The Master will report to the Harbour-master, St. Helier, and will obey his instructions.

(9) The sale of Motor Spirit is prohibited except for use on Essential Services, such as Doctor's vehicles, the delivery of Foodstuffs, and Sanitary Services, where such vehicles are in possession of a permit from the Military Authority to obtain supplies. The use of cars for private purposes is forbidden.

(10) The Black-out Regulations already in force must be obeyed as before.

(11) Banks and Shops will open as before.

(12) In order to conform with Central European Time, all watches and clocks must be advanced one hour at 11pm to-night.

(13) It is forbidden to listen to any Wireless Transmitting Stations, except German and German-controlled stations.

(14) The raising of Prices of Commodities is forbidden.

(signed) The German Commandant of the Island of Jersey.

July 2nd. 1940.

Orders continued incessantly during the next five years. Hardly a day went by without some new stricture or some extra regulation. As Sinel wrote in his Diary, 'Hitler once promised that he would bring a New Order to all Europe; at least we in the Channel Islands know what he meant – there is a "New Order" almost every day.' But like the Island authorities when they received the ultimatum to surrender, the Germans too often had problems with translation. They rarely got help from local people, and at times appeared foolish. The most memorable occasion was when they reported: 'German planes were over England again yesterday. Among other targets, they dropped bombs on the pier at Random!'

A notice on 8 July, 1940, acknowledged the 'loyal cooperation' of the civil authorities. There had been no overt antagonism. People were waiting to see what would happen. The words were no reflection on the Bailiff or his Officers, despite what some not there have written since. New instructions required all laws and regulations made by the Island authorities to be signed by the *Kommandant*. He replaced the authority of the Crown.

Church Services continued. We were told that we could pray for the Royal Family and for the welfare of the British Empire, and as one Jerseyman remarked in a BBC interview, "letting us pray for our own people made me believe that the Germans didn't have much faith in the power of prayer."

The Bailiff respected the first Kommandant, Hauptmann Gussek as 'a no-nonsense officer'. He dealt with matters promptly, and without a mass of paperwork. After the establishment of the administrative *Feldkommandantur*, he visited Coutanche before leaving the island. He said: "Now the paper war begins!" He was right. The mass of correspondence between the Bailiff and *Feldkommandantur 515*, which survives in the archives, is ample testimony to the accuracy of his prophecy.

✳

Slowly, our lives began to change. Things we had taken for granted vanished or took new shape. Cars disappeared. Public transport was almost non-existent, and when available ran on charcoal gas. Later, the buses disappeared altogether. Soon, many taxis, hearses, ambulances and similar forms of conveyance were horse-drawn. The humble bicycle became our main means of transport. We walked a lot too, and no doubt to begin with we were better for it. When the shops ran out of new bicycles, the cost of second-hand ones escalated and became exorbitant.

There was a run on chains and padlocks. Bicycles were a prime target for thieves. Later, when puncture outfits and tyres too ran out, we replaced the tyres with old hosepipe pulled tightly round the rim and held with wire. When brake pads wore away the only alternative was a foot in the spokes of the front wheel. I have a vivid recollection of a hair-raising ride with Basil Le Brun down the steepest part of Queens Road to Rouge Bouillon, with Le Brun on the saddle and myself sitting on the handlebars, the heels of my wooden-soled shoes jammed tightly into the spokes in a futile attempt to slow us down.

In the autumn of 1942, during protest riots, which took place when the enemy deported hundreds of Islanders to camps in Germany, I lost my bike. I was arrested, but managed to escape. It was a serious loss, but sometime later I passed a German billet near the Opera House, in the blackout, and through an open door saw a bike parked in the hallway. There was no sentry. The owner was occupied with other soldiers upstairs and a radio covered any noise. I sneaked in and stole it, and hared off in the dark to the Le Bruns' farm where I was able to disguise its military origins with parts from another old bike. The Gestapo traced me later and I was picked up again.

As far as I know, the *Geheime Staatspolizei*, the Secret State Police, or true *Gestapo*, were never in the Island, but the *Geheime Feldpolizei*, or Secret Field Police – 'The Gestapo of the Army' – were present throughout the Occupation. As in other occupied territories, they were always known as the *Gestapo*, whichever they were, and I shall continue to refer to them as such.

As the war years slowly passed and we grew towards adulthood, our thoughts and needs became the same as those of our generation in other parts of the world. Girls became important. The blackout was not totally without advantages.

Early in the war I cycled everywhere, particularly with Charles Gruchy. We were still at Victoria College then and often rode out to Vinchelez to meet Philippe Alexandre to go swimming at Grève de Lecq. We could still get to most of the beaches in the first year or two, and I remember our boyish excitement one day when a Blenheim flew over as we dunked ourselves in the surf below.

As the months lengthened, food became our main preoccupation, but I can't remember being really ravenous until the winter of 1941-42. The first shortage I remember was when chocolate and then sweets disappeared from the shops. The first German troops went on a shopping spree with 'Occupation Marks'. Deprived of many luxuries for so long at home, they bought up everything they could find and, among other things, stuffed themselves with our chocolates and sweets! It wasn't long before the *Kommandant* had to limit what they could buy. For a while we found cough sweets at the Chemist, and several of us developed a sudden liking for tubes of sweet, condensed milk.

As the months passed, our clothes began to wear out. The shelves and hangers in the shops soon emptied and weird and wonderful garments began to take their place. The States opened a clothing factory and a workshop, for making and repairing shoes with whatever material was available. Mother was a good needlewoman. She also had an old-fashioned but reliable Singer sewing machine. Vicarages are not wealthy places and in the years before the war, with a large family to provide for, she had learned thrifty habits. Now she put her skills to good use. She turned frayed collars. She patched shirts and trousers. She made new garments out of old ones. As my brothers and sister grew, clothes were handed on, or enlarged. She was particularly skillful at putting gussets in the seats of trousers – usually to the accompaniment of suitably ribald remarks. She unwound old woollen garments to reknit the yarn into something new. For grown-ups, like my father and Charles Duret Aubin, the Attorney General, the problem was not getting bigger, but shrinking. Both had been large men before the war. Both lost a lot of weight. Mother never threw away bits of cloth she removed, and she put old blankets and curtains to good use.

When leather and rubber ran out, shoes were made or repaired with bits of old car tyre or wood. Wooden soles clattered on the pavement and were hopeless for trying to sneak about after curfew. I often sidled home with my shoes in my hands. To begin with, it was like walking on stilts, and there were quite a few sprained ankles.

For a time, when I lived at the Le Bruns' farm and worked as a labourer, I wore wooden sabots stuffed with straw, like the old-time French peasant. Clacking down the road one day in my filthy, patched clothes, with several days' growth of beard, and leading four cows on chains, I passed a platoon of soldiers and overheard one mock as he laughed at me: *Das ist kein mensch* – That isn't human.

One of my father's parishioners – a kindly, retired Indian Army officer, Colonel Montgomery – emptied his old, leather, travelling trunks for the benefit of the vicarage children. For a long time I wore khaki army trousers, and in the winter, khaki woollen mittens. The mittens helped to keep my fingers warm when chilblains became a problem. With lack of food and heating in the winter of 1941, our toes and fingers itched incessantly. An old wive's tale said that soaking them in urine was the answer. Many tried it, but it never seemed to work for anyone I knew. One chilblain on my heel ulcerated and almost reached the bone. Even when it healed, the scar was tender for several months.

Like most youngsters growing up before the medical profession discovered the link between smoking and cancer of the lung, we puffed away whenever we could, but cigarettes and tobacco were strictly rationed, and when supplies ran out altogether, we smoked almost anything. For several months, the correspondence columns of the *Evening Post* were full of letters describing what the writers were currently using to still their craving for tobacco. Mainly from the hedgerow, the various weeds and herbs 'smoked hot' and tasted foul. Michael Ginns told me that coltsfoot, a plant of the daisy family, is a depressant and can cause delusions. His late father-in-law was hospitalised for a while after smoking it and turned to other leaves, including blackberry, for relief. Later, in 1944, when I lost my pipe at sea during a failed escape, I had to smoke 'cigarettes' in prison. After 'good morning', and 'good night', the first Russian words I learnt were for tobacco and cigarette paper. 'Tobacco' was anything we could get hold of and looked as if it would burn. Paper came from an old King James edition of the Bible. It was suitably thin for the purpose. To eke out the short supply of matches, I became highly skilled at cutting them lengthwise with a razor blade, which I kept hidden in the sole of my shoe. I also had a penknife. During searches I hid it somewhere very private.

For some unfortunate addicts, the comfort of smoking was as important as food, and the search for tobacco, or an acceptable substitute, loomed large in their minds. Though not addicted to that extent, I had a reliable source in the early years. Arthur Le Rossignol and his father kept a tobacconist shop opposite the market in St. Helier. When I left school towards the end of 1941, and worked as a clerk for a lawyer, Advocate P.J. Richardson, in Hill Street, one of my jobs was to go round town with the *rentes* book. I always made time to call on Arthur for a quick chat, and he never failed to find me something to smoke when I was too young to get the official ration. By the time I was old enough, Murphy's Law was in operation. It was too late. The ration had run out. And I was in no position to apply for it anyway.

For a time, the Le Bruns grew tobacco and we cured it in an old tin shed behind the stables at Beauchamp, where we also dried the haricot beans. It was processed at Germain's Tobacco Company and the States of course didn't miss a trick. Even under those conditions, they levied their share of *Impôt*.

Green tobacco plants contain dangerous levels of nicotine and we were not always as patient as we should have been when curing and maturing the leaves. I was sitting against a wall in the grounds of the hospital one day, talking to some nurses, when I felt my pulse take off and I passed out from smoking green tobacco.

Unauthorized sales of food and other luxuries flourished while they lasted. Rumour had it that an elderly lady approached a policeman and asked the way to the black market. I like to think it was true. Prices soon became exorbitant and eventually astronomical. Rich people could afford their little extras, but prices were soon too high for the poor and less well off, and vicarages are in that group.

It wasn't long before a barter system started. An advertising column appeared in the evening newspaper. Inevitably, before long it too was controlled by regulations. A typical advert read: 'Pair of man's shoes, brown, size 8. For what?' All sorts of things that would have been valueless in normal times were swapped or sold. Our dentist, Mr. Price, pulled teeth in exchange for eggs.

The Jersey authorities soon realised they would have to import most essentials from France and that they would need money available over there. Understandably, the French weren't falling over themselves to sell things they needed at home. Early in the Occupation, with the usual Island income from tourism and farm exports reduced to nothing, the States requisitioned civilian cars and sold them to the Germans to make some money. It was a wise, pre-emptive move. It was not a form of collaboration, as some ill-informed critics still claim. The cars would have been commandeered anyway in time. However, in 1940, most of us believed it was German-inspired, despite what we were told, and it seemed to those not-in-the-know a gross violation of the German promise to respect our property. With the proceeds, the States sent a buying commission to France and, at least until the start of the siege, some essential imports reached the Island. It should not be forgotten too, that under international law, the Island had to pay the Germans for the costs of the Occupation. They needed every penny – or *pfennig* – they could get when the usual sources of revenue no longer existed.

For many years I thought incorrectly that for some peculiar reason known only to themselves, the Germans wouldn't let the States open a bank account in France. In fact, it was the French. According to a Guernseyman on the Purchasing Commission from that island, the late Raymond Falla, they insisted on being paid in cash. This was partly because many of his purchases were made on the Black Market: but also because a States of Jersey bank account in France would have counted as a British-owned asset and would have been liable to confiscation. The money was taken over in one of the barges that sailed between the islands and the French ports. In a cumbersome and somewhat risky exercise, the notes were packed in old tea chests, counted on arrival in France, and then stored in a hotel bedroom cupboard until they were needed!

Very soon, shortages of almost everything made our daily existence difficult. Getting fuel to cook and to keep warm became an increasing problem. Later, when the electricity supply gave out, candles were in great demand but in short supply, and in the winter, people went to bed at nightfall. There was nothing they could do in the dark. Bed was the warmest place. The birth rate rose!

Housewives saved fuel by using hay boxes to complete cooking started by conventional means, and used them later to keep the food warm. By 1944, many people took their meals to be cooked at the bakery.

The States opened a soup kitchen and communal restaurant. It was run by a Miss Fraser whose devotion to her work throughout the five years earned her a well-deserved British Empire Medal in 1945. At the beginning, she served thick soup in milk bottles for those who wanted to eat at home. Initially, it was mainly the poorer people who used her restaurant, but as food got scarcer many more in the town survived on Miss Fraser's 'bottled stew'. It was pretty thin by 1944.

Salt was rationed or unobtainable for long periods. Food was then cooked in seawater. It took too much fuel to evaporate the seawater for its salt. When most beaches were off limits and their approaches mined, the authorities delivered it in a cart, like milk, or we collected it from salt water distribution points.

Townspeople suffered most, even though they dug up every bit of spare ground to grow something – mainly potatoes. Lawns and tennis courts disappeared for the duration. There was more land for cultivation in the country districts and most people living in rural areas were farmers, knew farmers, or worked for farmers. They fared much better. Food soon became the focus of our lives. It influenced everything we did, especially after the invasion of France in June 1944, when nothing came into the Island for almost a year. If it hadn't been for the Red Cross, many of us would have died.

Chapter Four

GROWING UP FAST

"I wish to speak to the School concerning the College cap."

At that moment, the boy in front of me blew a tremendous fart. The Headmaster was not amused and, as I fell about consumed by peals of maniacal laughter, his face turned puce and I was blamed for both the interruption and its musical accompaniment. I left school in 1942 and recall the circumstances with some clarity. I had already had several run-ins with him and, though not actually expelled, the Headmaster made it abundantly clear that my presence was no longer desirable. To my mind, school had become a waste of time. It is hard to study and to keep interested when cold and hungry and there is no clear road ahead. I was later to regret my truncated education.

At the beginning of the Occupation, the school stayed in its own buildings at Victoria College and we used the playing field until October 1941 when the Hitler Youth took over. We were then banished to a school in Halkett Place – a dull, dim building about as inspiring as Brown Windsor soup. Strictly speaking, the new tenants of Victoria College were no longer Hitler Youth. They were members of the RAD, the *Reichsarbeitsdienst*, a labour corps which youngsters joined for a year between leaving the Hitler Youth and going into the armed forces. They wore brown uniforms, marched everywhere with shouldered shovels and drilled with proper weapons. They were among the first to work on the extensive fortifications, which eventually encompassed the Island. They were very young. Few would have survived. Most would have shared the same patriotic ideals that we did, distorted though they were by Nazi ideology. They would have been impatient to get into a proper uniform and, within a year, many would have finished up on the Russian Front.

Rumours persisted for a time that we would combine with the Ladies' College, as the girls' school was then known. Our hormones told us it was a good idea, but it never happened, even when their school was taken over by the OT, the Organisation Todt, for use as a hospital.

During the war, Father taught Scripture at Victoria College and with several friends who shall be nameless – since they later became eminent in the island – I did rather well in the terminal exams after seeing the questions on his desk. To be fair, none of us took the future too seriously at that time.

It was difficult for the school to keep staff. Several masters joined up or left in the evacuation. The College closed for a time in the summer of 1942, when the Germans took five teachers as hostages. They deported two to Germany.

At the end of a year in Halkett Place, and some time after my somewhat precipitate departure, the occupying authority gave the College buildings back, so those still at school resumed in happier and more familiar surroundings.

The *Kommandantur* made German compulsory in all the Island schools, but despite backing of the project by the Dame of Sark in her island, the majority of children in Jersey, and no doubt in Guernsey too, resisted learning the hated language with a patriotic fervour which now seems if not a little stupid, at least a wasted chance. Our own masters taught it, in the same way they had presumably taught it for years in the Modern Languages Department. There would have been at least a little long-term advantage in acquiring something more useful than *Achtung minen*, or *Rauchen in kino ist verboten*. Or such vulgar expressions as 'Shit in your socks'.

Those who stayed at school had to put up with worn textbooks, shortages of paper, and stubs of pencils when ink ran out. I was told that, in some schools, they used slates again. School uniforms disappeared, including the dreaded College cap, which had precipitated my downfall. The Headmaster, P.A. 'Pat' Tatam – with whom I shared a mutual disrespect, was not an understanding man, and when regulation clothing disappeared from the shops, he had to placate several irate mothers before he realised that his pupils would now come to school in whatever their parents could find for them. Until then, he often held an 'inspection parade' after morning break. Michael Ginns was among the first to substitute a blue cricket cap for his regulation College cap, after having ruined it by using it to fish some whitebait out of a rock pool. As he remarked: "Food came first. Never mind the cap"

I must be fair to Pat Tatam. He displayed considerable courage. Throughout the Occupation, many anonymous letters from informers were incorrectly addressed to the *Kommandantur* at Victoria College, instead of at Victoria College House. The latter was the boarding house before the war. The Germans commandeered it as the headquarters of *Feldkommandantur 515*. Pat steamed open any letters that landed on his desk, and managed to give several victims at least 24 hours warning of an impending raid.

Food supplies continued to dwindle rapidly, especially in the town, and by the winter of 1943-44 children often took a potato to school for lunch. There was no mid-morning break. While there was fuel for the stoves, they baked their potato during morning lessons. When there was no fuel, they usually went hungry. In winter, they took blankets to school to keep warm. I remember sitting in Father's study one evening, my hands and feet like blocks of ice, trying to concentrate and to get that night's homework done before they shut off the electricity supply.

Growing up under German rule deprived us of many things young people take for granted, but it had advantages too. We made our own amusements. Television didn't exist, and for most of the war the Germans confiscated our radios. The local library and amateur dramatics took their place, and there were some superb stage productions. Dramatic clubs sprang up all over the Island and they went to endless lengths to get or to make authentic looking props, including very realistic suits of armour. Extensive reading helped to make up for my shortened time at school. I haunted the *Bibliothèque Publique*, and spent hours devouring everything I could get on astronomy, history, and such diverse topics as Islam and the 'British Raj'.

It was considered unpatriotic to see German films at the cinema. Having to look at German newsreels was bad enough when we saw old English and American movies, as we did, over and over again, but I was lucky enough to see many good German films – without suffering the opprobrium of my fellows – from behind the screen at the old Opera House. There, the film was projected onto the back of the screen and not, as is more usual, beamed down over the heads of the audience. I knew several of the stagehands and spent many evenings in their company. If we weren't playing cards, we looked at the movie, which always had sub-titles. Not many were propaganda films. The Germans would soon have got bored themselves if they had been. There were many good productions with first class acting, and with no political or racist content whatsoever. They were far superior to much of the rubbish put out by Hollywood.

In the early years, we youngsters seemed to have enough energy and time for sport and similar activities. The Medical Officer of Health stopped them when he began to worry what too much exercise might do to undernourished bodies. With the benefit of hindsight and medical training, I believe they went on far too long, but there was little else to pass the time and I don't think there were any lasting ill-effects. They probably kept the more restless spirits out of trouble for a little longer.

On a Sunday evening, we often played mixed hockey on the beach at Grève d'Azette. The tide goes out a long way there and the sand is firmly packed. A couple of coats, or a pile of seaweed, were used at each end for goal posts, and when the pitch got churned up we just moved along the shore. The girls proved more violent than the males and I had more injuries then than I ever got from playing rugby later on.

Cut off as we were from Britain there was no School Certificate Examination or Matriculation, no way to qualify for entrance to a university. To many of us it seemed futile to work for something unattainable and we left school. However, the Island teachers set an examination for those who stayed. They marked the papers and stored them until the war was over and the Oxford and Cambridge

Boards recognised them retrospectively.

My first job after leaving school was in legal chambers. My father hoped I would eventually study law and Advocate P.J. Richardson employed me as a clerk, at five shillings and sixpence a week, in his Hill Street office. Much of the work was in French. I wrote out contracts, and typed letters with two fingers, and sometimes went with PJ to Court, or looked up references for him in the law library.

Advocate Ogier had chambers in the same building. The Ogiers were family friends and Mr Ogier was one of father's churchwardens. They often visited the vicarage with their son, Dick – a large, gangling, happy, inoffensive sort of person with, I believe, some minor degree of intellectual impairment. It was no defence when he insulted a German officer, and a later search of the house revealed a map of the fortifications. His father had to share the blame. He was charged with harbouring a spy! They were transported to the notorious Fresnes prison in Paris to await trial for espionage. Dick was sentenced to a term of imprisonment and survived. His father was reprieved on the grounds of ill health and returned to Jersey. Once in the German prison system, however, it was hard to get out and he was deported to Biberach in July 1943. He was again taken ill and died in Ulm Hospital. His remains were cremated and his ashes returned to England with a party of sick and elderly exchange prisoners. Michael Ginns' mother was matron of the camp hospital at Wurzach and was on hand when the Gestapo searched the repatriates' luggage. When asked what was in the box, she replied: "Cremated human remains. Would you like to look?" – "No thank you, I'll take your word for it," was the polite reply.

By the winter of 1941-42, stores of food put by for harder times had nearly all run out. Until then, people used them to supplement the weekly rations, which got smaller month by month. Supplies from France became increasingly irregular and more uncertain and I began to feel real hunger. One day, when working for PJ, I repaired to an outside toilet behind the office after a scrap of food for lunch, and for the first time cried with hunger. Things got worse. Much worse.

I didn't last long as a law clerk. I wasn't cut out for office work and about then Captain Sowden started a nautical school. He had to be careful and could not let it seem at all military or in any way threatening to the Germans, because he had already been in trouble early in the Occupation. When Master of the *SS Normand*, he refused to carry ammunition for them. They first threatened and then arrested him in St. Malo. Then they took away his command. He lectured to us on navigation and seamanship, and taught us how to knot and splice. I can still remember disjointed chunks of the *Rule of the Road at Sea* in verse.

✳

Learning navigation and seamanship inevitably raised the possibility of putting it to practical use and I pored over charts, tide tables and the *English Channel Pilot*. I studied maps of the south coast of Britain, and worked out possible landfalls. My memory for that part of the Occupation is patchy, but it was then I joined a group who planned to escape, and was betrayed. Not to the Germans fortunately, but to the Island authorities. I didn't contact them again when I was back in circulation. It would have been too late anyway, even if it had been safe to do so.

I had been given the difficult task of finding petrol and asked help from a member of St. Mark's choir who worked in a garage. I thought I could trust him, but he told the Attorney-General and my father. I refused to say who the others were and they confined me to an upper room in the vicarage for a couple of weeks. A Jersey policeman patrolled the road outside for several days but, eventually, they had to let me out. I was made to give my word not to try again, but didn't feel bound by such a promise. It was given under duress.

Escape from a heavily fortified island needed careful planning. There were several basic problems to overcome before you could even think about setting out. The first and perhaps the most difficult was to find a seaworthy boat. The waters around the Islands are among the most dangerous in the world. On spring tides, the sea level rises and falls as much as forty feet. At certain times of the year, when wind and tide combined, water overflowed the old harbour and, if not prevented, swept up Conway Street and Mulcaster Street into town. Workmen built sandbag levees to keep the water back.

You had to find a safe place to work on your boat, to caulk it and make it waterproof, and if possible to paint it a dull colour. You needed a reliable engine and a good supply of petrol. You had to find a gap in the German defences at a point where you could get the craft into deep water and navigate it between the rocks and other hazards to the open sea. You needed some form of transport to get the boat to the shore and helpers to lift it over the seawall, or to carry it over the sand or between the rocks to where she would float. You had to do all this in complete silence, and with a constant watch for patrols.

Getting petrol wasn't easy. Sometimes it could be siphoned from enemy transport, as Peter Crill – later Bailiff of the Island – and his companions John Floyd and Roy Mourant did; or it could be stolen from one of the enemy fuel dumps or bought on the black market. But all such methods were dangerous.

You needed food and water for a journey of unknown length and time; and a compass and bailer; and some form of communication, such as a torch, to signal with. In 1944 we took a bugle!

The sea demands respect. You needed to know as much as possible about tides and currents when such a large rise and fall in sea level can generate currents of seven or eight miles an hour. As Harbourmaster, Captain Bullen, wrote in his introduction to Roy Thomas' book, *Lest We Forget*, such knowledge could make the difference between going in the right direction, or going backwards. Several escapes failed because of this. As Captain Bullen also pointed out, a combination of low speed over a number of high and low waters, over a long distance, could also catch the unprepared or unwary. To escape from Jersey to France was difficult enough, but for the earlier escapers who had to go all the way across the Channel, it was very much more hazardous.

Another danger was a sudden change in weather. Two American prisoners of war left in fairly calm weather, and sailed into a blizzard and howling gale. Wartime security prevented the broadcast of weather forecasts by the BBC. The Germans weren't likely to give their advice.

On top of all the other difficulties, you had to choose the right companions and to ensure total secrecy. Great care was needed when dealing with other people. Finally, you had to think about how the Germans would react and what danger there would be to family and friends. The Nazis had already made it clear that escape was a form of sabotage, not to mention its obvious potential for espionage.

And tragedy was never far away. In May 1942, Peter Hassall, Maurice Gould and Denis Audrain tried to escape but their boat sprang a leak and it sank about two miles off the island. Denis Audrain couldn't swim and drowned. They had collected military intelligence to take to England, but failed to weight the document container before setting out. It was washed up and the Germans found it. They took Gould and Hassall to Paris where the SS and Gestapo gave them a savage beating. For a time they worked in a mine near Warsaw, before being moved to a prison at Trier to await trial. Maurice Gould died of malnutrition and tuberculosis. They took Peter Hassall to Breslau, court-martialled him, and sentenced him to death. His sentence was reduced to eight years hard labour. He was eventually freed by the Russians.

Recently, Maurice Gould's body was rescued from – of all places – an SS military cemetery, and returned to Jersey. He was reburied in his native island with full military honours.

✳

Early in the Occupation, I started going to the Le Brun's farm, Beauchamp, on La Grande Route de St. Jean. It became my second home. I went first with a group of other youngsters to work on the land during the school holidays; I was the only one to stick it out.

After many years growing other crops for export, the Islanders suddenly had to grow cereals again. Workmen restored long disused waterwheels and cleared streams, and old millers came out of retirement to grind the grain and to teach younger men their art. Before the war the main crops had been early potatoes and outdoor tomatoes and at first there was no machinery to cut the wheat. We reaped by hand. We advanced in a line down the field, bent double, wielding sickles, sweeping an armful of stalks to one side – sufficient to make a good-sized sheaf – and then cutting off the stalks near the ground. It was back-breaking work.

During 1941 and 1942 I went to the farm at weekends and in the holidays, and more and more I stayed the night, partly because I was tired and wanted to avoid cycling back to St. Helier before curfew; and partly because I knew I would get more to eat. Dolly Le Brun was English, a real Cockney, born within sound of Bow Bells. She had a generous heart, and when I didn't stay, always sent me home with a small gift of food.

In the town, conditions soon went from bad to worse; to find enough food for a growing family became more and more difficult for my parents. Vicars are not well paid for what they do, and black market prices were too high, even if dealing with black marketeers had not offended Father's scruples. Like many other women, Mother sacrificed some of her own rations for her children. She lost weight rapidly and always looked tired and ill. A burst appendix didn't help.

We had a pear tree in the garden at the vicarage and one day I was so hungry I ate an unripe pear. It was like chewing wood. It took a long time to soften and to swallow, and I was still ravenous after all the effort. Unrationed olives appeared in the shops for a time; when I could find the money I sucked them slowly as a substitute for sweets.

My parents had kept a bottle of Gordon's gin hidden in their bedroom cupboard. I realised too late that Father hadn't kept it to drink, but had put it aside to barter or sell in an emergency. By gently working the foil, I managed to take the cap off, drain the gin, and substitute water. When I replaced the seal, it looked untouched. Father never noticed and sold or bartered it later in the Occupation. I can only hope it wasn't to one of his own parishioners. With an early curfew, young people began to hold all-night parties – strictly in the Australian tradition of BYO – Bring Your Own – food as well as grog. We met at someone's house and partied on until the early hours, usually crashing just before dawn on the floor, or in any old chair that was available. Stocks of real booze had long run dry, but we could occasionally get rough cider – at a price – and even less frequently on the black market, a little very rough red wine. Some enthusiasts began to distil cider into calvados, the apple brandy of Normandy, but what the Normans would have thought of some of those brews, I shudder to think.

In time, as food became even more difficult to find, I moved to the farm and became a full-time labourer. It was hard work, but I got more to eat. I put on weight, but was still growing and still felt hungry. I wasn't alone. The Medical

Officer of Health, Dr McKinstry, kept measurements of children up to 14 years of age. Not only were they several pounds less than the average for their age by 1943, they were two to three inches shorter. I don't know what the figures were for 1944 and 1945.

On the farm I got three meals a day and, at about ten o'clock at night, Dolly always cooked a big pan of wheat porridge. It warmed us in winter, and going to bed with something in our stomachs did a lot for our morale.

✳

I went to town to see my parents and take them some vegetables as often as I could. It was a tiring climb cycling back in the dark and one night I was half-way up the steepest part of Queens Road when there was heavy anti-aircraft fire against some marauding RAF plane. I pedalled on for a while, hunched forward over the handlebars, but paused briefly to catch my breath and look up at the sky. There was a sudden whirring noise and a loud clang as a piece of shrapnel bounced off the cross-piece of my handlebars, just below where my head had been a moment earlier!

There was always some risk of being hurt by our own people, particularly after D-Day. Allied aircrew were usually careful to avoid targets near civilian houses, but one day in early 1944, I was cutting mangels in an upper field with Harry Miller, another labourer, when anti-aircraft guns near the farm opened up and we were machine-gunned by their target, an American plane which flew low over our heads, pumping away at the offending gunners and, it seemed, at us. We hurriedly threw ourselves to the ground. Harry was an old soldier from the 1914-18 War and long forgotten reflexes took over as he got down much more quickly than I did. Bullets cut a swathe through the roots and leaves and threw up large lumps of vegetable flesh and clods of earth, but we weren't hit. We recovered to see Keith Le Brun standing with a horse and cart at the entrance to the field, firmly clutching the bridle with one hand, while solemnly holding an old tin bathtub over the horse's head as he yelled at the departing aircraft, and pleaded with them that we were British, that we were friends, and should not be shot at. In the next field, a neighbour milking a cow was caught by the tethering chain when the frightened animal took off and dragged him round and round. He was soon soaked in milk and cursing even more volubly than Keith.

During the time I worked as a labourer, I learnt a lot about the island farms and the way they are run. Jersey farmers fertilise their fields with *vraic* – seaweed – at the right time of year, and at other times they use copious libations of *purin*, liquid manure. They collect the liquid in a tank under the manure heap and it contains all the 'goodies' that drain from whatever lies on top. Friends in

Normandy told us it would dissolve a whole German soldier and all his uniform except for the *Gott Mit Uns* metal buckle of his belt.

One day I had taken several loads of liquid manure in the 'shit cart' to one of the lower fields and the last load was a bit short. As I went down the road the liquid slopped backwards and forwards in the tank in perfect counterpoint to the undulations of the horse's buttocks. I was relaxed and looking forward to knocking-off, and probably inattentive. All would have been well, however, if our friendly, local anti-aircraft battery hadn't opened up.

Lummy was usually a placid horse but, as all hell broke loose, he bolted. We bounced off a wall. Then off another. I was sitting on the front of the tank where it joined the shafts and, as we gathered speed, I felt the liquid take on an existence of its own. Suddenly the shafts snapped and the horse went up in the air. We came to rest in the middle of the village soaked in the offensive liquid. The cart was written off and Lummy needed stitches in his bum. I stank for several days and Le Brun's father, Clarie, was not amused.

There were sometimes safe and simple opportunities to get some of our own back on the enemy and to gain a little amusement at their expense. At that age, they were seen by my adolescent mind as a major triumph. Sometime in 1942, we were ordered to deliver a load of potatoes to the harbour for – so we understood – direct shipment to Germany. It is possible, however, that they were destined for the German garrison in Guernsey, where the vast acreage of glasshouses caused great difficulty in growing enough potatoes for the civilian population, never mind for the occupiers as well.

They told us to deliver them in barrels and to have the load checked at the Weighbridge before emptying the containers directly into the hold of the ship. Determined that the Third Reich would benefit as little as possible from the fruits of our labour, we put good potatoes at the bottom of each barrel, added a second layer of bad ones half-way up, peed on them, and then covered them with more good ones. We reckoned that most of the cargo would be rotten by the time it reached Hamburg. And since we also managed to get the back legs of the horse on the weighing platform before unloading, they paid for the horse's arse as well!

Such episodes were neither dangerous nor useful anti-German measures, but they gave us tremendous pleasure at the time, and did much for our morale.

There were other happy moments too. Life was by no means always dull and without incident, but it was not only our side which showed a sense of humour. From the perspective of over fifty years it is easier to see many of those we hated so fiercely in a kinder, more tolerant light. In 1944, I shared a cell with Eddie Langlois. Today he, like me, lives in Australia and he told me recently of two Germans with such a happy attitude. They were a couple of ordinary men who, no doubt like us, were fed up with the war and the Nazi regime. Late in the Occupation, they came to his farm with authority to take a pig, and on reaching the sty in which a black sow was the sole resident, came smartly to attention, clicked their heels in the best Prussian manner, and gave the animal an impeccable "Heil Hitler!"

The thought of food, the need for food and the search for food occupied our minds and activities each day. In the end, no patch of land was left uncultivated. Nothing was wasted. Gleaning after the harvest could produce enough grain to make a few pounds of flour. With others we scoured the stubble for what little we could find. Mother ground it in a coffee grinder, and made cakes and scones, sweetened with saccharines when they were available. We made potato flour, sugar beet syrup, and carrot jam; and ersatz tea and coffee from various toasted leaves and roasted parsnips, carrots or sugar beet. With carrageen moss, a seaweed, Mother made a disgusting jelly that tasted of iodine. We never peeled potatoes or other vegetables and to this day I harbour a deep resentment if boiled potatoes are put before me with their skins still on.

One day in August 1942, we were working in a shed behind the farm buildings when we noticed a lot of coming and going on the road outside. Military lorries and motorbikes roared up and down, and soldiers ran around and dug slit trenches in response to bellowed orders, and generally looked excited and martial. News filtered through to us of the landing at Dieppe and our hopes soared. The Second Front at last, we thought. We'll soon be free! Total despair followed when the British and Canadians withdrew and German propaganda made the most of it. At the cinema to watch 'The Wizard of Oz' for the tenth, fifteenth, or twentieth time, we saw khaki-clad bodies, burnt out tanks and wrecked landing craft and once again the German news-reels subjected us to the sad spectacle of long columns of Allied prisoners on their way to Germany. Once again, I wondered if there were any young men of military age left in Britain.

We know now that Dieppe was just a raid, but at the time it seemed to us a major strategic disaster, a failed invasion. Fortunately, we didn't know that a similar disaster nearly took place on our own doorstep. It would have done if Lord Mountbatten, who then commanded Combined Operations, had been given his way. Code-named Condor, the plan began with heavy bombing of the east and west coasts of Jersey. Parachute drops and infantry landings would follow, and once beachheads were secure, 'tanks would land and the enemy be mopped up by the fifth day.'

Ten miles by five. It would have been a massacre! Even if the Island had been taken and held for a while, it would have been bombed and shelled mercilessly from the nearby French Coast. There were no underground caves or tunnels to shelter in. It would have made the siege of Malta look like a picnic. Wiser heads prevailed.

Occupation historian, Michael Ginns, commented as follows:

> In regard to Lord Mountbatten's commando raid on Jersey, Churchill was just as eager as Mountbatten that this raid should take place. It merely serves to underline what you say about "let 'em starve" (Churchill's remark when refusing to allow relief food supplies into the islands in 1944. See Chapter 13). Like you, I am sure that he included the civilian population in that statement, and I am not alone in this. As far as Winston Churchill was concerned, I feel if it had been necessary to decimate the civilians through military action, then so be it. The Mountbatten plan would have done it too! The 'wiser head' that prevailed was Air Marshal 'Bomber' Harris, who said that there were too many anti-aircraft guns in Jersey and he was not going to risk losing valuable aircraft on an operation that would have little effect on the outcome of the war.

As conditions deteriorated further, the Germans took steps to prevent food and other essentials being diverted from their clutches. The Island Government also had a duty to the civilian population to see that food was collected and distributed as fairly as possible. Instead of missiles, both civilian and military authorities bombarded us with new Orders. New rules and regulations came out daily, and were often amended or rescinded before the print was dry. Sinel commented in his Diary: 'Hitler once stated that he would introduce a New Order in Europe. Here in Jersey, we know what he meant – there is a new order every day!'

When the threshing machine came to a farm, a soldier always came with it to see that all sacks of wheat, or other cereals, were accounted for. It was simple enough to get him drunk, or to seduce him with the prospect of a good meal. Rumour had it that some farmers even made a special brew of cider, almost as strong as calvados, just for the purpose. Many of the German inspectors were countrymen themselves and not unsympathetic to our needs. A strict Nazi, or someone incorruptible, however, had to be diverted for a few moments by other means, and it was usually easiest to appeal to his Germanic sense of efficiency. A concerned expression, and a request for him to check the tally board again – 'To make absolutely sure there were no mistakes' – was all the time needed to slip one of the sacks out of sight and to smuggle it into hiding.

Early in the Occupation, a farmer could often 'liberate' some pork for his Sunday roast by cooperating with another farmer on the other side of the Island. Provided they talked in Jersey French, a *patois* that even the French find difficult to follow, they could arrange matters by telephone. The first farmer rang the inspector to say a pig had died. The inspector came out from town to certify the animal dead. As soon as he had gone, the carcass was rushed to the other farm to be certified a second time.

After a while the inspectors got wise to this trick and clipped or cut off one of the animal's ears. Later, livestock were branded or tattooed when first registered, and other means were needed to fool the authorities. Farmers reported litters short or that a pig or cow had been stolen, and the 'liberated' beast was hidden until slaughter, often in the most unlikely places. Some even found their way into bedrooms. But getting the animal to maturity was only half the battle. It had to be killed.

A pig about to have its throat cut squeals. The deed was usually done at night in some remote outhouse or, if possible, at least away from the main farm building. Civilian food inspectors, informers, German patrols and nearby garrison billets could all be dangerous. One way to ensure silence was to quickly shove a bucket of straw over the pig's snout and just as rapidly expedite its demise. According to John Lewis, there was one slaughterman well known for his way with animals, and for his complete discretion. He walked up to the beast, rubbed its back for a few seconds, and then cut its throat before it knew what was happening. He always took payment in kind. Then there was the matter of disposal. First, the carcass had to be scalded and skinned. Then cut up. All this took time, and everyone pitched in. Unwelcome visitors could appear at any moment.

Late in the war, when food shortages became even more acute, the Germans took to raiding farms without warning. They swept through whole parishes, looking for unregistered animals. Such searches were dangerous for those on the run, and I had to move my place of refuge rather quickly on one such occasion.

John Lewis, who lived just up the road from Beauchamp, told an amusing story in his book, *A Doctor's Occupation*. A farmer at Trinity had a pig hanging when a breathless lad arrived from the next farm to say the Germans were doing a sweep, and that they would soon be closing in. With admirable presence of mind, the farmer's wife got her husband to amputate the pig's forelegs, cut it down, and put it on the bed in the best bedroom. She covered the carcass with a white sheet, and sprinkled the room with Eau de Cologne. Then she pulled down the blinds and completed the scene of mourning by putting a small table at the foot of the bed with the Family Bible between two candlesticks. Precious bits of candle were sacrificed and lit for the occasion.

The soldier who opened the door was completely taken aback. He closed it as quickly as he had opened it, mumbling something in German which was probably an expression of condolence, but no one understood; particularly not the farmer's wife, whose collapse and tears stemmed from utter terror.

There were few refrigerators in those days, and those that did exist were unused – *verboten* — forbidden by the authorities to save electricity. The farmer and his friends quickly salted any illegal meat, if they had any salt, and hid it away. If not, they and their relatives and friends ate it as soon as possible. There was no answer to the final risk. There is no way to disguise the smell of roast pork!

Most farmers and their families ate reasonably well for most of the Occupation, but not always as well as townspeople thought, especially towards the end. However, my country friends never knew real hunger in the way the poor and most people in St. Helier did, especially during the worst shortages of the siege.

Soap and toothpaste disappeared early on. For a time, local pharmacists made substitutes, some of which were quite good. Then they ran out of ingredients. The Buying Commission imported soap from France. It seemed to consist mainly of clay and sand, and no matter how hard you tried, it wouldn't lather. It was not much better than a pumice stone.

With difficulty in finding fuel to heat water, and eventually rationing of water itself, getting clean and keeping clean became more and more of a problem, especially for those with dirty jobs. Water in household pipes had to be pumped from the reservoirs. Pumps use fuel. Early in the Occupation the authorities limited us to two inches of bath water. Few houses had showers.

It was difficult to wash clothes. Many people started to hum a bit. Skin rashes and infestations with lice and scabies were common, and we were lucky there was no outbreak of typhus in the civilian population. It did break out among slave labourers.

When there was no more toothpaste, we used salt or bicarbonate of soda when they were still available, and then soot from the chimney. I think the rationale for using soot was that chimney sweeps were supposed to have very white, healthy teeth. Whether such a claim is true, or it was only because their teeth looked exceptionally white in contrast to their blackened faces, I don't know, but having vigorously rubbed my teeth and gums with soot for several years, I try to forget its carcinogenic effect which gives rise to 'chimney sweep's cancer' of the scrotum!

With blunt razor blades and little lather, shaving was particularly difficult and painful. An enterprising shop in St Helier ran a sharpening service with some success, but my greatest relief came when I was hiding at Les Fougères, and Frank Le Calvez introduced me to the cut-throat razor. He showed me how to keep it sharp and how to use it without cutting my face to ribbons.

It is difficult for those who have never had to make do, or to do without, to imagine what life is like without all the things considered essential to everyday living. It wasn't just food and soap and toothpaste and toothbrushes and shoes and clothes that were in short supply, or unobtainable, it was the little things as well: buttons, needles, cotton and thread, string, shoe laces, pens and pencils, ink, paper, envelopes, matches, elastic, batteries and bulbs for torches, electric light bulbs, etc. etc. When batteries ran out we used carbide lamps. When toilet rolls disappeared we managed for a while with small squares of pink paper that I believe came from Guernsey and were cut from sheets usually used to pack tomatoes.

In the corner of the yard at Beauchamp there was an old two-seater toilet, and when the pink squares too ran out, and the *Evening Post* shrank to a size insufficient for the family needs, we kept a pile of dock leaves outside the door. They were fine. Provided it hadn't been raining!

Michael Ginns tells me that fig leaves or mallow are a better substitute, and that is the reason many old Jersey houses have a fig tree lurking in the garden. Nearby, there would have been a *petite maison*, as a *vrais Jerriais* would have called it. Nowadays, wealthy tax dodgers from England often call their converted cottages *La Petite Maison* and wonder why the natives fall about laughing.

As well as the Le Brun brothers and Harry and I to work the farm, there was a cowman, an old Frenchman called Ted Matré, who for some unknown reason was known as Tits. Ted had been a *Poilu* in the First World War and was still wearing parts of his uniform in 1942. We reckoned they had never been taken off since 1918, except possibly once a year in spring, probably on the anniversary of his birthday, when he hung them on the line for a day to have a good blow through. Ted had ankylosing spondylitis, a frequently progressive disease that afflicts the spine and, if untreated, leads to increasing flexion of the back. Ted was bent so far forward that he was almost doubled over and could look backwards between his legs. He was the only man I ever knew who could lead a Jersey bull by a chain from in front without risking severe injury.

Ted had a good turn of phrase. In French, of course, but always colourful. When the *tas de fumier* – the manure heap – succumbed to its annual emptying, the two-seater communicated with the base of the heap via a short tunnel and became exposed at that time, at low tide so to speak, so that it could be cleared with one of those long implements French bakers use to extract loaves from the back of deep ovens.

Poultry love to fossick on manure heaps, and Le Brun and I were working in the yard one day when we heard an almighty roar from the toilet, followed immediately by the door flying open, and Ted appearing, red in the face, his French Army trousers at half-mast, howling obscene imprecations as he stumbled across the yard, closely followed by an irate cockerel which, finding the tunnel clear, had wandered in, flown up and pecked him on the arse.

I would probably have stayed at Beauchamp until the end of the war and never done medicine if I hadn't fallen in love. One day in late autumn, we cut back a hedge bordering the field across the road from the farm buildings and I got a thorn in my left middle finger. I pulled it out, sucked away a bit of blood and thought no more of it. That evening we were going to a concert in St. Helier, and as we went up to wash and change I said, "I'm too tired to have a proper wash, Mouse. Let's go."

I shall always remember his reply. "Go and wash, you dirty bugger. You never know when you'll end up in hospital." It was the only time he showed prophetic powers. I washed.

Halfway through the concert, I started to shiver and shake and staggered out. I made it to the vicarage with some difficulty, and from there Father helped me to the hospital. I had a streptococcal septicaemia, 'blood poisoning'. It was before the days of penicillin. There was only a limited supply of sulphonamides. They started me on a course of Prontasil, but I was still very sick when the tablets ran out and I might very well have died if Josie Mines, an Irish nurse from neutral Eire, hadn't sneaked up to the German floor and stolen some more.

During my time in hospital, one of the resident doctors, Ray Osmont, lent me a copy of a book called *Labrador Doctor*. I had never even thought of medicine as a career, but that book and daily dressings in Casualty after leaving the ward fuelled my interest in hospitals and, more importantly to begin with, in hospital workers. She was blonde, and very pretty.

Chapter Five

MEDICAL MATTERS

began to haunt the hospital and made various excuses for my presence. Almost overnight I had decided that one day I would like to become a doctor. How and when I had no idea. My parents could never find university fees and the money needed to live as a student, but somehow I knew something would turn up. It did. After the war, the British Government gave grants to ex-servicemen and women to help them back into civilian life. It paid the university fees, and my wife and I lived in some comfort, especially as she was able to work in the X-Ray Department of the Bristol Royal Infirmary.

As the war continued, unemployed Islanders risked conscription to work for the Germans. They had no right under international law to make us work on military projects, but there was nothing to stop them using us in other ways. In any event, they had already shown in France and other occupied countries that whenever they felt like it, they forced anyone they wanted into their labour organisations, and put them to work on anything they wanted done.

Unlike France, there is no *maquis* in the Islands. There was nowhere for a large number of *résistants* to hide. Those conscripted had little choice. They worked, or went to prison and their families starved. Few Islanders worked willingly for the Germans. Most who did work for them on non-military projects did so to survive, but many neutral Irishmen still in the Island did volunteer. At the time, I thought there was no way I would ever work for the Nazis except at the point of a bayonet, but over the years I have become much less critical of those Islanders who did. Mature reflection makes it obvious that family men in particular had no viable alternative. The States created a project which employed some of them to build a road in the north of the Island, La Route du Nord, but many bread winners remained out of work.

When surgeon Arthur Halliwell, ACH, learned that there were several young men who wanted to do medicine after the war, he took some of us on as 'medical students'. I had left the farm to convalesce, and instead of going back to Beauchamp, joined them.

We couldn't matriculate or pass any other form of university entrance examination, nor could we do the practical work needed to understand anatomy and physiology properly, but ACH and other members of the hospital staff gave lectures and lent us textbooks. Our first contact with patients – walking the wards as it used to be called – began with at least a modest theoretical knowledge of those subjects. What we lacked in science, we made up for with enthusiasm. We attended post-mortems. We did dressings in Casualty and assisted in the Operating Theatre. I used to go to the Limes Nursing Home to assist Claude Avarne, another surgeon. As far as the Germans were concerned, we were in an essential occupation.

Throughout the five years, there were desperate shortages of drugs and equipment. Anything worn out or broken couldn't be replaced. It was the pre-antibiotic era. The tragic results of untreated or untreatable infections were commonplace. When rubber gloves ran out, the surgical staff operated with bare hands.

There was only a limited supply of sulphonamides. They controlled some infections but many organisms are naturally insensitive to them, or quickly become resistant. There was a critical shortage of dressings and bandages and of all the other things needed to keep a busy hospital running. Sadly, we saw the full clinical picture of overwhelming and untreatable diseases in their inexorable progress towards death.

Without insulin, diabetics died. I remember a man who succumbed to the toxic effects of a fulminating sub-phrenic abscess, a collection of pus under his diaphragm, which followed surgery for appendicitis. Such abscesses are rare today. If they occur, they are treated rapidly with every prospect of recovery. I saw the same clinical picture later in my surgical career in Africa and Arabia, when patients arrived at hospital untreated after long journeys from up-country.

Dr Darling was Senior Resident Medical Officer at the General Hospital throughout the war. Just before the Occupation, Ray Osmont was studying at St. Bartholomews Hospital, Barts, in London. He was on holiday in the Island and failed to get out in time. He joined Dr Darling and they worked long hours under difficult conditions. They were always there when needed.

Poor nutrition gradually undermined the health of the population and lowered resistance. Infections became more vicious and less predictable in their outcome. There were several outbreaks of diphtheria and scarlet fever. Both are serious in normal times. Under such conditions, they were often devastating.

Throughout the Occupation, several doctors and other members of the hospital staff risked their freedom and lives to help escaped prisoners of all nationalities. The first care I got for my injuries after escaping from prison in 1944 was from Ray Osmont and physiotherapist, John Le Sueur.

Working in the General Hospital had advantages. Until the final winter of the war, it was almost always warm: not surprisingly, as the Germans had taken over one whole floor. Sometimes we got a little extra food, but not all sick people lose their appetites. It wasn't often. The greatest pleasure was to have a proper bath. Most of the time there was plenty of hot water, even if there was little or no soap.

We students all had girlfriends, often among the nurses, but as a group we got on particularly well with some Irish nurses who stayed on in 1940 when they could easily have left. They were from neutral Eire. They were not part of our war. To begin with they didn't consider the Germans enemies in the same way that we did, but when they saw what the occupiers did to people, especially to slave labourers, that changed.

Sometime in 1943, we made friends with a Czech who told us that he was a medical student. He was a wild sort of fellow who had been conscripted into the German labour force despite his occupation. He had reasonable freedom to move around, and one night after curfew he robbed a German liquor store. There was a sentry at the front of the building, but he got in by making a hole in the roof. He lowered himself down a rope and liberated a whole crate of Cognac. We celebrated by renting a cottage at St. Brelade's for a long weekend and the Irish joined us. We had a great party, but it was strictly platonic. On Sunday morning, we walked with them all the way to St. Aubin so that they could go to Mass. I had a terrible hangover and the only thing I remembered from the night before was passing out from a surfeit of Cognac. I couldn't abide the smell of it for years, never mind drink it.

By today's standards, anaesthesia was still primitive in the war years. Towards the end of the Occupation the hospital began to run out of anaesthetics and any left were kept for essential operations only. Blood transfusions were much less common than they are today, but I saw at least one example of direct blood transfer from donor to recipient. They lay in beds side by side, their veins connected by a red rubber tube. The compatibility of their blood had been roughly determined by mixing small specimens from each on a white tile. To patients who were just dehydrated, the nursing staff gave frequent, small amounts of water by mouth, or a slow infusion of tap water into the rectum.

Towards the end, the Germans used paper dressings. They weren't available to the civilian population and we spent a lot of time during slack moments in Casualty rolling freshly laundered bandages. In those pre-antibiotic days, hospital staff was more aware of the dangers of getting infected, or of passing organisms from one patient to another. They were much more careful than their modern counterparts, who had to relearn the lesson the hard way when HIV Aids and hepatitis began to spread. In the pre-antibiotic era, nasty infections, amputated fingers, even death, were not uncommon among pathologists, surgeons and other staff who accidentally pricked or cut themselves during post-mortems, or when operating on or dressing septic lesions.

A thoughtless moment in Casualty showed me how dangerous carelessness could be. I replaced a dirty dressing, and on my way to the washbasin forgot for a moment what I had been doing, and rubbed an itchy eye with an unwashed finger. I developed a roaring conjunctivitis. It spread to the other eye. The only treatment was stinging silver nitrate drops and I lay in bed for several days.

In *A Doctor's Occupation*, John Lewis described his difficulties running a busy General Practice. Not least of his problems was to avoid being shot after curfew. On one emergency call at night he had a round through the back window of his car. Fortunately, the soldier concerned was used to drivers sitting in the left-hand seat. The petrol ration was soon cut to a minimum, even for essential services. In 1944, it stopped altogether. The only alternative for a busy a GP was to cycle or walk to see his or her patients. For a time, one enterprising lady doctor who lived in Val Plaisant visited her patients on horseback!

When the Germans commandeered large parts of the General Hospital, the Health Department decided to use a small cottage hospital on the outskirts of St. Helier, the Dispensary, as the new Jersey Maternity Hospital. According to Dr Lewis, who was put in charge, many admissions were 'in poor shape.' He found that several had puerperal fever – a dangerous contagious septic condition which spreads easily from mother to mother and which can be lethal to both mother and infant. Sulphonamides were unsophisticated and in short supply. There was no such thing as penicillin.

There is no doubt there were many babies born to Jersey girls from German fathers. However, Dr Lewis puts the absolute maximum at 100 over the five years, and some had more than one. He was in a better position than anyone to know but it is always difficult to estimate that sort of thing and to refute outrageous claims. A Ghanaian Nursing Sister once told me why inheritance of tribal status in their society is through the female line. She said "you can always know for certain who the mother is, but you can never be sure about the father."

No doubt also, some babies with German fathers were attributed to local men, and vice versa. As John Lewis wrote: 'The locals did not abdicate from all sexual activity for the duration.' Foreigners, who volunteered or who were forced to work for the Germans, were also free to meet local girls socially in their spare time, and many of the volunteers were very well paid. Later, some married their girlfriends of the time and still live in the Island. But scandalous claims by the British Press show how readily they distort the truth to make a story.

Such a perversion of the truth occurred in 1945 when Peter Curwood, Hugh La Cloche and I were approached by reporters and filmed for one of the news-reels. I doubt this saw the light of day, never mind reached a cinema screen, but one of the London Sunday newspapers took three different stories, combined them into one, and put our names at the top. Among other things, we were credited with blowing up the Palace Hotel, a building I had been in only once, and that unwillingly, much earlier in the war. Out for a walk with friends one evening, we wandered by mistake into the hotel grounds. Somehow we didn't see the sentry, and he didn't see us until we were well inside. We were arrested and questioned. Halfway through the interrogation, I remembered that I had incriminating papers in my pocket. They included a photograph of some military installations. I pleaded an urgent need to go to the toilet and fortunately the guard who took me let me close the door. I flushed away the evidence. In the event, they didn't search us, but I was badly frightened. They released us soon after with a warning not to trespass on military property again.

Shortly after the war, a British reporter asked John Lewis how many babies had German fathers. He gave the figure suggested above. He was upset when the number was distorted to 400 babies for Jersey alone. He thought that was bad enough, but a few days later a major London Daily claimed the true figure was three thousand; a thousand more than all the babies born in all the Islands during the Occupation.

Such newspaper stories must take much of the blame for the suggestion that there was widespread collaboration by Islanders. With the recent release by the Public Records Office of secret intelligence transcripts dating back to 1944, the Press has once again distorted the figures to an alarming extent, largely, I believe, on the unsubstantiated evidence of a few of the young men mentioned in the secret papers who had just escaped from the Island.

During those years, most of us accepted all sorts of terrible judgements, which were just not true. Innocent women were called Jerrybags. Loyal men and women were condemned as collaborators or informers without any evidence. Many times, when our own civilian authorities issued an unpleasant regulation, the reason for the order itself was conveniently forgotten, or considered the fault of some poor official who had no control over the matter whatsoever. Living and surviving as we did, in an emotionally charged and hostile environment, it is not surprising that States officials in particular – but almost anyone else as well – were considered fair game, especially if they were, or seemed to be, better off than we were. Such nastiness is not unknown even in peace time in small, relatively closed communities. The Channel Islands are no exception. Their own historians have long accused the inhabitants of being some of the most litigious people in the world. How this 'island madness' can intensify under stress is well illustrated in the fictional autobiography *Ebenezer Le Page*, written by G.B. Edwards, a man who himself experienced the Occupation in Guernsey.

✳

Pharmacies soon ran out of all essentials. There was little chance to restock from France or Germany, but a Gestapo search for anti-Nazi literature in the library of the Guernsey branch of Boots the Chemist had a fortunate if temporary result.

According to the Woods, they confiscated over a hundred books, but their interpreter had worked for a Hamburg drug wholesaler in civilian life and recognised their difficulty. For a while, he managed to get at least some supplies of new stock by taking money when he went on leave, and arranging for the drugs to be sent directly from Germany. £50,000 worth were imported in this way and distributed in all the Islands. He was an honest man. On his first leave, he was given Occupation Marks. They were useless in Germany. He took the train to Belgium during part of his precious furlough and changed them into Reichsmarks. Despite an obvious commercial advantage to the firm he worked for before the war, and would no doubt like to return to when it was over, his actions can only be described as decent and cooperative.

The greatest tragedy due to the shortages of medication was on insulin-dependent diabetics. Many took the advice of their doctors and evacuated in 1940. About 30 stayed. All but one died.

The Medical Officer of Health, Dr McKinstry, tried repeatedly, but with little success, to get insulin and other essential drugs through the Red Cross. When he realised insulin was running out, he admitted all the diabetics to hospital for strict bed rest and a carefully controlled diet. One by one, they went into coma and died. At the time Dr Lewis wrote his book in 1982, the survivor was still living, but Dr Lewis didn't mention his name. Recently, I saw a BBC programme in which Maurice Green – whose father survived Buchenwald – told how a German soldier gave him insulin. The soldier's mother was diabetic and he had scoured Occupied France for insulin, only to be told when he found some that she had been killed in an RAF raid on Hamburg. He arrived weeping at the Greens' house, thrust the insulin into Maurice's hands and left, still weeping, and without giving his name.

During the Occupation, obesity became a thing of the past, though a few managed to stay somewhat larger than the rest of us. Two of those were the Chief Surgeon and Chief Nursing Officer of St. John Ambulance, an organisation which, strangely, since they suppressed everything else, the Germans not only allowed to continue, but let its members wear their distinctive black and white uniform throughout the war.

In late 1944, an anxious population waited for the Red Cross parcels to arrive. When they didn't turn up as expected, a joke went round St. Helier that the boat had been delayed because when it neared the Island the captain, through his telescope, had seen these two large people waiting on the quay and had turned back, remarking as he did so, "there are no starving people here."

John Lewis told of a patient who weighed 24 stone before the war. Multiple specialists in France and England failed to help. His excessive bulk was attributed to 'glands' and 'was nothing to do with his eating habits.' He lost 14 stone very rapidly!

Under such conditions, it was not surprising that resistance to infection was low. I wrote earlier of the infected chilblain on my heel that ulcerated almost to the bone, but all infections became more serious. Cuts and grazes took longer to heal. We all suffered on the vegetable diet from excessive wind, made more intolerable by painful attacks of colic, which could strike at any time and double the victim over in his or her tracks. The mixed smell of unwashed humanity, intestinal gas and home-grown or substitute tobacco was unpleasantly pervasive at times in public places.

Tuberculosis took advantage of the harsh conditions to strike indiscriminately. A soldier, who returned with the relieving force in 1945, found his wife had died of TB while he was away. It was difficult to control worms, skin diseases and the predatory attacks of lice, fleas and scabies without proper medication and with little or no soap and only a little rationed, unheated water to wash in.

It may be asked why water had to be rationed in an island surrounded by the sea and with adequate rainfall. The answer lay in the lack of fuel to work the pumps, which normally lifted water from the reservoirs into the domestic supply: and, as one would expect from Murphy's Law, just when we wanted it most, the rainfall decreased.

Dr Lewis described how, towards the end, swollen legs became common, and not just in the elderly. Gums became spongy and teeth loose.

More important matters took precedence after D-Day, but until then I continued to work in the hospital. I am grateful for what I was taught during that time. I am particularly grateful that I didn't have to work for the enemy. Most of us hated the Germans with a deep, dark loathing. Not because they were the enemy. Not because they had bombed us and taken away our freedom. Not because they were still killing and wounding our relatives and friends beyond the sea. Those things were important, but the main reason for that overwhelming hatred was something I can never forget and can certainly never forgive.

In some places, being in the Island during those years was like looking over a barbed-wire fence into a concentration camp. The slave labourers, those tragic victims of Nazi brutality and the way they were treated, were only too obvious. They were living skeletons. Some had bloody bandages. Others were covered with sores. They arrived in rags, many without footwear. Some with only a sack for upper body clothing, so that they looked as if they were wearing the pointed hoods of a monastic order. They were covered in cement dust.

They begged at the back door of the vicarage for the few scraps of food mother could spare. An Orthodox priest among them took my father to see the conditions they lived in. For many years his gift of an icon hung in Father's study. On the work gangs, which were in plain view of passing civilians, OT guards beat them and left them for dead. Near First Tower, I saw a man hit across the side of his head with a shovel. I told an Intelligence Officer about it after the war. I had the feeling he didn't believe me. Perhaps the most awful thing was the way ordinary-looking German soldiers laughed at them.

My hatred lasted several years and, as I wrote before, I am still afraid of what I know some Germans can do, but there are good and bad in every race and perhaps my eventual change of heart owed something to several sobering incidents at the hospital in the final stages of the war, as well as to a few simple acts of kindness from individual Germans.

Soon after the Invasion, we sat on the roof of the hospital one morning and watched an armada of Allied planes pass overhead. Suddenly a flight of Spitfires peeled off and dived to attack German vessels running for the relative safety of St. Helier harbour. We cheered and clapped as the attack went in, completely insensitive to the blood and anguish of those on the receiving end. Shortly afterwards, I had to go to the mortuary. The bodies had been brought in. There were about forty, stacked like logs of wood. They almost reached the ceiling on three sides of the room. They had the bloodless pallor of those who have died violently and in shock. Some were horribly burned. All but one were sailors, young men. The exception was a Luftwaffe pilot who lay on top of one of the piles by himself, as if disowned by his comrades. He was covered in dust and streaked with soil, but otherwise unmarked. Except for one eye. It lay like an oversized grape in the middle of his forehead.

From time to time, it has been my lot as a surgeon to triage and then look after battle casualties. The near dead and the dead all had the same look those Germans had. They too looked exsanguinated, bled out. They too were nearly all young men.

After the fall of St. Malo, wounded Americans arrived in the hospital, including one whose name was Malo. We slipped into their ward for a quick chat as often as we could – when the guards weren't looking, or were willing to turn a blind eye.

Soon afterwards, the German part of the hospital filled with the wounded and dying. The moans and screams were terrible. The fear was palpable. Over 200 arrived when the hospital was already full. There were beds and cots and mattresses and stretchers everywhere. The wounded lay in the corridors and anywhere there was a bit of space. There was little room to move between them.

Some died where they lay. Many died before they could be treated. It is impossible to feel hatred under such circumstances.

Michael Ginns told me how his late first wife, after sharing the same initial hatreds I felt, came to change her mind. She was deeply affected by all the wounded from St. Malo littering the corridors and stairs at the General Hospital, but never more so than when she looked out of a top window one day and saw an 18 year old German soldier being put out in the sun; he had no legs, and only one arm.

John Lewis also told how from time to time the German surgeons came out of the operating theatre and leaned or sat against the walls, drained by fatigue and the emotional stress of dealing with so many badly injured and dying men. Their surgical aprons were wet with blood. Their faces no doubt showed the tight skin and prison pallor that surgeons acquire after endless hours of strain – cutting, stitching, draining, dressing, putting on plasters, amputating. From time to time, orderlies took out big panniers filled with arms and legs. When they ran out of anaesthetics, fit soldiers helped orderlies to hold down their wounded comrades. The screams and moans increased. The most awful thing was that when Arthur Halliwell, a veteran of the Battle of Jutland, and other members of the Staff, offered to help the Germans. The German doctor in command, who was an out-and-out Nazi, refused. When a distressed Halliwell volunteered a second time and was once again rejected, he went home.

Dr Darling and Dr Osmont also offered their services, and were refused. However, Ray Osmont asked for and got permission to go around the German wards to see if there were any British, French or Americans among the wounded. He stuck his head round the door of a small ward at the top of the stairs on the first floor and called out: "Are there any British or Americans here?"

Back came an immediate reply: "God dammit to hell, I sure never thought I'd be so glad to hear a Limey voice!"

Chapter Six

DEPORTATION: A FIRST BRUSH WITH THE ENEMY

When we awoke on 15 September 1942, there was nothing to suggest it would be a day any different from the one before nor, for that matter, from any of the other 807 days since the beginning of the Occupation.

I can't remember what kind of day it was. But whatever the weather, it was a bleak day from every other point of view. I have a vague recollection that when the news broke I was in St. Helier and not out at the farm though, like Sinel, I do recall the wretched state of the Islanders, even those unaffected by the 'Proclamation' which appeared without warning in the *Evening Post*.

> NOTICE
> By order of higher authorities, the following British subjects will be evacuated and transferred to Germany:
> (a) Persons who have their permanent residence not on the Channel Islands, for instance, those who have been caught here by the outbreak of war;
> (b) All those men not born on the Channel Islands and 16 to 70 years of age who belong to the English people, together with their families.
> Detailed instructions will be given by the Feldkommandantur 515.
>
> *Der Feldkommandant;*
> *KNACKFUSS, Oberst.*

Equally upsetting was a second order that the first deportees would leave the next day. They had less than 24 hours to get ready. They had to get someone to look after their homes. They had to let employers or employees know that they wouldn't be coming to work – to make arrangements about practices and businesses; to sort out medical or family problems; to get in touch with their lawyers and bank managers; to give away pets or have them destroyed; to make arrangements for safe storage of anything valuable; to pack for whatever lay ahead. They did not know where they were going. They had no idea what sort of camp they would be in. Nor did they know how long they would be away.

There were several suicides. More predictable was that the Germans were now breaking the solemn promise they had made in 1940, 'to protect the lives, property and liberty of peaceful inhabitants.'

Our names weren't on the first list, but little did we realise then that I would soon be involved in an episode which would make my family prime candidates for a later deportation; a deportation which was largely made up of people in special categories: retired Army officers and Islanders who had fallen foul of the German authorities.

As Sinel wrote, the Islanders were in shock and people asked each other, "Why are they doing this?" There was no logical explanation. Rumours circulated that it was in revenge for the bombing of German cities and they were going to put us in the centre of target areas.

German propaganda had kept us well informed about the bombing of Britain, though it was less forthcoming about what was happening in the Fatherland. The troops on the other hand were less reticent. It was not uncommon to hear of Germans grieving or committing suicide after a whole family had been wiped out by *Terror-Flieger*.

Such unpleasant rumours were a constant feature of the Occupation. They were readily believed by many and, at the very least, intensified our general hatred of all things German.

The *Feldkommandantur* always referred to the Deportation as an 'Evacuation'. We only found out the real reason long after the war, when captured papers showed that, in late 1941, Berlin learnt that Iran was handing over Germans working there to the British. Britain wanted this potential Fifth Column well out of the way in case Rommel's Afrika Korps defeated them in the Middle East and made its way up through Turkey into the soft underbelly of the Soviet Union. Success in such a venture would have given the Nazis both the Iranian and the Russian oil fields. Hitler was incensed and ordered immediate reprisals. In particular, 'action was to be taken against the people of the Channel Islands.'

The *Kommandantur* ordered the Bailiff to give them a list of English nationals, of those born outside the Islands. To their amazement, they were also asked for details of any Iranians. They found a 69 year-old man who had been born in Smyrna. Somehow the Germans overlooked him and he stayed in Jersey, probably never knowing that he was in any danger of being sent away.

Hitler's orders clearly contained a punitive element. He demanded that ten selected Englishmen be deported from the Jersey Islands to the Pripet Marshes [of Byelorussia] for every German interned, and that they should include prominent British civilians; and in particular, 'Churchill's nephew', some unfortunate man with the same surname who was not even distantly related to the Prime Minister.

Hitler used the word Deportation. He said it should be made clear to the world why it was taking place and should be accompanied by confiscation of the deportee's property for redistribution to Jerseymen of French descent.

Cruickshank explained how the Führer's order worried the German Foreign Office. They estimated that, apart from Channel Islanders, they only held about 3,500 British internees. There were more than 18,000 German citizens in British hands. They were also concerned about what the Protecting Power would say. The Swiss Red Cross had access to the camps and would soon let Churchill know what was going on, especially if the deportees were treated badly.

The Pripet Marshes were on the Russian Front. The German Army would have had to build camps and find guards for the deportees. Not surprisingly, they didn't want to feed, house and guard hundreds of civilian prisoners close to fierce fighting in an active service command. It would have been the height of stupidity. However, graver dangers threatened our safety. By the time of the last deportation in February 1943, Hitler had put *Reichführer SS*, Heinrich Himmler, in charge and ordered him to take full responsibility for the prisoners. The consequences, if they had fallen into Himmler's hands, can be imagined. Fortunately, Hitler's order was somehow forgotten. Cruickshank wrote that, 'it was submerged in a welter of signals and paper work.' It came up again, but only briefly, as part of a study of potential security problems when Hitler began his plans to fortify the Island into an impregnable stronghold. On that occasion too, the Germans differentiated between English-born and Island-born people, as if the former were in some way more liable to be a problem for the garrison. According to Cruickshank, the whole affair was forgotten for a time, and probably would have been altogether if it hadn't been for a well-intentioned but unfortunate approach by the Swiss.

About ten months later, the Protecting Power tried to arrange an exchange of sick and badly wounded prisoners-of-war. Michael Ginns wrote: 'They wanted to balance the figures and asked if Channel Islanders could be included in the exchange.' When Hitler suddenly found out his order had been ignored, he flew into one of his well-known rages and declared that 'immediate steps must be taken to remedy the situation.' Though the Iranian problem had long been overtaken by other events, he again ordered the immediate evacuation of British subjects who were not indigenous Channel Islanders.

As Cruickshank pointed out, throughout the whole sorry episode both Hitler and the German Foreign Office failed to understand that there was no real difference between those born in the Islands and those born elsewhere. They persisted in the belief that the Islands were British colonies and retained the quaint idea that they were ruled by members of the English upper class and prominent Colonial Officers.

The Germans in the Islands, who had to organise the deportation, soon recognised that sending men only to the Fatherland would not make up the number they needed. Women and children would have to go as well.

Sinel pointed out that in fairness to the Germans and the *Feldkommandantur*, evidence suggests they were as puzzled by the order as the deportees themselves, and that a few were almost equally upset. They were being forced to dishonour the promise they had made in their surrender ultimatum of July 1940.

Michael Ginns pointed out that perhaps we should have expected something similar even earlier. The German sections of the *Evening Post* and the *Guernsey Evening Press* reported in 1941 that German nationals in the Middle East were being rounded up and put into internment camps in Palestine and hinted at reprisals. In his unpublished diary, the Reverend T. Ord of Guernsey, wrote: 'We fear that people in the Channel Islands will be the subject of these reprisals.'

It is said that many ordinary soldiers and sailors who had to carry out the deportation shared the same opinion as the *Feldkommandantur*. In a BBC programme at the time of the 40th Anniversary of Liberation, Ginns gave particular credit to a young German who came up to him on the boat and apologised for what was being done. The man was going on leave. He was about 22 years old and wore horn-rimmed spectacles. 'He spoke English, and was genuine,' Ginns told me in a recent letter. 'I thanked him, but did not respond at the age of 14 as well as I now think I should have done. Ridiculous as this seems, it still bothers me today.'

Place of birth is an indiscriminate and inexact criterion from which to select people for anything. An ethnic Jerseyman was deported to Germany with all his family because he had been born in England. He was described in those less tolerant days as illegitimate. To avoid gossip at home, his mother had gone to England to have her baby. Incredibly, and with true Germanic efficiency, they also deported a German whose parents were interned in Britain, in the Isle of Man. Cruickshank reported that even when *Reichführer* Himmler himself said that the man was a German, the German Red Cross was still fighting bureaucratic incompetence a year later, trying to get him out.

I am again grateful to Michael Ginns for more up to date information. He wrote: 'Cruickshank did not dig deep enough and follow the story through. The man's name was Martin Schultz. He had been born in London, and claimed British nationality. He was deported with his family to Biberach, where on February 24th, 1942, his wife gave birth to twin boys. On April 14th, Schultz and an older child were released. Mrs Schultz, who was English, followed with the twins on June 5th. They went to live with Schultz's stepbrother, Karl Bucholtz, in Baden Baden. It raises the interesting question of how Mrs Schultz was received by her new neighbours.'

Ginns continued: 'The family wanted to return to Jersey, but were not allowed to do so as OKW *Auslander Abwehr* (High Command of the Forces, Foreign Security) decided that Schultz had been in touch with the British Secret Service.

The German love of bureaucracy determined that their release was only provisional, while various authorities continued to argue over who should make the final decision about their disposal. It was not until September 1943, that higher authority decided that *Oberegierungsrat SS und Chef der Deutsch Polizei (Abt. 1V Gestapo)*, i.e. Himmler, was responsible. But even Himmler had to refer the matter to *OKW Auslander/Abwehr*, because of the military importance of the Channel Islands.'

Ginns raises another interesting question. Since Schultz was under 45 years of age, was he called-up into the German Army in 1944 when they began to scrape the barrel?

✻

The first deportees left on 16 and 18 September. Another group of 560 went on 29 September. Later deportations, in February 1943, were a reprisal for a commando raid on Sark, Operation Basalt, which took place on the night of 3 October 1942. Major Geoffrey Appleyard and a small raiding force of 12 commandos ran into five Germans and, according to their report, they killed four and took one prisoner. It was less than accurate. One source suggests it may have been deliberately untruthful, but there is no evidence that such was the case.

The German account claims an officer and four men were captured as they slept. Their hands were tied and, when they tried to escape, the officer was shot and stabbed to death. Two soldiers were wounded and got away. One died later. A third, Obergefreiter Klotz, escaped unharmed. They presumed the fourth was taken to England.

When Hitler heard about the raid, he was enraged, particularly when he learnt that the dead prisoners had been found with their hands tied. He ordered the immediate manacling of all Allied POWs. He also ordered that all captured commandos be 'treated as bandits and ruthlessly eliminated in battle wherever they appear.' This took away their protected status as prisoners-of-war. The Germans murdered many of them after they had surrendered.

There were serious consequences for the civilian population of the Channel Islands. Hitler ordered further deportations. According to Cruickshank, 'the categories to be deported were to include people who had offended against the German regime: communists and others politically suspect, work-shy people, young men without important work in the German sense, former officers and reserve officers, Jews and high-ranking Freemasons, people prominent in public life, rich men who were considered to be anti-German, and, finally, people on Sark not engaged in agriculture, and those living in the centre of the Island.'

The final, rather mysterious demand may have related to that part of Sark where the commandos took their prisoners. German orders were frequently obscure, especially those first promulgated in France. For example, if one regulation that barred civilians from within a certain distance of the coast had applied to Jersey, it would have left only a tiny area in the very centre of the Island for the population to live in; probably on the Le Bruns' property, in the main field behind Beauchamp.

On 15 September 1942, Sinel described how the Island was in chaos. The Germans summoned the Bailiff and Parish Constables to the *Feldkommandantur.* They were told about the order and told to distribute evacuation notices to those selected to go. The notice read:

In pursuance of Higher Command, British subjects are to be evacuated and brought to Germany.

You have to appear, therefore, on 16-9-42 not later than 4 o'clock at the Garage, Weighbridge, St. Helier with wife and minor children.

You have to take with you all papers proving your identity.

It is necessary to outfit yourself with warm clothes, strong boots, and provisions for two days, meal dishes, drinking bowl, and if possible with a blanket.

Your luggage must not be heavier than you can carry and must bear a label with your full address.

It is further left to you to place ready, for each person, a trunk packed with clothes to be sent afterwards, labelled with full address.

It is also left to you to take with you an amount of money not exceeding RM 10 in German notes for each person in Reichcredit notes.

All valuables (jewels) must be deposited as far as possible with the banks.

Keys of houses are to be handed over to Constables.

Should you fail to obey the order sentence by court martial shall be effected.

Der Feldkommandant;

gez, KNACKFUSS, Oberst.

Sinel refers to the great distress amongst Islanders and to some Germans who were unhappy at enforcing such deportations. Coutanche protested to Knackfuss. The *Kommandant* said it was a direct order from Hitler, and could not be disobeyed. Coutanche refused to let the Constables select the names of those to be deported and, with other members of the States, he threatened to resign. Fortunately for the Islanders, they did not carry out their threat. As Cruickshank pointed out, it would have left the population unprotected and at the mercy of complete domination by the military government.

There has been much unfair criticism of the Bailiff and of the parish Constables for delivering the deportation notices. Until she died, my mother would not accept that it was not an act of collaboration. John Lewis tells with evident satisfaction how when one Constable delivering an order asked, "Do you know who I am?" he received the reply, "I'm not sure of your name, but I think it is Judas Iscariot."

At first, the Bailiff refused to let the Constables carry out this unpleasant task but, when they told him that many of those who had to go lived in country areas and that the Germans did not know their way around and that those leaving had less than 24 hours to get ready, he reluctantly gave permission.

Those Islanders staying behind did what they could to help those leaving. Some families got their deportation notice in the middle of the night. They had even less time to get ready. Several witnesses agree that most of the deportees reacted with dignity and showed by their demeanour that they could put up with anything the Germans might do to them. Neighbour helped neighbour. People who couldn't afford to do so gave away shoes and warm clothes because they thought those who had to go would need them more. The Woods tell how women stayed up all night, mending and making children's frocks, pants and coats out of blankets and curtain material, and how Island officials and tradespeople combined to give the deportees a good send-off with hot meals, hot soup and rich and rare presents of tobacco and cigarettes. They went on to tell of an incident at St. Peter Port, which showed something about the harder times ahead. When a can of soup was accidentally knocked over, so that it lay in puddles on the rough quayside, some OT slave workers standing nearby were down on their knees in a flash, scooping it up in their hands. Other witnesses, who saw the deportees reporting to the Weighbridge, recall their dignity and cheerfulness, but there were some who were obviously distressed.

Crowds lined the roads to the harbour. Complete strangers, as well as relatives and friends, shouted words of sympathy and encouragement to those going. They booed and jeered at the Germans. The military were certainly out in force that day, but I can't confirm the truth of one account, which described how the Germans sited machine-guns at various points. I didn't see any myself, and I haven't heard of anyone who did. I suspect it was just another Occupation rumour. The more reliable Sinel told how some of the soldiers appeared shamefaced and didn't look anything like as cheerful as the people being deported. We did not see the brutal, aggressive herding of the deportees onto the boats as happened to the Jews and others rounded up for concentration camps, but our friends and relatives were taken away under guard. Neither they nor we knew their fate, nor did any of us know the reason for their deportation. We could only guess.

In the event, though they had to put up with harsh conditions and hunger when they first arrived in Germany, once they had settled into what were standard internment camps and had managed to organise themselves life became bearable, if extremely boring. The Red Cross soon supplied them with food parcels. They were better off than we were. Supplies were so reliable that until the last year of the war, when the siege cut off all communications, they often sent small parcels of food and cigarettes to relatives and friends at home in the Island.

The first deportees left on 16 September. They sailed in the *Minotaur* and *La France*. Because of the short notice, only 280 left and there was no overcrowding. Crowds formed on Mount Bingham, above the harbour, but there were no violent demonstrations. 460 more left on 18 September in *La France*, but another 300 were sent home. They were supposed to sail in the *Robert Müller*, a general cargo ship. It had just unloaded coal and Dr Shone, representing the Red Cross, protested to Colonel Knackfuss. Knackfuss, who was on the quay, agreed and they went back home. Some found their houses stripped by neighbours who hadn't expected to see them again.

As the crowd increased, the Germans closed off the main roads down to the harbour. We couldn't see what was going on at the Weighbridge, nor could we see the embarkation point on the quay, but we heard the deportees in the holds of the ships shouting and singing patriotic songs. These were echoed by those of us who watched. 'God save the King', 'Land of Hope and Glory' and 'There'll always be an England' thundered and reverberated across the harbour, sung in turn or together by those going and by those staying. There was an emotional outpouring of grief, of anger, and of frustrated patriotism. In such an atmosphere, it was not long before the crowd became sullen, and then dangerous.

The Germans became less and less patient in the face of continued insults and jeers. They moved us from place to place, using rifle butts and bayonets, but we knew the town better than they did and each time they moved us on we found a new vantage point. Again the crowd shouted and sang defiantly, and the singing went on long after the boats had left. I remember feeling terribly flat as the ships disappeared out of sight behind Elizabeth Castle. Many in the crowd cried openly.

In *Three Years Behind Barbed Wire*, Joan Coles describes the journey to Germany. At the Weighbridge, from their emergency supplies the States gave each deportee a loaf of bread, a tin of milk, a jar of paste, a slab of chocolate and, for adults, a packet of cigarettes. The deportees travelled in a small ship to St. Malo. Some were tied into their lifejackets by German sailors, 'who were considerate and sympathetic, especially with children and old people.' They travelled by train to Biberach-Riss, in Württemberg; not in cattle trucks, but 'in cramped but civilised carriages.'

Until the transport system broke down towards the end of the war, for most of the time they were in Germany they each received a Red Cross parcel every week. The parcels were intended to supplement the German rations, which by international law were supposed to be the same as those of military POWs and their guards. Joan Coles painted a word picture of life in an internment camp and gave a graphic description of some Jews who were lucky enough to be transferred from Belsen to the deportees' final camp, Schloss Wurzach; and there is a moving account of their liberation by Free French troops in 1945.

At the vicarage, we waited for our notice to be on the next boat, but nothing happened. Mother believed it was because we were too high up the alphabet, but there were many taken with surnames well beyond ours. Several authors mention three conscientious objectors who volunteered to go instead of a clergyman's family. We have no knowledge of it and do not think it was us. It could not have been because father was a clergyman that we did not go. The Reverend Atyeo, vicar of St. Luke's, went with his wife and son, Paul. Mr Atyeo died in Germany.

✳

It is still a great mystery why we weren't deported, and particularly why we were not included in the third batch which contained the recalcitrants who had already been in trouble. I was picked up by the *Feldgendarmes* and later by the *Gestapo*, after the second deportation on 18 September. It was a much less peaceful affair and could so easily have been a personal disaster. Moggy Hill was arrested in the rioting and deported at that time but, like me, Joe Mière, Hugh La Cloche and Dennis Le Cuirot were overlooked. Father was arrested at the time of the Canon Cohu tragedy, which I shall describe shortly, and he should have been a candidate too. The troublemakers who eventually disappeared to Germany included a few real petty criminals.

On that occasion too, crowds lined the streets. They filled the roads around the harbour and spilled onto Mount Bingham, which overlooks the quays, and once again they shouted and sang, and defiant chants echoed back and forth between the watchers and those being deported. "One two three four, who the hell are we for ... CHURCHILL." The Prime Minister's name was like a red rag to a bull, and infuriated German soldiers cleared Pier Road with fixed bayonets. One soldier hassled a young woman carrying a child and when he pushed her savagely against a wall, I punched him in the face. He recovered more quickly than I anticipated, or I was a bit slow, and he bayonetted me in the upper part of my right buttock before I disappeared into the crowd.

As it was pushed and prodded away from the harbour, the crowd became more angry and vocal and the Germans increasingly worried for their own safety when faced with such angry numbers and such obvious hostility. They reacted accordingly. Carried along on a high by the inflamed emotions, which take over the minds of rioting crowds and provoke them to uncontrolled and uncontrollable violence and madness, we spat and cursed at some Luftwaffe officers outside the Barra House Hotel. Three or four of them grabbed me and pulled me into the doorway and for several minutes punched and kicked me before I managed to break away when I again disappeared into the crowd. Some time later, I recovered my bike, which Moggy Hill had rescued for me during the fracas outside the hotel, and we moved up to the Parade.

When reinforcements arrived, the Germans split the rioting mass into small groups and, outside the north side of the General Hospital they arrested me again. Once more, I was about to lose my bike and it may have been the numberplate that enabled them to trace me later. Several friends arrested at the same time were imprisoned that night. I was surrounded by a group of soldiers and an officer began to scream and yell. A rifle butt thudded into the small of my back and was quickly followed by another. Then a stunning blow found my neck and right shoulder and threw me forwards with some force. I felt sick and dizzy and, without thinking what I was doing, I jammed my bike against a soldier and slammed my fist into the officer's face. He toppled backwards, taking another soldier with him. It broke the cordon and I took off.

Pain and panic gave me strength. I ran towards the West Park end of the Parade, past the turn-off to Rouge Bouillon, and then bolted up the hill, expecting a round in my back at any moment. I have no idea why they didn't shoot. I had committed the capital offence of striking a German officer. I was escaping from arrest. They had every right to fire. It happened on the edge of the crowd, which made some sort of avenue for my escape, and people milling around were probably in the line of fire. But I don't really know if that was the reason. I didn't hang around to find out.

Sheer terror added speed to my retreat as I ran up St. Johns Road, continually looking over my shoulder and sometimes stopping briefly to listen for sounds of pursuit; but no one seemed to be following and at the top of the slope I sheltered in a doorway and vomited. My heart pounded like a steam engine and I was badly out of breath. I felt sick for several days afterwards, though fear probably had more to do with it than being unfit.

When I rejoined Rouge Bouillon at the other end of St. John's Road, I walked slowly back to the vicarage, partly because of pain, but also giving myself time to make up a story of theft to explain my missing bike. I hurt all over from the beating and there were a couple of tears in my shirt. I did my best to tidy up. The bleeding from my buttock seemed to have stopped, but the wound was very sore and there was blood in my sock and shoe, and the whole leg soon became stiff. I think I managed to say good night to my parents, without causing concern, by leaning round the edge of the living room door and without actually going into the room.

My neck stiffened quickly and was soon very painful. Large bruises came out there and on my shoulder and soon spread to most of my back. Fortunately, my clothes concealed most of the damage. I contorted in front of a mirror and found the bayonet wound – it looked to have closed off. There was dried blood on my trousers and down my leg, but I don't think it could have been as deep as it felt when the blade went in. At the time, I thought it was almost through into my pelvis.

✳

I didn't sleep that night. Beside the pain, I was frightened by what I had done. I was even more unhappy the next day when I heard how many friends were already in prison, and even less reassured by rumours going round the town which blew up events out of all proportion to the truth, and firmly linked my name to the most damaging ones.

Until now, I have always blamed the bicycle number plate for the Secret Police tracing me but, thinking about it dispassionately after a long interval, it could have been a result of those rumours or the work of an informer in the crowd. The patrol that arrested me would have been far too busy to bother about wheeling away a bike or noting down its number. Some bystander probably 'liberated' it anyway. If so, he or she can easily be excused for thinking I would have no further use for it.

Nothing happened for a couple of days and I vaguely began to hope that all was well. At least I tried to tell myself that it was. I was rudely disabused when two large *Feldgendarmes* (Military Policemen), Schmeisser machine-pistols slung across their chests, called to take Father and me for interrogation in a mock-Tudor villa on Bagatelle Road, just above the *Kommandantur* HQ in College House. I was very frightened. Father was no better. He was as pale as I was. They sat us in a waiting room under guard and we were not allowed to talk. My main worry was that I had hit an officer. The penalty was death.

I decided the best thing to do was to face them out and to deny it, deny it and deny it again, but to admit to lesser offences almost willingly. Perhaps it would make them think I was being honest. They might accept my word that it was someone else who hit the officer. It seemed the only hope. The interrogator's opening words didn't reassure me. He stood at the back of a large desk. A huge portrait of Hitler dominated the wall behind him. For a while he just looked at me, his expression one of utter contempt. Then suddenly he shouted something in German and came round the desk and put his face close to mine as he spat out in guttural English, "We don't know whether to shoot you or to put you in prison for a long time." My heart hammered in my chest. I felt sick. I couldn't have said anything just then if I'd tried.

I was standing with my hands in my pockets and he walked round and stood behind me. The hairs on the back of my head stood up and my skin began to prickle. The next thing I knew was a vicious pain in the back of my neck. I staggered upright from against the desk. He hit me exactly where the rifle butt

✳   79   ✳

had landed. He yelled: "Take your hands out of your pockets in front of the Führer." Then he punched me in the mouth. The blow loosened several lower teeth and took another chip out of an upper one damaged earlier. That was the last thing I remember clearly. I was obviously concussed.

I don't know how long I stayed in that room. Several interrogators came and went and seemed to want to out-shout each other. My head was pounding and my lips felt like footballs. I don't think they hit me again, but I have no clear recollection of being taken back to the waiting room or of being released to go home. I do remember saying over and over again that it was not me who hit the officer. I admitted shouting and abusing officers outside the Barra House Hotel. Reluctantly, I said that I might have spat at one of them. When I got back to the waiting room Father was so relieved to see me again, he didn't comment on my appearance. I have a vague recollection that on the way down the stairs I had tried to clean my face with spit and a handkerchief. For the next few days, I was very careful how I ate. I could only chew on one side. My teeth hardened up with time, but the lower ones have been crooked since.

Two or three days later, as I walked along St. Saviour's Road, a car pulled up and two leather-coated gentlemen hustled me into the back and sat each side of me as the driver pulled away. I had been vaguely aware of a car since leaving home and was already feeling nervous. It was not the last time I rode in the back of one of those low-slung, black Citroens with the long bonnets and big inverted Vs on their radiator grills. Ever since, when I see old movies about the Occupation of France and they show those cars and the men in leather coats, I am reminded of the fear.

They took me to Gestapo headquarters at Silvertide in Havre des Pas. They ranted and raved and repeated the same questions over and over again. They shouted threats and generally intimidated me, but nothing dreadful happened. There was no physical violence, but I was very frightened. They threatened me with imprisonment on Alderney. It was the first time they hinted at such a possibility. I can remember being disturbed at the thought, but we didn't know then the full implication of what it meant. We slowly came to know that it was something to be feared, but it wasn't until well after the war that we learned the true horror of that 'Island of Death'. The questions went on for what seemed hours. They repeatedly went over the same ground as the Military Police. They didn't believe me, but I continued to deny that I hit anyone, never mind a German officer. They let me go.

I didn't tell my parents where I had been, nor of their parting shot: "You will be hearing from us." In retrospect, I am certain they thought the Military Police hadn't questioned me properly, and wanted to interrogate me themselves. Paradoxically, the violence I experienced was not from these men whom we feared most, but from the *Feldgendarmes*. Another beating later in the Occupation was also by a naval policemen, not by the Gestapo. Thinking back about that hour or two in Silvertide, except for the shouted abuse, my main recollection is one of silence, as if the rest of the building was empty. I passed a woman coming in under escort as I went out. I don't know who she was. I didn't recognise her as one of the rioters. She had her gaze firmly on the ground but glanced up briefly as we went by. I can't remember if her eyes showed fear or, for that matter, any other emotion, only that she was there.

Meanwhile, several friends were having their first taste of life in prison. Most were my age. There were a few adults, including café owner Emile Barbier. He got the longest sentence at our court martial. I only learnt recently that he survived his three-year sentence in Germany. He is on the list of those who went to concentration camps from Jersey. Thanks to Joe Mière, and to Paul Sanders in his book, *The Ultimate Sacrifice*, the names of those 172 prisoners are now public property. I find it sad that it has taken such a long time for so many anonymous people, reported by Sinel and others as taken to France or Germany for punishment at various times during the war, to be recognised; that until now, more than 50 years later, there was nothing to say what they were punished for, nothing to say they ever returned. It is a scandal for which the States must take full responsibility.

The next couple of weeks were spent in unpleasant anticipation. Apart from my bruises, I had a nasty bout of diarrhoea and was laid up in bed when they came. I have always wondered why they let me remain at liberty until the trial. The only explanation is that the prison was already full and they probably thought that since we were on a small island there was nowhere to escape to, and little chance of hiding out for very long.

It was 12 October when the black Citroen pulled up again outside the vicarage. They took me to the States Building to be arraigned with my co-defendants in what I believe was an old committee room. If I remember correctly, it had tiered seats like a lecture theatre, but I wasn't thinking very straight that morning. I felt terrible. My parents weren't allowed to come with me. They must have felt even worse than I did, not knowing if I would ever come home again.

The equivalent of a Lance Corporal came in just as the trial started. He barked a staccato Heil Hitler and sat down. They were the last words he uttered. Apparently he was our defence counsel. I do remember the cold-faced Judge Advocate, and the way he and the members of the Court stared at us. In comparison, the little interpreter seemed positively benign.

They asked me time and time again about escaping from arrest, and about hitting the officer. Repeatedly, I said it had not been me. I did admit abusing and spitting at an officer outside the Barra House Hotel. I added to my admission, "like everyone else." I don't know if they believed me or not, but it must have confused them. To our amazement, they sentenced the younger ones to a lenient two years on probation. My adolescent friends were released from prison. The adults were less fortunate.

There is no doubt some senior German officers in the Island were severely embarrassed by Hitler's order to deport the English. They saw it as a broken promise and a matter of honour. Their Leader was making them break a pledge given in their ultimatum for the surrender of the Island in 1940 'to guarantee the lives, property and liberty of peaceful inhabitants.' The deportation was an affront to their honour. They must have decided to redress the wrong by treating our reaction to their Nazi master's brutality with understanding leniency. It is the only explanation I can offer. We would never have got away with it in France or Poland. We were very lucky.

Chapter Seven

COMMANDOS, RADIOS AND CONCENTRATION CAMPS

The only commando raid on Jersey took place at Christmas 1943. Lieutenant A.J. McGonigal and four soldiers landed on Sark the same night but were unable to get up the cliffs in Derrible Bay. The same raiding party landed on Sark again forty-eight hours later. Tragically, they strayed into a minefield and two French soldiers were killed.

A party of ten, with Captain P.A. Ayton in command, got ashore in Jersey at Petit Port. They knocked at a house and their report stated that a terrified young woman directed them to a nearby farm. According to local sources, she told them she had elderly parents and couldn't leave, but Cruickshank wrote that she refused to tell the commandos where they could find some Germans. Brothers at a nearby farm were also described as being too terrified to speak, but were eventually prevailed upon to give some information.

The commandos found an empty strongpoint at Les Platons, but saw no Germans. Going back to the boat, Ayton stepped on a mine and was severely wounded. His men got him back to England, but he died in hospital.

Cruickshank reported the two brothers as telling the commandos: 'There is no resistance movement, and the people are not really hostile to the enemy.' Such a statement, especially in conjunction with comments made about fear and lack of cooperation, might easily have been misinterpreted in Britain. Accepted at face value, it could have led to false assumptions about the Islanders in general. Later, wild claims about the level of collaboration made by some young escapees could only have reinforced such a belief, and may have contributed significantly to subsequent criticism of our conduct and attitude towards the enemy; in particular, to how Churchill thought of us. He never visited the Islands after the war. A very strange omission.

It is true there was no organised Resistance Movement of the type and scale found in France. That does not mean there was no resistance. The word hostile can also be misinterpreted. To a commando, it might mean something quite different to what a civilian might imply. Open aggression against the occupiers was clearly impossible for civilians in a tiny island, but the attitude of the majority was most certainly hostile towards the enemy. It is a matter of semantics, but only a small step from such innocently conceived statements for those more interested in a good story than in telling the truth, to the distorted picture of 'widespread collaboration' and 'lack of resistance'. Churchill could easily have been influenced unfavourably by this report.

Rumours about the landing spread quickly, but we had no reliable information. In view of the German warning that the penalty was imprisonment or death for even knowing of and not reporting the presence of enemy soldiers in the Island, never mind helping them, the civilians concerned were remarkably foolish to tell anyone what had happened. As far as I know, they were not discovered. They were very lucky.

Once again, Michael Ginns has provided a postscript and put me right. He described how the commandos were directed to a nearby farm but, in the first instance, their knocks at the door of La Geonnière were answered by an old lady who told them to push off. The next day, she told the Le Breton brothers: "We had some Jerries round in the night banging on the door – *but talk about they spoke good English!*" The words in italics are real Jersey-speak – from someone probably more used to communicating in *patois* – for something like, "my word, but they could speak good English."

✳

When we saw in the New Year, 1944, we hoped the next few months would bring the Invasion and our liberation. On 2 January, the Germans searched a large area for a deserter who had shot an officer. They concentrated on the eastern part of the island, but didn't find him. He tried to get civilian clothes from an innkeeper. The licensee refused, but found himself in trouble for not reporting the matter. They caught the soldier later. Eventually, they court-martialled and shot him, but not before he caused tragedy to another Jersey family.

The Germans couldn't get typists, and in the New Year they visited several schools to look for records of girls who had been taught to type, so that they could conscript them into their labour force.

11 January began 'Rat Week', an attempt to kill off some of the large number of rodents attacking our precious food stores. They had to compete with hungry humans for every scrap of food. Inevitably, Rat Week inspired a spate of remarks and stories in which vermin of another kind were the main objects of derision.

Many people hid radios and spread the BBC News. The Secret Police caught many of them and they were sentenced by court martial to various terms of imprisonment. On 16 January, the Gestapo arrested Stanley Green. His awful journey took him all the way to Buchenwald. He never recovered his health, even after the war.

His story began much earlier. At the beginning of the Occupation he joined an intelligence gathering organisation run by retired British Army officers: an organisation I will discuss later in this chapter. I originally wrote that the group was never discovered, and it was for something he knew nothing about that Green was eventually arrested and court-martialled, and nearly lost his life. The latter is true, but recent research suggests the Germans knew a great deal about the espionage ring run by Major Crawford-Adams.

When we formed our own resistance group after the Allied Invasion of Normandy, we tried to get someone with experience to lead us. Somebody approached several retired soldiers. I was not one of them and can't recall who was, but I believe Bernard Cavey was involved. Equally, I don't know which officers they asked. But I do have an odd incident to recount. Just after Liberation, one of the hospital porters called me to say there was a gentleman who wished to speak to me. He was waiting in the front hall. We shook hands. I can't remember if he introduced himself, but if he did, I didn't note his name. He was tall and wore a bowler hat and an expensive looking coat. He had a furled umbrella. He carried himself like a soldier and looked distinguished. He was well fed and not dressed like the rest of us. He did not look like we did after five years of occupation.

He said: "On behalf of British Intelligence, thank you for what you and your friends did." He shook hands again, turned on his heels, and disappeared. I have never seen or heard from him since. I don't think I said a single word. I found it hard afterwards to believe that anyone in Intelligence would do such a thing and I often wondered if he was a nutter. I can only tell it as it happened, and vouch for its truth. Nevertheless, since I originally wrote those words in 1995, the British Public Records Office has released more secret papers and, having read some of those that refer to our group, it no longer seems quite so far fetched. Also, Michael Ginns recently referred to my "Man in the Bowler Hat". He wrote: 'Just such a person was described in one account of the Liberation as coming off a landing craft. It was assumed at the time that he was a Civil Servant from the Home Office, coming to look at conditions in the Island.' He added: 'But I'll bet he was your "Man in the Bowler Hat," which reinforces my opinion that somewhere in the Island there must have been an agent – and here we are back to the man Holmes again."

Ginns continued: 'In about May 1940, a man called Holmes arrived in Jersey with his Austrian-born wife. He got a job at the airport, but was dismissed following receipt of a letter from the Home Office stating that he was not to be employed anywhere that there was a security risk, as he had been involved with the British Union of Fascists. He was sacked, but found alternative employment and stayed in the Island.

Soon after they arrived, the Germans told the States to provide transport for officers. They demanded twelve cars and drivers in the day, and four by night.

They were to be at instant readiness. This transport pool operated out of St. Helier Garage in Bath Street, and Holmes was among the drivers.

More than a year later, he resigned and opened a stamp shop in King Street. Many German officers were keen stamp collectors. They were always in and out of his shop with their briefcases, and Holmes was noted to be on good terms with them. Yet, at the same time, Norman Le Brocq and his communist colleagues were using the shop to meet and to leave messages. Holmes never betrayed them. His wife, who had initially taken up employment with an OT Firm, suddenly left the island and went off to Berlin to work for the German Radio network.

Shortly after Liberation, his shop window was stoned and smashed. On 11 May, Norman Le Brocq met Holmes in Broad Street, and said: "I'm sorry to hear what happened to your shop after all you did for us." He replied: "Don't worry about that, I'll be leaving the island soon." The next day, he was seen leaving the harbour in a naval pinnace, which headed for a destroyer anchored in St. Aubin's Bay. Some two or three years later, Holmes was discovered working and living in an English town, re-united with his wife who had surfaced in Berlin. No charges were laid against her, unlike Pearl Vardon and Lingshaw, who had also gone to Germany from Jersey to work on radio.'

Ginns continued: 'Two questions then arise. Firstly, if Holmes was an agent, how could British Intelligence have been certain in 1940 that the Germans would occupy the Channel Islands? Was it a calculated guess? Secondly, if he was an agent, how was he getting his information out? There were no clandestine radios operating, and in 1940, Intelligence would have had no idea whatsoever that foreign workers of the OT would one day be in a position to smuggle out information to the Resistance in St. Malo or Granville. The whole thing is very odd. There are still about six files at the Public Records Office with a one hundred years ban on them. They may hold the key.'

Not all retired military men were as spineless as those we appealed to for help. Major Crawford-Morrison, formerly of the Black Watch, and three other retired officers, also majors – two brothers called Manley, and Major L'Amy M.C. – collected intelligence wherever they could. They deliberately asked reliable men to work for the OT so that they might get on to the construction sites. Some did, noted all they saw, and passed it on to Crawford-Morrison who collated it and had it smuggled out.

Crawford-Morrison was Controller of Air Raid Precautions before the Occupation and kept the post after the Germans landed. It involved frequent contact with the Germans and he always tried to memorise any maps he saw in their offices. He deliberately called on new battery commanders and asked them when they were going to fire their guns so that he could warn owners of nearby houses to open their windows. In that way he gathered a lot of information. One of his informants, Frederick Cook, was a gardener who worked at Linden Court, where the *Feldkommandant*, Oberst Knackfuss, had his quarters. The *Kommandant's* name was immortalised by the comedian, Tommy Handley, as 'Fussknack', in the popular wartime BBC programme, 'Itma'.

Stan Green, who also worked for Crawford-Morrison, was a skilled photographer. He reduced photographs of German fortifications, with their map references, to the size of postage stamps. Crawford-Morrison later smuggled them out when he made several trips to France for the Buying Commission. Mrs. Green sewed the photographs into the lapels of his coat, and he passed them to the French Résistance for onward transmission to London.

Later, the Germans deported him to Germany. They searched him thoroughly before he left. He had hidden more photographs in the lining of an old hat, which he managed to toss to one side when the search began, and they never examined it. A patient, who was repatriated from Germany as part of an exchange of sick prisoners, took the photographs to London.

The Gestapo arrested Stan Green in 1944. He was the chief operator at Wests cinema and they would not believe that he knew nothing about wireless equipment his assistants had hidden in the roof of the theatre. They took him to France, without trial, to the notorious prison at Fresnes. The 'White Rabbit', Wing Commander Yeo-Thomas, was there at the same time. Green saw he was in a bad way after brutal questioning but he had not lost his spirit, and on one occasion heard him shout, "Go to Hell! God save the King!" He later saw him beaten with a rifle butt for shouting out news of the invasion.

Stan Green couldn't sleep at night because of women crying in the same block. He saw a young boy with his hands tied behind his back, shot by one of the guards. He travelled in a cattle truck to Buchenwald with five young French women who had been captured helping the Maquis. They had been subjected to unspeakable torture. An old woman, who'd had her nails pulled off, died on the journey. For six weeks, he slept on a pile of stones without cover in cold wind and rain. He met Bill Symes from Guernsey. Symes travelled naked for several days in a cattle truck after the guards took away the prisoner's clothes because someone tried to escape.

Britons were rare in Buchenwald and to avoid the attention of SS guards Green crooked his hand over the 'E' for 'Engländer' on his prison uniform. His release from Buchenwald was miraculous. He managed to smuggle out a letter. It reached Sherwill, who persuaded the Camp Kommandant to arrange Green's transfer to Laufen, where most of the male Channel Island deportees were interned. Bill Symes managed to smuggle out a postcard to his wife with French prisoners' mail. By an incredible stroke of good fortune it was delivered to his wife in England. The British Government was able to secure his release and transfer to an internment camp.

Stan Green's son, Maurice, was interviewed in recent years for a newspaper article. He told how his father was a changed man when he returned, his hands permanently disfigured by torture. He also told how two local Jerseymen betrayed his father for a reward of 1,000 Occupation Reichmarks. The Gestapo forced him to stand behind a door in the prison and listen to what the traitors had to say about him. He knew who they were, but they were never investigated, never brought to trial. Stanley Green received £1,800 compensation in 1948 – not a vast sum.

Such infamy was not restricted to one or two cases. Most of those who died in the concentration camps started their terrible journeys because of informers, but it is important to remember that the vast majority of the population was intensely patriotic and loyal. They should not be blamed for the actions of a few.

Another tragedy struck very close to home. Canon Cohu, the Rector of St. Saviour's, had a radio hidden in the steeple of his church and was arrested with two other men, Nicolle and Tierney. The Gestapo also arrested and interrogated several of his parishioners, among them an elderly lady, Mrs Inverness-Bathe. The radio was originally hers.

❊

Mrs Bathe was a family friend. My father frequently played bridge at her home. He was picked up by the Gestapo on his way back from Evensong and questioned. The story I remember is that Mrs. Bathe wrote him a note that said something like: 'We are in great trouble. Please come and help us,' and that she gave it to her gardener who was arrested as he left the grounds. My mother remembered it differently. She could not recall a note. She believed Mrs. Bathe was forced to make a list of everybody who had visited her house. Father was arrested outside the vestry by plain-clothed Secret Policemen and bundled into the back of the inevitable black Citroen. They took him to Silvertide for questioning, but fortunately he was able to convince them that he knew nothing about the radio and had never been told the news. They let him go. Cohu, Tierney and Nicolle died in prison or in concentration camps. According to my mother, they sentenced Mrs. Bathe to a term in prison, but because of her advanced years let her pay a big fine instead.

I remember Clifford Cohu as a kindly, jovial man, but he was over-trusting and rather naive. He spread the latest news too publicly. He was both Hospital and Prison Chaplain and the risk of doing this in the Maternity Hospital, where some of the women were having German babies, must have been obvious. It didn't deter him. He was more interested in keeping up the spirits of those in his care than he was in his own safety.

My brother remembers Cohu greeting him enthusiastically in the street and telling him in a loud voice the latest BBC news. Stan said: "He was very prone to do this when the news was good. He was not exactly the soul of discretion!"

Eventually, Cohu was taken to Spergau concentration camp where, according to *Islands in Danger,* he became an immediate object of malice from the guards. Amongst other things, they blamed him for the bombing of German cities, and one particularly brutal guard used to call out *Welcher is der Engländer?* – which is the Englishman? And then shout at Cohu, *du wirst da krepieren* – you will die here.

Sick and weak, so that he could hardly lift a shovel, he was made to work every day. At night he often slept in a tent. When he died of dysentery lying in his own filth on a dirty palliasse, they found a tiny Bible hidden inside his shirt.

All sorts of people were arrested for such diverse offences as being in possession of stolen German coal or brandy, for having RAF leaflets, for dealing on the black market, for failing to register pigs, or for fiddling the amount of wheat or potatoes they handed over to the Germans. As the number waiting to go into prison increased, the *Kommandantur* made a list of those who would have to serve their sentences after the war! But for some of those who served their sentences on the Continent, the outcome as we shall see was much more serious.

As D-Day approached, the Allies became much more active over and around the Islands, and on the neighbouring coast of France. In late January, the RAF attacked two patrol boats off La Rocque. They sank one and badly damaged the other.

As petrol became shorter, more and more the enemy used horse-drawn transport and the number of tumbril-like carts crossing the town and seen on country roads increased dramatically. A couple of youngsters, adept at leaping on the rear step of the carts and avoiding the driver's whip to steal a loaf or two of bread, had a rude shock one day when they pulled back the canvas flap and found a dead Russian lying in the back. On another occasion, a boy climbed over the tailboard to find a soldier waiting for such an invasion. He got a good hiding on the spot. The practice of jumping onto carts probably dropped after that.

More and more Allied aircraft flew over the Island. We saw hundreds of planes at a time going to targets in France. The sound of heavy bombing became a daily event. Shockwaves radiated through the rocky strata so that houses trembled and shook. At times, the Germans put up a fierce anti-aircraft barrage.

At others, and for no apparent reason, the guns kept silent. By now, German aircraft were rarely seen over the Island, but they were sometimes heard at night. Sinel recorded for 27 March: 'The largest number of German planes heard for some time passed over the Island; the BBC next morning announced that Bristol had been bombed.'

On 8 April, German gunners shot down one of their own planes. All four of the crew were killed.

On 19 April, there was a torchlight procession and two military bands beat *ein Grosse Zapfenstreich* – a tattoo – to celebrate Hitler's birthday. The heavens responded with heavy rain and the Allies with heavy bombing in France, which shook buildings on the Island to their foundations.

In late April, there was a naval action south of the Island, near St. Malo. We saw and heard even more Allied planes. We saw 'Windows' for the first time – strips of silver foil dropped by Allied planes to jam German radar. We didn't know what it was and rumour had it that some people even tasted it!

On 27 April, a firing squad executed the German soldier who had shot an officer in January. They buried him in the Strangers' Cemetery. He was probably called David, a German deserter who was given clothes by a Jehovah Witness and his wife. The Gestapo arrested the husband and he died in Buchenwald. Until recently, I thought him another of those faceless, nameless people whose memories go unrecorded in any worthwhile way, but Michael Ginns tells me that his name is now among those of others who died in the camps, names recorded on a new memorial tablet outside the Occupation Tapestry Gallery on New North Quay.

From time to time the Germans held practice artillery shoots which damaged windows, and on 4 May, they cleared several districts. But they damaged eight houses at Mont-à-l'Abbé and Saint Aubin when shells fell short. They closed and mined the remaining fairways of the Royal Jersey Golf Club. On 8 May, a German ammunition ship blew up between the Islands. The shockwaves were like an earthquake. There were three survivors.

According to Sinel, the German garrison was always on manoeuvres. 'It roamed over farms and around the coastline, trampling crops and damaging property. Soldiers slept fully-armed in slit trenches in the north of the Island. They put twenty-four hour guards on the telephone exchange and sentries patrolled outside all important buildings. They turned families out of their homes, with little or no warning, for military reasons.' In May, they arrested James Houiellebecq for stealing weapons and ammunition. They arrested his family too, but released them later. James withstood severe interrogation and protected others involved. He died in a concentration camp just before his eighteenth birthday, another example of the resistance the British Press and others claim did not exist.

The enemy treated the bodies of Allied sailors washed up after battles at sea with respect and honour, but they usually buried American and British servicemen without publicity to avoid demonstrations. At earlier funerals, the local people had made their loyalty only too plain by the hundreds of wreaths and bunches of flowers that they sent or put on the graves.

When British MTBs attacked German shipping in St Aubin's Bay, a barge finished up on the Dog's Nest rocks. Allied aircraft came over every day. Sometimes the guns roared. At other times, they kept silent. We became more and more impatient. We asked each other: "When are the Allies coming? How much longer have we got to wait?"

Among the more bizarre robberies were those of horses' tails. They were used for making shaving brushes.

It was now forbidden to paint woodwork unless the building was used for growing food, such as a glasshouse. As if there was any paint anyway!

The anti-aircraft guns shot down an American plane and the pilot told locals who got to him before the Germans: "Everything is ready for the big event."

Chapter Eight

INVASION: THE WAIT IS OVER

For almost four years, the Germans subjected us to a barrage of propaganda that mocked the Allies for their failure to open a 'Second Front'. When D-Day finally arrived, we greeted it with relief as well as with indescribable joy.

As each month, and each week, and each day passed, we waited for something to happen. People conjured up all sorts of unlikely reasons for a certain date: a quotation from the Bible, the anniversary of St. Crispin's Day, St. George's Day, the King's birthday, even magic. But as each propitious occasion passed and all the forecasts proved false, we became used to disappointment.

We reassured each other it would come one day, but as the months and then the years went by, doubts crept in. We had never seen a defeated German soldier. Victorious enemy troops had occupied the Island for four years. They boasted that they would throw any invasion back into the sea. We were surrounded by the same kind of fortifications the Allies would encounter wherever they landed. They were formidable. Apart from the Pas de Calais, the fortifications on the Channel Islands were stronger than any other part of the Atlantic Wall.

In early June 1944, Von Schmettow went over to Normandy for a War Games conference at Rennes. Two days before the Invasion, he inspected fortifications at the mouth of the River Vire. He was shocked by what he found and remarked to his Corps Commander that they were nowhere near as strong as the defences in the Islands.

We asked ourselves: "Will they never come? Shall we never be free?" More importantly, we wondered: "And if they come, will they be successful?" We had thought that the landing at Dieppe was the Invasion. We didn't know it was just a raid. We didn't know that our troops didn't mean to stay. The memory of that disappointment fuelled our uncertainty. We had waited so long.

I can't remember what time on 6 June it started. Soon after midnight, I think. I woke from a deep sleep and rushed to the window. Instantly awake, I opened it as wide as I could and stared up at the sky as it pulsated with the noise of aircraft. They were too high to see, even in the flashes of the shells. I had never heard anything so intense before. Nor have I since. I had no doubt. This was the Invasion. The wait was over.

The old vicarage was a substantial building, but it felt as if it were falling to pieces. The noise of hundreds of planes, the anti-aircraft barrage and, later, the shock waves through the rocky strata from the bombing and shelling in Normandy itself, caused the whole building to quiver and shake as if it were being buffeted by a hurricane. In my bedroom just below the attics, my bed trembled and jumped and took on a life of its own.

I didn't know we had a radio in the vicarage at that time. My brother, Stan, didn't tell the rest of the family that he had one, so that we couldn't be blamed if it was found. It was under the floorboards in his bedroom. I can't remember where or from whom I did get confirmation of the landings, but it certainly wasn't from my brother. In fact it has taken until now, writing this book, to realise that in the months just before D-Day, I never even knew for certain who did still have a radio. There were those I suspected, but I never asked. It was not the sort of thing you talked about.

I knew of several radios after the Invasion. Their owners became less discreet when they thought that liberation was imminent and, when the Allies were well ashore and started to broadcast from just across the water, many people built crystal sets. They were small and easy to hide. We even had one in the prison. My brother, Stanley, also built a crystal set and hid it in a drawer. It was found by the Gestapo when they searched the house for me the following February but, fortunately, their search was incomplete. The electricity supply had run out and they had to make do with torches. They failed to find a second radio, a weapon, some ammunition and photographic material, all hidden under the floorboards.

Before D-Day though, I never seemed to be out of touch with what was going on, even if I didn't know where the news came from. Although the Germans threatened the death penalty for keeping a radio and for spreading the BBC news, I don't think it was ever imposed. The danger in being caught was that those convicted had to serve any sentence longer than two months on the Continent, not in the Island. Then it was only too easy to get caught up in the German concentration camp system.

There was nothing on the early news on 6 June, but by 9 o'clock everybody in the Island knew. It is impossible to describe how we felt. It was a heady mixture of joy and hope for the future, but tinged with anxiety and the fear of disappointment. The waiting was over. Would the landings succeed? We would soon know.

✻

Looking around Jersey today, it is difficult to imagine how heavily fortified the Island was in 1944. After the war, some experts described the defences the Germans built as the greatest feat of military engineering in history. Even today, one only has to look at the blockhouses, radar towers and gun platforms that do remain as tourist attractions, and to see the Underground Hospital, to get some idea of how extensive they were.

Why were the Islands so heavily defended? Only the fortifications along the Pas de Calais were as formidable. Cruickshank explains how Hitler saw the capture of the Channel Islands as a triumph out of all proportion to their military significance, and how he was able to exploit the initial propaganda value of their fall in 1940. They would also be useful forward bases for an invasion of Britain. When Hitler postponed Operation Sealion, the invasion of Britain, he believed the English would try to get the Islands back. He demanded the construction of formidable defences and issued an order that: 'They must therefore be made so strong that no force can land there, even if the Luftwaffe cannot help the defenders.'

As Cruickshank pointed out, it was the start of his preoccupation with the only British territory he was able to conquer, a preoccupation that was to continue almost to the end of the war. When he invaded Greece and Russia he expected the British to react and to attack the Channel Islands or Norway. He personally and carefully studied the defences of the islands. He demanded more strongpoints and that the garrisons of Jersey and Guernsey be increased to a reinforced regiment on each. He ordered the construction of terrifyingly strong defences against both air and sea attack. He sent in tanks and heavy coastal batteries.

Hitler believed an attack on the Islands was a logical step for the British to take to show their support for Russia. It would pin down German forces in the west. He wrote: 'We must be prepared for skilful handling on the enemy's part. Moonless nights and bad weather can favour such undertakings.' As previously explained, his fears were not without foundation, but the German High Command did not share his opinion. There was little they could do though when the Führer gave them a direct order.

In later directives, he demanded that batteries on the French coast have a range of 25 kilometres, so that any enemy vessels which dared to use the Channel between the Islands and France could be shelled from both sides. He told the OT to model the Island coastal fortifications on the West Wall – the Siegfried Line – and to make them just as impregnable. Even German female workers and construction labourers were armed. The infantry was reinforced. He increased the strength of 319 Division to well above that of a normal front line unit. To give better air cover, Hitler also reinforced the Luftwaffe in neighbouring France. Flame throwers and extensive minefields supported the other defences.

By October 1941, Hitler believed that if the British did invade and were successful, he would be unlikely to dislodge them again. He cited Malta, 'where, in spite of thousands of bombs, they still held on.' He now wanted even bigger guns on the French coast: at Cap de la Hague, at St. Malo, and on Guernsey. He wanted between 200 and 250 strongpoints on each of the larger Islands and to build them he would use the local population as well as foreign workers. Our worries about having to work for them on military projects were not without foundation either.

'Spiders' appeared in several places. A large shell was put in the middle of a field; the detonator was connected through a ring to overhead wires that extended, like a web, to the edges of the open area, so that a paratrooper or glider that landed on one would set off a huge explosion. The wires were high enough for people and cattle to move around underneath.

They put roll bombs at the tops of cliffs, and engineers built anti-tank traps and mined the exits from the beaches. There were extensive underwater defences, and slave labourers built long, concrete anti-tank walls in several bays. The biggest guns were at Le Frie Baton in Guernsey, the so-called Mirus battery. Four 30.5 centimetre guns, which had been part of the armament of a First World War battleship, had a range of fifty kilometres. The gun emplacement alone took almost two years to build.

By 1944, the Germans had laid 67,000 mines in Jersey alone. Compared with a total of 6,100,000 cubic metres of concrete for the rest of the Atlantic Wall, they used 484,000 cubic metres in the Islands. Cruickshank suggests that if this concrete and the labour used to lay it had been used elsewhere, the mainland part of the Wall would have been about 10% stronger over its entire length.

The Germans built two railway lines in Jersey to carry all the concrete and other building materials. They garrisoned Elizabeth Castle and Mont Orgueil Castle, and built new strongpoints into the original fortifications. In the same way, they fortified the Round Towers and Martello Towers that surround the Island and which were originally built to keep out the French. Cruickshank wrote: 'To the work of castle builders in the times of King John and Queen Elizabeth, they added reinforced concrete gun emplacements and bunkers.' Some have been retained as tourist attractions.

As well as standard fortifications, German engineers disguised strongpoints inside houses and other buildings, on quays and around the coastline. The most complicated feat of military construction was the Underground Hospital. They cored a similar one out of the rocky base in Guernsey.

In Jersey, they didn't finish the tunnels. Originally intended as an artillery barracks, they used them after D-Day as a hospital. Slave labourers and other workers dug out over 14,000 tonnes of rock to give a final floor area of 2,565 square metres. There was enough space for a complete medical staff and five hundred patients. It had its own power. It was both air-conditioned and heated. It is now an Occupation Museum. Any visitor should try to imagine the misery and death that went into its construction.

The above description makes it obvious that any invasion of the Island would have been extremely costly to the Allies. As a *Führerweisung* – Führer directive – of October 1941 stated: 'Counter measures in the islands ensure that any English attack fails before a landing is achieved whether attempted by sea or air, or both' – an early echo of Rommel's dictum that any invasion must be defeated on the beaches.

✳

While one can admire the skill that contributed to these engineering feats, the means by which the Germans achieved them remains the most obvious reason why it took so long for us to stop hating them. North Africans, Russians, Poles, Czechs, Frenchmen, Spaniards and Jews of all nationalities made up the labour force. The Spaniards were refugees from the Spanish Civil War. It is not commonly known that thousands of these former anti-Franco, Spanish Government supporters who were interned in France were later deported to Germany. It has been estimated some 10,000 were worked to death or exterminated in the camps. Many were ordinary refugees. Many had no particular political loyalty, but the Nazis considered all of them were 'Reds'.

The slave labourers who joined the volunteer and conscripted workers worked 16 hours a day on a starvation diet of thin soup. It was rumoured that many Russians had walked all the way across Europe. In fact, they travelled in closed railway wagons for three weeks, with no sanitation. What little food they had was thrust in to them through the barred windows or partly opened sliding doors. They suffered the same treatment while they worked in Alderney and Jersey.

The Nazi Party classified people of Slavic origin as *untermenschen*, sub-human. They considered them only fit to work as beasts of burden. They were the 'living dead'. Mere skeletons. The first I saw were in rags. Some wore cement sacks over their heads and shoulders, like monk's hoods. They were gaunt, and grey all over, coated with cement dust. Some were only children. Many had no shoes, or only bits of sacking tied around their feet. The Germans herded them like cattle. OT guards beat them with whips and sticks. They were ruthless and immediately attacked anyone who fell or failed to keep up.

A witness told a BBC series how he saw a young girl drop a small bundle. As she stooped to pick it up, she was struck such a powerful blow that her scalp was laid open. An old lady at First Tower was heard to exclaim when she saw them for the first time: "Oh God! Oh my God! Where are you?" Perhaps the most awful thing was the way ordinary German soldiers seemed devoid of pity. Some laughed at what they saw.

There has been much said in defence of 'decent Germans' since the war – and rightly so – but we should remember that those Germans who were in command of the Island and who are now considered by some to have been in that category knew very well what was going on in the area they commanded, just as well as we did. They did little or nothing to correct the situation.

It is pertinent to recall what Von Schmettow said at a time when the war was still going reasonably well for Germany. On the third anniversary of the surrender of the Islands in July 1943, he told his troops: "It is three years today that a few bold airmen took possession of the British Channel Islands. Looking back on the total operations of the war, it was only a small enterprise, but of singular importance. The oldest possession of the British Crown was lost. The German soldier entered British territory for the first time. This led to the dissolution of the British Empire, whose breaking-up becomes more evident year by year. The German soldier, with building pioneers, supported by the OT men, has made this Island impregnable. As a result of hard work and iron execution of duty, the Atlantic Wall is the best defence work in history, which is what our Führer ordered. The German soldier, true to his flag, will hold the position to which the Führer has appointed him, until the last drop of blood. We, the Occupation Forces in Jersey, are today conscious of the warriors of Stalingrad and trusting in our power and strength, and in our faith in our Führer, and, pledging increasing devotion to duty and preparedness, we will hold the Island in the coming fourth year. When the hour of trial comes it will find us ready. Heil Hitler!"

Von Schmettow was not blind. He could see what we could see. His words need no further comment but, in recording them it is essential we put aside the emotions of long ago and recognise there were other Germans and, on at least one occasion Von Schmettow himself, who reacted differently and who, when they could, tried to alleviate some of the suffering.

Most labourers who worked on the defences were OT workers: some volunteers, some conscripted victims of the STO – *La Service du Travail Obligatoire*. It was an unpopular program in which young Frenchmen were compelled to work in factories in Germany. By volunteering for the OT, instead of waiting to be called up, some managed to stay in France. Many, the more courageous ones, took refuge in the *maquis*. The Resistance told some to volunteer for such work so that the information they gleaned could be passed to London. There were some that worked for the Germans because they wanted Germany to win.

When the Germans needed to build such fortifications all over Europe, to defend their conquests, they soon found there were not enough volunteers. They began to force people to work for them. Out-of-work North Africans were among the first to arrive in the islands. Pétain turned them over as a gift from Vichy France to the Nazi cause. They were so hungry when they arrived in the Islands they ate anything they could find. They were seen trying to catch fish at the sea end of sewage outflows. Four died after eating hemlock. Others succumbed to typhus which, not surprisingly, broke out in their insanitary camps. Other forced labourers were civilians rounded up when going innocently about their business:

on the streets of their home towns, in cinemas, or in similar public places. They came from France, Holland, Belgium, Poland and other occupied territories. Many slave workers were Russian prisoners-of-war, denied the protection and dignity usually accorded to such military personnel.

At the peak, some four to five thousand of these labourers worked in Jersey alone. We do not know exactly how many died of overwork, starvation or untreated sickness or injury. To see those who were slave labourers was in some ways to share a tiny portion of their misery. We were never as badly off as they were, never approached it even, but in the final year we came close to starvation too and, perhaps more than others who have never been really hungry, can appreciate at least to some degree how they felt. To some extent also, as I wrote before, in some parts of the Island it was like living on the edge of a concentration camp, but without being a part of it. There were no double-layered barbed wire fences and there were no watchtowers as there were at Belsen and other camps. It was more like a prison without bars.

Desperate for food, the slave labourers often managed to break out of their camps. During the day they begged, and robbed when they had the opportunity. They broke into houses at night. They stole food and clothes. Householders barred and bolted their doors and windows. They frequently took all their food and clothing up to bed with them. One lady told how her mother used to take her silver to bed with her, but after the foreign workers arrived she took up her food instead.

Their clothes were tattered and inadequate, but even in winter they preferred the harsh conditions of living rough to the brutality of the OT guards. Unfortunately, after more than two years of occupation, we too were so short of many essentials that we had to protect our own stores from these poor wretches. That was the dilemma. They were robbing us, but they were our allies.

The Germans asked the civilian population to help catch them. There was no way we at Beauchamp would have assisted in such a way, but we had to defend the farm. Keith Le Brun pulled me from my bed one night when he heard noises at the back. It was a bright, moonlit night and very still. We armed ourselves with clubs, which we kept handy and crept round the building to look. Fortunately, the intruders must have heard us and disappeared. We were more than somewhat relieved. Such visits always caused anxiety. You could never be sure the intruder you were stalking wasn't a soldier with a firearm.

During the siege, matters became even more desperate. As one man said in a BBC broadcast, you could be feeding one lot at the front door, while another lot robbed you at the back. In St. Ouen, neighbouring farmers organised what amounted to an early edition of Neighbourhood Watch. The farmer being raided raised the alarm by leaning out of his bedroom window and banging on a metal jug or basin. Intruders killed a Mr Le Gresley when he tried to defend his poultry.

They wounded another farmer with a pitchfork. Another farmer and his sons killed an intruder who attacked them and injured another so severely that he too died later.

The Germans reported the incident in the *Evening Post* but no charges were laid. The article stated: 'It is a fact that the population does not enjoy the presence and behaviour of these allies of the English Government. Many islanders anxiously ask themselves what would become of law and order if Bolshevism should conquer and send more of her representatives here.'

It completely ignored the fact that it was the Germans themselves who brought the Russians to Jersey in the first place. With crops being torn out of the fields and their homes being robbed the farmers were in an invidious position. Most, but not quite all, felt sorry for the Russians and the manner in which they were starved and treated. But not only was the farmer's livelihood at stake, the food supply of the island was at risk. Something had to be done. Special night patrols were set up in country parishes. Yet the participants knew if a Russian was caught and handed over to the Germans he would be severely beaten and sentenced to punishment at Elizabeth Castle.

One farmer in St Ouen, after going out on patrol to look after other people's property, got back home to find all his next season's seed potatoes had been stolen.

✳

Bill was employed at L'Etacq Quarry. He lived in *Lager Immelmann* at the bottom of Jubilee Hill in St Peter. The OT man in charge of the camp had the reputation of being particularly brutal; the treatment was dreadful, the food watery soup, sickness was endemic. Bill decided to escape. He was recaptured. He was made to strip naked in the camp compound in front of the entire workforce and then to push a wheelbarrow loaded with stones over the rough surface, at the double, until he collapsed. He was made to stand, first in a water butt, and then outside all night. It was mid-winter. In the morning he was allowed to dress and join the column of men shuffling to work at L'Etacq. Believing he was probably going to die anyway, he decided to escape again and jumped over a low wall when nobody was looking. He was picked up by a bread delivery van.

He was sheltered initially by a farmer called René La Motté, then by Mrs Gould at La Fontaine. An informer betrayed her. Thanks to an anti-Nazi sergeant in the *Feldgendarmerie*, who tipped off Norman Le Brocq's communist resistance group, Bill was smuggled to safety by Bob Le Sueur. Michael Frowd and René Franoux, two conscientious objectors, took him in. He survived the Occupation.

The overseers in Jersey were brown-uniformed OT men instead of black-uniformed SS but, as this episode shows, they could be just as brutal. The prisoners were the same. Living skeletons.

It is incorrect to say, as the Woods did in *Islands in Danger*, that the islanders only had occasional glimpses of them. One only had to walk along the barbed wire that divided the construction sites from the road, along St Aubin's Bay, or at St. Brelade's, or visit St. Ouen's, or the north coast around Ronez quarry, to see what was going on. For some, like Jersey artist Edmund Blampied, there were more vivid horrors. He saw a prisoner hung by his feet and beaten. A house in Guernsey, ironically called 'Paradise', was particularly notorious for the bestiality of the man in charge. Reports describe the screams that came from this prison for OT workers. They describe the man in charge as a sadist who took particular delight in flogging his victims with rope before hanging them upside down from banisters.

It is important, however, when trying to assess the total picture of what actually happened, as opposed to what journalists and others more interested in sensation claim happened, to be as unbiased and truly analytical as possible.

In October 1993, R.W. (Bob) Le Sueur spoke to the Channel Islands Occupation Society on 'Foreign Workers of the OT.' He befriended many Spaniards during the Occupation and risked his life to hide several escaped Russsian slave labourers. He began his talk by saying: "Of German misdeeds (towards the OT workforce) there were plenty, but it is a pity when inaccurate stories, which can be disproved, rob authentic accounts of their credibility. It is the essence of an historian's work to consider only reliable facts and then to deduce opinion from them; too often, people first make up their minds on an issue and then select the evidence to support those views whilst ignoring what does not suit them. Now, 50 years on, we can I hope, and certainly among the membership of this Society, look at this period of the Occupation and consider plain, unvarnished facts with a certain detachment and complete objectivity."

The number of prisoners was nowhere as large as in the major concentration camps in Germany. There were no gas chambers or furnaces for mass destruction. But the misery and degradation for some was the same. In his book, *The Holocaust*, Michael Gilbert wrote that inside the labour camps conditions were savage. He told how on the night of 15 August, nearly a thousand Jews, most of them born in Poland, were taken to a camp in Alderney. One survivor, Albert Eblagon, described how when he and the other Jews reached the port, they were forced to run the two kilometres to the camp, while the German guards continuously stabbed into their backs with bayonets and kicked them. Many of the men were over 70 years of age but nobody was spared. There was hard physical work for 12 and 14 hours a day, every day, building the fortifications. The prisoners were beaten every day, their arms or legs broken. They were starved and worked to death. Many died from total exhaustion.

Gilbert told how hundreds of Jews died on Alderney of exhaustion and ill treatment. 384 are said to be buried in the camp itself and many others dumped at sea. Among the names recorded on the few marked graves are Chayim Goldin, Robert Perlestein and Lieb Becker. They all died in December 1943.

The number of foreign workers who died is one of the most emotive subjects of any concerning the activities of the OT in the Channel Islands. It will always be open to question and debate. From official German records in Jersey, from the Parish of St. Helier burial records for the Strangers' Cemetery and from the records of J.B. Le Quesne, the funeral director who held the German contract for burials during most of the Occupation, it appears that in Jersey 116 foreign workers died during that time. There were 11 German OT deaths. Of the former group, 2 were Belgian, 2 Dutch, 18 French, 6 North African, 5 Polish, 9 Spanish, 1 unknown, and 73 Russian. Similar records in the other islands, show that 96 foreign workers died in Guernsey and 397 in Alderney, a grand total of 609 deaths for the three islands.

There are two schools of thought about the accuracy of these records. Firstly, that they are totally misleading: the true number runs into thousands with stories of mass graves and bodies dumped in the setting concrete, flung over cliffs, or tipped off the end of the Alderney breakwater by the lorry load. These are the claims grasped at by sensationalist journalists. Secondly, that the official German records are roughly accurate. This is the view expressed by Cruickshank in his official history of the Occupation.

The first foreign workers to die in Alderney were buried in St. Anne's Churchyard, but as the Russian death rate rose to well over 300, they were all buried on Longy Common. Burials in Jersey took place in the Strangers' Cemetery. Apart from the interments of Muslim North Africans and Nazi-classified *untermenschen* – Russians – they did not lack dignity. Canon Cohu, the Hospital Chaplain, conducted funeral services for the first burials in the Strangers' Cemetery. They were the workers drowned when the *mv Hermann* and *mv Schleswig-Holstein* sank. My father took over his chaplaincy when Canon Cohu was imprisoned and taken to Germany; where he died in Spergau concentration camp.

There was usually no ceremony for the Russians. Le Quesne makes no mention of wreaths or religious services. Most died at work. Other workers took the body to the camp at the end of the working day. It was collected from there and taken to the Strangers' Cemetery. It is believed that on occasions four of the victims' workmates were allowed to attend the burial. In March 1943 a Bishop of the Russian Orthodox Church visited the islands. He left behind two Russian priests. It was probably one of them who visited the vicarage and gave my father an icon.

Very few Russians worked in Guernsey. There is only one Russian death recorded for that island. A higher number of deaths among French, Dutch,

Belgian and North Africans workers in Guernsey was due to tunnelling accidents, a severe outbreak of typhus in February 1943 and the bombing of St. Peter Port harbour by the RAF in January 1942. The RAF tried to hit the vessel bringing in the Mirus battery guns. The bombs fell on the wrong ship and killed many foreign workers.

Immediately after the D-Day landings, uniformed OT personnel were armed. About a hundred Frenchmen failed to turn up for work and were imprisoned in Fort Regent. Armed OT men rounded up others, and they were locked up too. As soon as the Germans realised they were going to be surrounded and by-passed, they sent back as many OT personnel as possible to France. Not all went quietly. On 15 August, another of the all too familiar *Bekanntmachung* appeared. In translation, it read:

NOTICE

Re: Search for wanted persons.

As already ordered, foreigners who wish to take lodging, or local persons who are wanted by the German authorities, must be reported immediately to the nearest German unit or authority or to the Constable of the parish. Any person who hides, supports, or conceals their whereabouts, is liable to severe punishment.

In the event of the concealing of those persons by the civil population or part of it, measures will be taken against the whole population or the part concerned.

At present the following persons are wanted:

Denis Clery, born June 12th, 1928, in London. Irish nationality, Electrician, last residence 22 Charing Cross St., St Helier

Bernard Turpin, born September 8th. 1918 at St Helier, fitter, last residence New-Land House, St Brelade's.

Besides the above, 13 Russian subjects are in hiding. Therefore, farmers particularly are warned not to give those persons work or to shelter them;

DER FESTUNGSKOMMANDANT

(gez) Heine

Oberst.

In late November 1944, another Russian escaped from a work party. Late in the Occupation, some Russians had been on the run for almost two years. They often spoke good English. Some had Jersey girlfriends. They went to cinemas and mixed with German troops at the swimming pool at Havre des Pas. Dr McKinstry provided many with false ration books and identity cards. Local informers betrayed some, but many avoided capture.

The following *WARNUNG* appeared after the latest escape:

WARNING

At 1p.m.on Nov. 27th a Russian prisoner named Ogaurenko, sentenced to five years imprisonment, escaped while at work. As Ogaurenko will try to hide in among civilians the population is warned not to lodge, feed, or in any way help the escaped prisoner. His whereabouts must be immediately reported to the nearest military post. Attention is drawn to the fact that farmers in Trinity and St Mary have already been sentenced to long terms of imprisonment for aiding escaped persons.

A description of the missing Russian followed, and Oberst Heine signed as *Kommandant Festung Jersey*.

Who were the farmers at Trinity and St Mary? It is clear there were numerous Islanders who risked their lives when they resisted the Germans in this way. The names of many, if not most, go unrecorded.

According to Gilbert in *The Holocaust*, on 4 July 1944, 250 prisoners from Alderney were put on board ship to be sent back to the mainland. British warships attacked and sank the vessel. He wrote: 'All the prisoners drowned. Most of them were French Jews.' He is probably referring to the near sinking of the *Minotaur*. On the night of 2/3 July, about 500 passengers, mainly volunteer and forced foreign workers were aboard. They were not 250 concentration camp prisoners. The Jews were on another vessel that was not sunk. A torpedo blew off the *Minotaur*'s bow, but her Captain saved his vessel by going astern and beaching her. Of the foreign workers on board, only 100 women and 75 men survived. In the three days or so before they left, these workers had wandered around St Helier; the *Evening Post* interviewed several of them.

Among the survivors was Dennis Le Cuirot. He escaped to France by pretending to be one of the foreign workers. I will describe his adventure later, but he would not have been able to mingle with those people and get aboard the *Minotaur* if they had been concentration camp prisoners with SS guards in charge.

In a personal communication, Michael Ginns told me that Gilbert has made other mistakes. He wrote: 'The Holocaust gives the figure of 1,000 Jews in Alderney, because that was the complement of the SS concentration camp there, but the prisoners were by no means all Jews. They included anyone of any nationality who had upset the Germans, as well as Germans who were anti-Hitler, and German officers who had been disgraced because they ignored Hitler's ridiculous orders that every soldier should fall where he stood and not retreat.' Ginns added that it is clear from the German War Diaries that the main body of Jews was kept as a separate entity, and did not mix with the other concentration camp prisoners.

Fifty-six Spaniards were still in Jersey at Liberation. They were valuable witnesses, particularly if they had been on Alderney. They were intelligent, articulate young men who had no reason to love the Nazi regime. Bob Le Sueur acted as interpreter when needed. He described how one after another, over days, the Spaniards were brought in, one at a time, and after the initial formalities of asking names, approximate dates of arrival in Jersey, work place and camp, the interrogation would go something like this:

Question: "Have you heard the stories of killings of Russian workers by OT guards?"
Answer: "Oh! Yes."
Question: "Can you give us some particulars of one such murder?"
Answer: "Well, there were so many."
Question: "Yes, but let us start with just one."
Answer: "Well, I didn't see one myself, but everyone knew it was happening and all the time."
Question: "Did one of your friends see such a murder? If so, can you give us his name?"

"And so it went on," Le Sueur said. "It was always someone else, a friend, or a friend who could not be identified. We got absolutely nowhere beyond rumour, and there was no evidence whatever on which anyone could have been arrested. This is not to say that there was no truth in these stories, it is simply that we were unable to establish any."

✳

We were only on the fringe of the horrors that did occur among slave labourers and in the camps, but we saw enough to understand some of what those people suffered. Some of our friends were drawn into it. We cannot know the full enormity of what they suffered. There have been descriptions, some so vivid as to be almost unbelievable. Others are almost more damning by their restraint. When Stan Green was in Buchenwald, he made a camera. At great risk, he used it. Some of the awful pictures he took secretly were used at the Nuremburg Trials.

Despite the recent publication of more secret papers from the Public Records Office, we shall never know the exact truth about Alderney, nor for that matter what happened in some parts of the other Islands. That, however, is not an excuse to invent and exaggerate, nor to ignore properly researched evidence. We shall never know how many actually died, either in the islands or when taken away to Germany, nor what unspeakable suffering some of them experienced along the way. We can only hope and pray it will never happen again.

Soon after the invasion, we saw the OT workers being shipped back to France. On 22 June, several small boats took away a large number. Sinel wrote: 'On the 28th some 1500 prisoners arrived in Jersey from Alderney. Most were taken to Fort Regent, but some were penned in clear view on a vacant strip not far from the harbour.' When the guards weren't looking, I spoke to some through the wire. I shall never forget the state they were in. Nor can I block out the look in their eyes.

Those not locked up in the Fort, and who were provided with at least some bedding, were not concentration camp prisoners. They were forced labourers, conscripted from all the occupied territories of Hitler's vast empire.

On June 29th, Sinel wrote, 'Indignation has been caused in the Island because about twenty local residents who had been sentenced by the Germans for 'political' crimes were sent to France; they were people who were serving or under sentence to serve more than two months imprisonment. They were taken from the prison in motor lorries, and many people gathered to cheer them up.' It was learned at a later date that a German concentration camp was the destination of these poor unfortunates, some of whom were never to return.

I didn't see those people leave the prison, but I recall an incident in the hospital that I believe to be accurate. 50 years plays havoc with the memory and things tend to become distorted and blurred but, as I remember it, the Germans gave these 'political' prisoners a medical examination before transporting them to Germany. It is the sort of bizarre efficiency one might expect of the Nazis. Among those due to go was Mrs Forster, sister of Harold Le Druillenec and Mrs Louisa Gould, two prisoners who went to the mainland for hiding the escaped Russian prisoner, Bill. Mrs. Forster had also sheltered him. Archives Book No 8 of the Channel Islands Occupation Society describes how Mrs Forster 'eluded prison [on the Continent], thanks to the staff of the General Hospital who faked tuberculosis for her (an illness of which the Germans seemed to have a particular dread).'

My recollection was different: I thought incorrectly that Ray Osmont had smuggled a precious lump of sugar into the prison to put in Mrs Forster's urine to make her appear diabetic. Faking tuberculosis saved her life. She was still in prison when I arrived there in September.

Soon after D-Day, Harold Le Druillenec and Mrs Gould were housed in the military wing of the prison. At the same time, *SS Baubrigade* I prisoners were in transit from Alderney to the parent concentration camp in Germany. The 'close confinement' SS prisoners, the *Schutzhäftlinge*, were also locked up in that part of the prison. The SS had to delay their transfer to St. Malo because of Royal Navy activity near the Island. When they eventually got away, the SS cleared out all the prisoners in the military section, whether they were due to go to Germany or not. Harold Le Druillenec was the only Briton to survive Belsen. Mrs Gould died in the gas chamber at Ravensbrück.

Before describing the reason for these tragic deaths, I must tell of a particularly daring escape that took advantage of the German transport used to take away the foreign workers. Dennis Le Cuirot was 17. He was imprisoned at the time of the deportation riots and tried by court martial at the same time as myself. He too escaped deportation to Germany as a 'troublemaker'. He believed, however, that he was still being watched and, in late June 1944, made friends with some of the workers being taken from Alderney to France. He found there was little check on their descriptions or number. To protect his mother from blame when his absence was discovered, he told her that he had been ordered to report to the *Feldkommandantur*, as he was being 'taken away.'

On 3 July, he calmly walked past the guards and onto the ship, the *Minotaur*, as if he was one of the workers. Off Chausey, British Motor Torpedo Boats attacked their small convoy. They sank all four escort vessels and torpedoed the *Minotaur*. It was also hit by a shell. Thinking the vessel was about to sink, he dived overboard and was in the water for some time before he climbed back onto the ship, which was still afloat. They reached St. Malo without further incident. He saw that there were only about 100 women and 75 men left out of the original 500 who left Jersey. These are probably the deaths Gilbert refers to in *The Holocaust*. He thought they were Jews, but research has show they were other foreign workers.

Housed in barracks at St. Servan, Dennis escaped over the wall with two Frenchmen and got through the lines to meet up with advancing Americans at St. Lo. As Roy Thomas commented in his book, *Lest We Forget*, 'it must have taken more than a modicum of nerve to have attempted such a venture which successfully utilised transport supplied by the enemy.' I can only add that it took even more courage to literally put himself in the lion's mouth by joining those workers. He might very well have finished up in Germany. With no papers and no satisfactory explanation for his presence, he might have ended his life in Belsen, or somewhere just as evil.

The German War Diary entry for '30.6/1.7.44 reads as follows: Jersey to St Malo: mv Klaus, Wilhelm, Gerfried, Georgi, Spinel, Franka, with 1 SS Baubrigade, with 634 prisoners, 58 SS men, 458 OT workers, 28 personnel under arrest (soldiers and civilians), 43 foreigners, 46 women and 1 English prisoner of war.' This transport also took away Harold Le Druillenec and Mrs Gould.

Louisa Gould ran a small grocery shop. One of her sons had been killed serving with the Royal Navy. A Russian, about the same age as her son, escaped and hid in a shed at René Le Motté's farm, La Villaise, at St. Ouen. Le Motté was already sheltering one Russian and couldn't manage to hide and feed two. He asked Mrs Gould if she would help. When she agreed, Bob Le Sueur took the fugitive there after dark. Louisa Gould knew the penalty for hiding an escaped prisoner.

The Medical Officer of Health, Dr McKinstry, who at great risk helped many escapees, got Bill false papers and a ration card. He became so fluent in English that he took a job and even joined Boots Library, but an informer betrayed them.

A telephone call in *patois* warned Mrs Gould and Bill got away but, when the *Gestapo* searched her house, they found a Russian dictionary. They searched the houses of her brother, Harold, and her sister Ivy Foster; in both, they found a radio. Bill survived.

We do not know the details of Louisa Gould's journey into degradation and death, but her schoolteacher brother survived to describe the horrors he experienced. They were parted when they got to France. After three days in a closed cattle truck, without sanitation, Harold reached Neuengamme concentration camp. The Woods wrote: 'Starving and caked in his own filth, he entered a world of its own, split off utterly from the one he had left – a world were the abnormal became the normal, where sadism and torture and hunger so transformed men that, within weeks, some were incapable of remembering that there was any other world.' They moved him to Wilhelmshaven. There, he was told that one Kapo – prisoner chief – had beaten more than a hundred prisoners to death, often for such an apparently trivial offence as stealing a potato. Harold learnt how to survive, immediately obeying any SS order. To conserve his energy, he shuffled, and 'marched' to work without looking to right or to left. He avoided drawing attention to himself in any way. The horrors he saw included a young boy beaten to death for stealing food in the kitchen. Another inmate was driven mad by torture before being killed. The Woods describe how he saw a young French poet cradle a louse on the back of his wrist and refrain from crushing it, saying "No! Let it live! They are the only creatures in this camp who are living their natural life." On Christmas day, in front of a tree bedecked with lighted candles, sadistic Kapos sang *Stille Nacht* – Silent Night.

As the Allies advanced into Germany he was moved to Belsen. Once again he travelled in a cattle truck. For five days and five nights, there was no food or water. There was no sanitation. In the camp at Belsen, the food supply had already ceased. Prisoners ate grass and leaves. If they could find any. Dead and dying prisoners littered the compound. Small children played among the corpses. When British troops rescued him, Harold weighed 7 stone. The first time he shaved, he looked over his shoulder to see whose face was in the mirror.

There were other Channel Islanders who made a one-way journey to death in German camps. Others survived. But for the present I must return to Jersey at the time of the Invasion. It was the moment we had waited for, but as the progress of our troops into France and towards Germany gained momentum, there was no sign of an attack on the Islands. We slowly understood that the war had passed us by. Little did we realise that there was another year to go before Liberation. It was a year of increasing shortages and near disaster and of possibilities about which, fortunately, we were unaware.

✳   ✳   ✳

Chapter Nine

THE SIEGE, ESPIONAGE AND ESCAPE

By July 1944, the question everyone asked was: "When will they come to us?" The Island was a turning point for many of the planes that dropped American paratroopers on Normandy in the early hours of D-Day. Early accounts of the Invasion in the British Press and on German and Swedish radio claimed that landings had already been made in the Islands. The *Daily Express* for 7 June published a map on its front page that showed airborne landings on Jersey. A headline trumpeted: LANDINGS ON CHANNEL ISLANDS.

The day after the Invasion, guns at Noirmont on the south coast of the Island opened fire on targets beyond the horizon, and our hopes soared as we imagined Allied ships closing in and that there would soon be a landing. The Germans put guards everywhere. Sentries or patrols moved us on if we slowed down or stopped anywhere near German billets, on the sea front, or near their fortifications. They painted Red Crosses on the gates and walls of hospitals and medical aid posts and Red Cross flags fluttered in the breeze above such buildings. German medical staff wore Red Cross brassards, but carried weapons! Troops dug and manned slit trenches and weapon pits. Allied planes flew overhead but the anti-aircraft guns didn't open fire unless the planes came in low and looked as if they were going to attack.

On 10 June, Allied planes machine-gunned six patrol boats lying outside the harbour. They dropped bombs at Les Landes in the north-west of the Island and destroyed gun emplacements. German guns at Noirmont were again in action the next day against more invisible targets out to sea. The BBC warned us to stay away from military installations. But there was no sign of an invasion. On the 12th the RAF attacked the harbour area in St. Helier. Bombs fell near patrol boats moored off Elizabeth Castle, but there was no obvious damage.

The atmosphere became more and more tense as we expected to be invaded at any time. The Germans remained on constant standby. Sinel wrote that soldiers kept hold of their weapons even when having a haircut. At any moment, we expected to be shelled by the Royal Navy and bombed by the RAF in preparation for a landing.

But two more days passed. Still nothing. Sinel reported that on 14 June, British and Polish destroyers sent three minesweepers to the bottom, and that they probably sank another and left two more burning. German casualties were heavy. Ambulances took them to the General Hospital and to other casualty reception centres. The RAF also bombed Elizabeth Castle. Michael Ginns corrects Sinel's account: the War Diary of the 24th Minesweeping Flotilla shows that only one boat was sunk; three others were badly damaged. They came into St. Helier Harbour to unload casualties and undergo running repairs. Then they sailed to St. Malo for dockyard repairs, and were back in full service within a week.

Shortages became more of an everyday problem. Hunger was our constant companion. The weekly ration for an adult at the beginning of the siege was 500 grams of bread, 500 grams of potatoes, 20 grams of meat (when there was no meat, there was a small allowance of butter), 85 grams of sugar, 200 grams of breakfast meal, 30 grams of salt. At that time, the Germans allowed themselves 2,800 grams of potatoes, 2,100 grams of bread, 500 grams of meat and 245 grams of fat.

Many potatoes were rotten. Meat was seldom on our menu. Those with rabbits and a secure place to keep them got some protein. We were grateful for the Jersey cow. At least we had some skimmed milk and a little butter. It wasn't much, but it helped to keep us alive. People living in the town who had enough money to buy them, or a small plot to grow them, eked out their rations with vegetables. We all ate a lot of fart-provoking swedes and turnips. They weren't brimming over with nutrition but their bulk filled our bellies, at least for a short time. As the official ration shrank even further and the ratio of root vegetables to other foods increased, griping colic and diarrhoea were more frequent. Families and individuals, men and women, walked or cycled into the country parishes to try to buy vegetables from the farms.

When the Battle of Normandy reached the coast opposite Jersey, we cycled to the north-east corner of the Island to watch. It was like 1940 again. But now it was the Germans who were beaten back. When planes attacked another convoy off Corbière and damaged several ships, we saw them limp into harbour and the casualties being brought ashore.

On 19 June, poor old La Rocque got clobbered again! This time, bombs destroyed a dozen houses. Civilian casualties were light and most of the wounds weren't severe, but the bombed-out householders had to find somewhere to live. They found it harder to replace all the necessities they had lost. Michael Ginns told me that the aircraft was a Marauder of the US Air Force, which had been cruising up and down, probably taking photographs. The sentry on Platte Rocque Tower was so unwise as to open up with his machine gun. Having finished what it was doing, the aircraft dropped a couple of bombs. They were supposed to land on the Tower, but hit the houses instead. Fortunately, it was a Saturday and most of the residents were in Town. Later, during the last winter of the siege, all the woodwork was ripped out of the ruined houses and used as fuel.

On 21 June, German-friendly fire from one of the flak ships lying just off the harbour hit one of their own bombers. It crashed in La Rue de Samarès. One of its engines broke free and somersaulted along the ground. It finally stopped in the gap between two bungalows opposite Brig-y-Don children's home. There were no civilian casualties. On 22 June, the RAF bombed Alderney. The next day, there was another naval battle just south of Jersey and the Germans brought more wounded men and corpses ashore.

The Parish Constables met to decide what to do when fighting spread to the Island. It was the day the Germans court-martialled Mrs Gould and her brother, and they started their terrible journeys to Ravensbrück and Belsen.

Sonderführer Wolchen listened to our telephone conversations, if we could get through on the limited service that still worked. German engineers turned the backs of cranes on the quays towards the water when they were not in use, so that if they had to blow up the harbour, the cranes would topple in.

The States made plans to cope with the increased demand for communal feeding, and members of St. John Ambulance sited First Aid posts at various places. They were still allowed to wear their distinctive black and white uniforms. Dolly Le Brun put hers on once a week and cycled into town to do an evening duty at the General Hospital.

The continuous rumble of the guns and the endless concussion of heavy bombs exploding somewhere inside the nearby French coast were music to our ears. The flashes and smoke were clearly visible, but there was still no sign the battle would spread to us. We feared an Allied attack and the cost in lives it would bring, but we longed to be free. We expected it to happen. We wanted it to happen. Liberation would come only at a price, but we would be happy to pay.

The Constables drew up plans to billet fellow Islanders with the rest of us if their houses were destroyed. The RAF dropped leaflets in English. They warned us to keep away from gun emplacements and to take cover in case of attack, but they didn't say when they were coming. The Germans requisitioned several hundred bicycles, and more people had to walk. There was no public transport. It became more and more of an ordeal for people to get to and from work or to forage for food when an empty stomach left them weak and faint. But life went on. It had to go on.

※

On 7 July, the Germans warned 'that a state of emergency would apply in the Island if the military situation demanded it.' In that event, they ordered all civilians to stay in their homes. The notice added that the distribution of foodstuffs would be suspended. As a result, the States issued an emergency ration 'to be used only if necessary.' They told us to eat any perishables in the reserve and to replace them from the normal ration. The bread went mildewed. For a while we ate it and replaced it from the weekly ration as they told us to, but then more and more people registered with bakers to have it made into rusks. Rusks kept longer.

A BBC broadcast told us how to make crystal sets – as if we didn't know! 20 July was my 17th birthday. Hitler survived Colonel Claus Von Stauffenberg's bomb in the Wolf's Lair at Rastenburg, but he wouldn't see another July.

Following the attempt on Hitler's life, all German personnel were ordered to give the Nazi salute instead of the normal military greeting. The BBC warned fishermen that the French coast and waters round the Islands were unsafe and that a free bombing policy was now in force, and we asked ourselves whether it meant they were coming at last?

The Germans slaughtered any horses they could spare for sausage meat and some ate cats and dogs too. Islanders who still had pets watched them carefully. They weren't always successful. Parties of Germans carried buckets to the beaches and collected limpets from the rocks and seawalls. Everything was running out. Soon they made nettle soup, but at that stage they still had more food than we did. It was only when we got Red Cross parcels that the balance changed.

The surrounding waters and the neighbouring coast became a *son et lumière* of war and we sat in the front row. It was almost like watching a war film from the safety of a cinema seat, a war that all but passed us by.

The BBC told us there were resistance movements in all the occupied countries and Colonel Britain's broadcasts encouraged us to resist the Germans in every way we could. It started early on with V-signs. Now we began to ask each other, "What can we do? How can we help when the Allies do invade?" We couldn't see any other way to freedom.

I talked quietly to Peter Curwood and we began to sound out those friends we thought might be thinking along the same lines, but we had to be careful. Secrecy was essential to avoid the attention of informers and the Gestapo. We had to be certain of the loyalty of anyone we spoke to, even if they didn't want to be involved themselves. Sometime in late 1943 or early 1944, I had a long talk with André Dubras and two other men in an empty house in the Georgetown area. I can't remember who the other two were, but I do recall that it was a very hot day and with windows closed and curtains drawn, the room in which we talked was stuffy and uncomfortable. We met for an hour or two and agreed to cooperate, but nothing came of it. It was too soon. It was not the time.

One evening in early 1944, I met James Houillebecq outside the General Hospital. It was late, just before curfew. He was on foot and I had my bike and we kept moving to avoid drawing attention to ourselves. We discussed stealing weapons and he told me that he already had, or was about to get, an MP40, a Schmeisser machine pistol. He had something wrong with one of his eyes and when I asked him about it, he said something about injuring it with the spring mechanism of a weapon he was cleaning. Fortunately for me, nothing came of that meeting either. A few weeks, later he was arrested. He was betrayed by an informer or came under suspicion for some other reason, and the Gestapo found ammunition and a list of stolen weapons in his house. He died in Neuengamme concentration camp.

Peter and I made careful progress in our search for others. Eventually we formed a group with Bernard Cavey, Oscar Horman, Charles Bondis, Ed Le Corre, Doug Davey, Hugh La Cloche, Charles Gates, Mark Burger, Denis Poignard, John Picot and Arthur Marett. There may have been others I have forgotten and I apologise if I haven't mentioned their names.

It is too long ago to remember who contacted whom, or exactly when or in what order. Other writers have described Bernard Cavey as our leader, but I don't think we thought in terms of anybody being in command. It was a pretty democratic organisation. We met several times after dark at Oscar Horman's house and later at Curwood's Stables in Palmyra Road, just off Rouge Bouillon. For a while our only weapon was a swordstick that my father had acquired as part of the metal collection before the Occupation and had been left with it when the Germans arrived. Playing D'Artagnan, I shattered it against a railing in the blackout one night and reduced it to the status of a dagger!

To begin with, we didn't try to add to our 'armament.' We decided early on that the time to get weapons was when the British did attack. To steal weapons in large numbers or to engage in active sabotage too soon would only lead to reprisals. However, Bernard Cavey did manage to liberate a Luger and three German potato masher hand grenades. There wasn't much ammunition for the pistol. We couldn't find a retired army officer to lead us and I had the impression that as a group the former military men didn't want to know. I might have been wrong.

We decided to concentrate on plans to help Allied troops when they got ashore. It would be easier to get weapons once the fighting started, but we thought we could be most useful as guides and made plans accordingly. The Island was divided into sectors. We paired off to map the strongpoints and garrison billets, and also tried to estimate the number of German troops in each area.

At further meetings, we discussed sabotage again and once more decided that, to protect the civilian population, we could do nothing active until the attack began. Only then would there be suitable opportunities, because in the absence of explosives – which we didn't know how to use anyway – we would be restricted to cutting telephone wires, and disabling German transport. There was still some phosphorus in the chemistry laboratory at Victoria College and we made plans to steal it. We could start fires and put sand in petrol tanks. We could cut telephone lines at many points, and we could kill isolated Germans for their weapons.

Peter Curwood and I explored and mapped the south-west corner of the Island. We spent several days cycling and walking around St. Brelade's and Corbière; we took care not to loiter too long near strongpoints or German billets. From time to time we sat in a field, or on a fence or wall, and pretended to eat, spinning out the little food we had. In case we were stopped and searched, we memorised as much as possible to write down and put on the map later, and anything we did put on paper, we kept as small as possible so that we could swallow it or get rid of it quickly by other means. At further meetings, the group coordinated all the information and someone, I think Oscar Horman, hid it somewhere safe. We had no reason to know where it was concealed so we didn't ask.

✳

The days and then the weeks passed with no sign of an invasion. Slowly we realised the Allies weren't coming: at least not until they had dealt with the Germans on the mainland. We became more and more despondent. We had no idea the Allied advance into Germany would be so swift. We could only see more months or even a year or two of increasingly harsh conditions, starvation and little chance of survival. We never thought it would take the ending of the war to secure our freedom. We never even considered the Germans would surrender the Island without a fight. The very nature of their fortifications made such a supposition ridiculous.

When the truth sank in, we began to discuss alternative plans. The Allies were in Brittany. Brest was under siege. The neighbouring coast had been liberated. It was less than fifteen miles away. If we could get our maps and other intelligence out, they would be useful when the Allies did invade. We never thought it would be unnecessary, but even if we had known, I think we would still have tried to get to France.

To escape and get the information out would be difficult and dangerous, and there were several significant problems to overcome before we could even think of breaking through the coastal defence line. Not least was the question of who and how many should go. And we had to find a boat. It was soon obvious that everyone wanted to go if a large enough boat could be found, but we agreed from the start that every member of the escape party must be able to swim. That meant Mark Burger had to drop out. He was bitterly disappointed but, given what happened to three of us later, it was a wise decision. We also decided that if anyone got into trouble on the way, the others would go on. We could not let such problems compromise the operation as a whole.

We tried to find a boat big enough to carry the whole group, or smaller boats seaworthy enough to get us to the mainland. We also needed transport to get the boat, or boats, to the embarkation point, and we had to find the best place to leave from, an area where the defences were less extensive, and where we could get past them onto the beach in the dark with the least risk of being shot or of stepping on a mine. I don't think any of us knew about Bill Bertram's embarkation point at Fauvic from which so many later escapees got away. It reflects perhaps the good security maintained by those who left from there.

The stables on Palmyra Road were secluded. They were around a corner from the main street and would make a good temporary hiding place. There was plenty of room and privacy to work on any boats or engines that we could find. Our main problem was solved fairly soon, though not as we would have liked. We couldn't just go around openly asking people if they knew where a boat was hidden, and even if we didn't make the fatal mistake of talking to an informer, there were plenty of blabber mouths who would not be slow to tell all their friends what was going on. Although we tried hard, making discreet enquiries, we couldn't find a boat big enough to carry the whole party. However, we found three canoes. They were not what we wanted, but they would have to do. We split into three crews.

We were lucky to find the canoes at all, tiny as they were. The Germans had confiscated all small boats in early 1941, and they guarded any licensed fishing boats and other craft still in the water in three small harbours. That didn't totally exclude the possibility of cutting one or more of them out, but it would have been much more dangerous. Both Mark Burger and Peter Curwood hid canoes away in 1940, and Ed Le Corre and Doug Davey found a 14foot Folboat. They were hopelessly unseaworthy and our first job was to make them watertight. Experts among the friends we could trust told us it was much too dangerous to use such small craft, but we couldn't find anything better.

Cavey, Bondis and Horman made up one crew. Shortly afterwards they managed to buy a better canoe from a dealer called Kenshole in St. Aubin. Clinker-built, it was made of Canadian pine, but only 21 feet long with an 18 inch beam, and designed for two people and the relatively smooth waters of a Canadian lake. With a crew of three, the freeboard was less than 3 inches!

I crewed with Peter Curwood and Bells La Cloche. In his book *Lest We Forget*, Roy Thomas described our canoe as made of wood and canvas, but it too was all wood, and also clinker-built. Peter Curwood and I spent two days caulking it with oakum, and then filled it with water to expand the wood that had dried out during storage.

The Folboat was the most unseaworthy and its crew had to patch several holes in its fabric. It says much for the courage of Ed Le Corre and Doug Davey that they agreed to put to sea at all in such a flimsy craft, never mind cross one of the more dangerous stretches of water in the world. I don't think I would have gone in their canoe.

Peter Guiton, a States pilot, and John Picot from St. Ouen told us all they could about the tides and navigation and Charles Bondis, who worked in the States Transport Office, forged the papers we needed to get a charcoal-burning lorry. Arthur Marett volunteered to drive the canoes to the embarkation point. Peter, Hugh and I spent several days reconnoitering the coast and we soon discovered that finding the best place to leave was far from easy. We walked for miles, trying not to look suspicious. That wasn't easy either. We needed to find a reasonable gap between the close-packed fortifications and weapon pits and as far away as possible from the direct view of any sentries. We would have to avoid frequent German patrols moving up and down the sea wall and the beach and its approaches had to be clear of mines and, if possible, of barbed wire. Finally, we needed a house to hide in close to the shore.

We spent about a week looking at the beaches and slipways along the south-east coast before deciding on Pontac. Those few days are finely etched in my memory. We were so hungry. Cycling out from St. Helier and then walking for long stretches by roundabout routes to avoid the curious gaze of German guards and patrols made us weak and dizzy. The Islands were cut off from all supplies after D-Day. There was just not enough to eat. I also remember being thoroughly frightened by what I had got myself into. That fear grew as the time to leave drew near and the night before we left I hardly slept. I lay awake, cursing myself for getting into such a situation, and wrestling with conflicting notions of pride, self-respect and downright cowardice.

Before leaving home on 19 September, I left a letter for my parents, thanking them for everything and apologising for giving them so much extra worry at such a time. It may be asked how I could have contemplated doing such a thing, especially when I had promised not to. The answer? We were young men of our time. We were fiercely patriotic. We had an unassailable belief in where our duty lay. Such emotions may seem outmoded now, but they were very real then and I make no apologies.

Some Germans and several local people saw Arthur Marett load the replacement canoe onto the lorry at St. Aubin, but he got it safely to Pontac without being challenged, where Dennis Poignard put it into a temporary hiding place. For many years I thought Arthur Marett and Ed Le Corre had stolen the lorry from a guarded German lager. Indeed, I said so during a BBC broadcast in 1985. I didn't know then, or had forgotten, that they got it by using false papers forged by Charles Bondis.

With final preparations complete and the tides right, we decided to go on the night of 19/20 September. Disaster struck soon after we met at the stables to load the other two canoes onto the vehicle. We had just put them on the back of the lorry and covered them with a tarpaulin and were waiting for Bernard, Charles and Oscar to join us for the journey to Pontac. It was dark when they arrived, about half-an-hour before curfew. An armed German soldier who was billeted in a house nearby challenged them just outside the stable. He had probably heard the lorry, become suspicious, and decided to investigate.

It is well known that descriptions of traumatic events vary from witness to witness, often in the most bizarre ways, and do so even shortly after the ordeal. My memory for the early part of that night is distorted and fragmentary, though it is sharp for most of what happened later. Over the years, I believed it was a two-man patrol that found us. I was mistaken. I remember at some time jumping from the hayloft-loading door into the road. It was round a corner from the main doors. I was obviously in a panic, but must have recovered and gone back in because I also have a distinct memory of being in the stable again and joining a chorus of voices saying, *Kartoffels, kartoffels* – Potatoes, potatoes, to explain the lorry. The soldier was not impressed. He looked under the tarpaulin.

While this was going on, Charles, Oscar and Bernard slipped away in the dark. They picked up their bikes from their homes and rode to Pontac. They didn't think they would see us again. They presumed that we were already under arrest, but expected us to keep our mouths shut until they were safely out to sea.

I cannot really understand or give an adequate explanation for what happened next. The only logical conclusion is that the soldier knew very well what we were up to and decided to take no action. If that was not the reason, he must have been extremely stupid. His name was Gretz. He was an *Unteroffizier* in the German Garage Stores and knew both Ed Le Corre and Arthur Marett who had to visit the store almost daily as part of their employment.

Gretz asked for our Identity Cards and, after examining them, ordered us to report to the *Feldkommandantur* – the next morning! He then turned on his heels and left! It seemed too good to be true and in our hurry to get away before he changed his mind, Arthur drove out too quickly. The end of our canoe was sticking out from the back of the lorry and hit the doorpost as he swung too widely, an accident that would prove disastrous.

The ride to Pontac was uneventful. It was impossible to avoid main roads and we sat in the back expecting to hear shouts of *Halt* at any moment, or to run into a roadblock. We had decided to make a dash for it if challenged and, as we drove through the darkened streets of the town and out into St. Clement's as quickly as the charcoal burner would let us, I felt terribly vulnerable and frightened. But we made it safely. There were no shouts. There were no shots. I am always amused when I see war films about Occupied France which show Germans every few yards. For dramatic effect, patrols crisscross the scene every ten seconds. The reality was different. It was a question of luck. They could not be everywhere.

We unloaded the canoes at Pontac and hid them in deep shadow close to the sea wall, then moved quietly into a bungalow belonging to Len Le Cuirot to settle down to wait. Dennis Poignard had arranged with Len to hide us until the time came to leave. They would get the canoes onto the beach for us earlier, hide them in the rocks and seaweed, and then help us to carry them and guide us through the gullies to the open sea. The tide goes out a long way at Pontac. We could not find our own way safely through the maze of rocks in the dark.

Arthur took the lorry back to St. Helier. The Gestapo arrested him soon after, and he was interrogated and imprisoned. Bernard, Charles and Oscar arrived a short time after us, without being stopped or shot at, and were more than a little surprised and happy to find us already there.

It was going to be a long night, so we settled down as best we could to wait until the early hours, when the tide and currents would carry us out to sea and, hopefully, sweep us towards the French coast. We were too keyed up to rest. I'd developed a severe headache, a real thumper, probably due to nervous tension since I don't normally get headaches, and when I asked Len if he had anything he came back with a large French Aspirin. It looked like a cross between one of those Bassett's Liquorice All Sorts covered in hundreds and thousands and a Horse Pill. I didn't know whether to swallow it or stick it up the other end and, as the French are somewhat unpredictable in such matters, I asked to make sure!

It was nearly 3am when we put out the lamp to avoid showing any light, and quietly left the bungalow. We crouched for a while to listen for approaching Germans and, hearing nothing, crept in complete silence across a patch of open ground towards the shore. We lowered ourselves as noiselessly as we could over the sea wall, and then waited in its shadow for the next patrol to pass above our heads.

It was a clear night. There was no moon, but the sky was bright with stars. There was an open stretch of beach to cross before reaching the rocks, and the nearest defence posts were only metres away, much too close for comfort. We couldn't afford to make any noise. Starlight made getting to the rocks easier, but added considerably to the risk of being seen, and it was with considerable trepidation that we crossed that first naked patch of sand.

We retrieved the canoes from under seaweed among the rocks, where Dennis and Len had hidden them earlier, and started our long walk to the open sea. Once into the gullies, it was relatively safe. As far as we could tell, the Germans had withdrawn their watchposts from Icho and Seymour Towers that lie well out from the shoreline. We followed our guides in single file, keeping complete silence, and it took until nearly 5am to reach the water. The strain of carrying the canoes and keeping quiet began to tell and we were glad at last to thank our guides, quickly shake hands all round, and put out to sea.

Dennis and Len reached the beach without incident, avoided the patrols, and got safely back into the bungalow to wait for curfew to end. Going back across that empty stretch of starlit sand must have been hair-raising. Coming from the sea, any sentry or patrol seeing them would have considered them enemy invaders and fired without warning. Bernard, Charles and Oscar took the lead. We went next, and Ed and Doug followed in their flimsy Folboat. For a while we paddled down a long gully, the rocks a few feet away on either side. Then the channel widened and, as we left Icho Tower and the last line of the reefs behind, we felt the swell, the rise and fall of the open sea.

We had done it! We had escaped! We were on our way! Only those who have made an escape know the elation success brings. At that moment we had no fear. The treacherous waters ahead were nothing compared with getting through the gap in the fortified coastal fringe. We might have expressed some concern for Ed and Doug in their fragile little Folboat if we had been asked, but for ourselves there was no such worry. How wrong we were!

I don't know how long we paddled before we felt our backsides getting wet. We were well clear of Icho Tower and a good distance into open water. We could still see a few outlying rocks over our shoulders, but they were fading into the dark silhouette of the Island landmass. As more water came in we tried to bail, but there wasn't room. The canoe began to list heavily and we knew there was no alternative to trying to get back to the Island. The blow against the doorpost as we left the stables must have opened up a seam. Our chances of getting back to shore at all, never mind making it across the sand without being spotted, were hopeless. We were a long way out. It would be daylight by the time we reached the beach. If we did reach it!

We wished the others good luck and headed back towards the rocks. We had all agreed not to stop for anyone in trouble, but we had to be firm in our refusal of help. I've been told since that we used some pretty bad language. It was a sad moment and I can only imagine the worry our friends must have felt, as they had to leave us, thinking that we had little chance and would almost certainly drown. We tried to paddle as quickly as the waterlogged canoe would allow, but it was not long before she slipped away from under us. It was a gentle, passive, almost graceful movement – a reluctant parting – as if she didn't want to let us down.

The sea was cold, but not intolerable to begin with. Fortunately, the tide had turned and began to sweep us in towards the shore as the water rose rapidly.

Bells La Cloche was a long-distance swimmer. Before the war he had represented the school and, I think, the Island as a junior. Peter and I were strong swimmers too, and were not overly concerned at first. Peter found our paddles and for a while they helped us stay afloat. We took off most of our clothes, but I kept on a tatty, khaki woollen pullover. When I found something floating nearby, I grabbed it and stuffed it up the front to give me greater buoyancy, but sometime later I lost it: it was washed away with the paddles when we were swept from a rock. I couldn't tell what it was in the dark, but it was probably part of a lifejacket from one of the ships sunk in naval battles around the Island.

Paradoxically, it was Hugh who got into trouble. He may have been swimming less strongly so as not to get ahead of Peter and I, or the cold got to him more easily than it did to us. He got severe cramps in his legs and was in such pain that to stop him going under we had to hold him up for several minutes at a time. We were relieved to get to another rock. It gave us time to get our breath back and massage his limbs.

With the turn of the tide, the water became choppy and it wasn't long before it washed us off our rock. There were plenty of other rocks at low tide, but as the water rose further, they too were soon covered, and our resting-places became fewer and further apart.

The next two hours are a blur. I remember being washed off one rock after another, and swimming for long periods between them, but I can't remember being very frightened. I think we were too numbed by what had happened and by the worry of what lay ahead when we reached the shore. When the sky began to lighten we were still a long way from the beach and by then we were really cold. We hadn't much spare flesh. There was no insulating fat on us to keep us warm. Very soon, we were dangerously tired.

We decided to call for help. It was obvious that once it was light we would not stand any chance of getting across the beach and through the fortifications without being spotted and Peter and I became more and more worried about Hugh. He had frequent severe attacks of cramp and even if we could get close to the beach without being seen, it would mean spending the day hiding in the rocks and seaweed up to our necks in freezing water; and then waiting for enough darkness to slip past the patrols. We were already close to exhaustion. Each time we made a new rock, we called for help.

Sinel wrote: 'Residents at Le Hocq were awakened by cries for help coming from the sea before daylight; these gradually grew stronger and, as visibility became clearer, three figures were seen – two in the water and one marooned on a rock. The Germans at Rocque Berg could not provide much assistance, but focused searchlights as two local residents made attempts at rescue. A canoe was found to be useless, but a ship's raft was obtained and with this, the person on the rock [Hugh] was rescued; the two others managed to get ashore by themselves, all being in an exhausted condition.' I can't remember searchlights. I think it was light enough already not to need them, but they could have been probing the water earlier and in our numb, disorientated, hypothermic state we hadn't noticed.

The other two canoes got to France. Once, they heard a boat engine further out to sea and thought it was probably a German E-Boat on patrol. Once, they saw a searchlight in the distance, but after that they saw no further evidence of enemy activity, and with mounting confidence paddled into the night. At about the time we dragged ourselves ashore, they changed course towards the east and took advantage of the tide and current that swept them towards the French coast. The water was still relatively calm, but a sea mist cut down visibility for a time. When it lifted at last, the two canoes were within a hundred yards of each other and they paddled towards France together, taking turns to rest. At one time they closed up and later remembered how pale and exhausted they looked to each other. 'Not surprisingly,' Roy Thomas wrote, 'with such hard physical effort after more than four years of Occupation diet.'

When they saw seagulls, they knew the French coast was near. Shortly afterwards, an American aircraft flew over and dipped its wings. About half a mile from the shore, they closed on a fishing boat and found that they were near Blainville-sur-Mer. As they ran through the surf towards the beach, waves swamped both boats before they could reach dry land, and after they pulled the canoes up the beach they were so exhausted they could hardly stand. Bernard Cavey lost his shoes in the landing. It was about 11am. They had done the crossing in something like six hours. As Roy Thomas commented, it gave them a strong claim to the Blue Riband of the Jersey-France escape route!

Cold, wet-through and very hungry, they walked into Blainville-sur-Mer and gave themselves up to the Mayor's secretary who provided them with a permit to get food at the town hotel. The French locals gave them a warm welcome. They were amazed at the short time they had taken to make the crossing.

When an American officer arrived, he took them by Jeep to Coutainville. Bernard was able to give the Americans the number, rank and name and other personal details of various US soldiers captured and taken to Jersey. It helped to remove any suspicion the Americans might have. Bernard's sister was a nurse at the hospital and got the information directly from the wounded Americans.

The Royal Marines then took charge of the party. They were debriefed and transferred to Bayeux before evacuation to England. Ed Le Corre stayed in hospital for a few days. He was totally exhausted. He lost most of the skin from his hands and strained his heart; the doctor who examined him told him, "It's going like a train."

After more interrogation, the Royal Marines put them in a Transit Camp near Arromanches before they travelled on to England in an LST commanded by a Jerseyman. When he heard they were on board, he took them to his cabin for a beer.

At their debriefing, Bernard was amazed to find out how much British Intelligence already knew about the fortifications in the Islands. They told him most of the information came from liberated Russian Slave Labourers. Much of the intelligence we collected was already known!

Douglas Davey joined the RAF. Bernard Cavey and Ed Le Corre went into the Fleet Air Arm. After the war, Bernard joined the Rhodesian Police. Later he became Secretary General of what is now Zimbabwe's Catering Industry Council. He still lives in Zimbabwe. On a recent trip to East Africa, I caught up with him for the first time since that night in 1944. We sank an alarming amount of beer at Meikle's Hotel in Harare, and finished up eating liver and bacon at one o'clock in the morning.

Ed Le Corre now lives in France. When they were still out to sea, he threw his coat overboard to make more room. It was washed up in Jersey, and identified. Until the end of the Occupation, his family thought he had drowned.

Arthur Marett and Len Le Cuirot both served time in prison. They kept Dennis Poignard's involvement from the Germans, so that later he was able to give other escapees the same kind of help he had given us.

Chapter Ten

BEHIND BARS

The next few hours are something of a blur. Odd moments, disjointed incidents and confused impressions stand out against a background of faded memories. I have a vague recollection of being dragged up the beach. I can remember standing under guard in some kind of German Mess, with hard-faced men staring at us and sometimes laughing. Until recently, I always thought it was a Gestapo Mess because they were in civilian clothes. However, they were probably OT officials. Although most had left the Island by then, there were still elements of the OT firm, Olbricht & Co, in the island. Their headquarters was at Craigie Hall in La Rue du Hocq near to where we came ashore. We were not questioned there, nor were we roughly treated, but we shivered with cold and shock. We were too exhausted and too relieved to be ashore to feel fear.

I remember lying in some form of transport, possibly a military ambulance, when something happened outside the open back door. There was a lot of shouting, but I couldn't see what was going on. It was probably an incident when a young woman, one of the Mossop sisters, shouted good luck and was arrested.

They took us to the OT Hospital, formerly the Ladies' College, and made us stand in a large room for a long time. All I had on was my old, worn pullover, and I was bursting for a pee. They gave me a tin Jerry – no pun intended – and I had to perform in front of a group of mocking German nurses. The fact that we were taken to the OT Hospital suggests the Mess did belong to that organisation. They didn't examine us or give us any treatment. After about an hour, they took us to La Folie Inn and separated us before the Naval Police interrogated us.

My first interrogator was brutal and unpleasant. He shouted at me repeatedly in broken English. He didn't ask any questions, but pushed my face into the edge of an unpainted, deal wooden shelf and kicked the back of my legs. My mouth was slammed repeatedly against the wood below a line of books and pamphlets. Then he made me stand against the wall and slapped each side of my head with his palms. They were hard blows and after a while I felt as if my head was coming off, and there was a build up of pressure in my ears so that I thought the drums were going to burst. I was still shivering with cold and shock. This interrogator was notorious and probably part of the *HafenÜberwachungsstelle*:

on another occasion, he knocked out Joe Mière's teeth.

They separated Peter and Hugh from each other as well as from me. They were questioned somewhere in the same building. It seemed a long time, but was probably no more than ten minutes, before an interpreter and another officer arrived. They said something sharply to the first man, then let me sit. To my relief, the original interrogator disappeared. The formal questions lasted some hours, but there was no more violence. I can't remember what they asked, or what I said, but I became more and more aware of painful grazes and bruises, from the buffeting against the rocks, and I ached and throbbed all over.

Sometime later, they too went away and left me under the guard of an elderly Marine who covered my shoulders with a blanket and brought me a bowl of soup. In sign language, he told me to drink it quickly. I have always remembered his kindness. He wasn't the 'soft' part of the interrogation because he didn't ask any questions, and the interpreter, at least, had been restrained. After a few minutes, the Marine turned on a radio and I heard part of the news. Then he warned me the others were coming back and quickly turned it off. I can't remember what the announcer said, or whether it was the BBC or the Allied Expeditionary Forces Network, but I think it was already tuned to the right wavelength.

The interpreter seemed to be in charge now and he continued questioning me without intimidating shouts or threats. I felt better after the soup, and quite strong by the time we left La Folie. They took us in a black Citroen to the prison in Gloucester Street. We were not allowed to talk. The forbidding entrance, which I had passed so often and never really noticed before, stands out in my mind as do the metal studs that festooned its massive, wooden doors.

As we drove along the pier from La Folie Inn, I was horrified to see Mouse Le Brun, in broad daylight, pushing a boat on a handcart, and I had to stop myself giving any sign of recognition. I looked the other way until we had passed, but I knew he'd seen me and managed a surreptitious V-sign out of the back window. He got away that night with Roger Lerouilly and with another Frenchman whose ticket to go with them was to steal the boat.

Roger had been getting out intelligence to the French *Résistance* for at least two years. He regularly took plans of the fortifications in his bicycle pump or sewn into the lining of his clothes, and the *Résistance* network – *le réseau O.C.M.* in Caen – sent them on to London. Mouse joined the Royal Navy and saw service in the Far East before the war against Japan ended. Roger received a citation from de Gaulle as a *Soldat sans uniforme des Forces Françaises Combattantes*.

✳

The clang of the cell door as it closed behind me that first time has left an indelible memory. Every time I hear the same noise in films, or on television shows like 'Porridge', the memory floods back. It is an awful sound. So final. I am surprised to remember though how cold I was. I was still freezing, and shivering intermittently some hours afterwards, even though outside the sun was warm. When they locked me in a cell at the prison, it was still shining through a small, high window and motes of dust danced in its beam. I have retained an impression of musty dryness.

My first glance around was not reassuring. The cell was about 10 feet wide and 16 feet long. The floor was bare timber boards and an uncomfortable-looking wooden bed lay alongside one wall. In the corner by the door there was an old jam tin still half-full of the previous occupant's contributions. There was no other furniture. An unused heating pipe ran across the back of the cell and disappeared into the wall on each side. The scrofulous walls wore peeling whitewash on stone and were decorated with new and old graffiti: the calendars and sadnesses of previous prisoners. A thick plate glass window covered an external light bulb which could only be turned on and off from outside. A small slit-like window opened, flap-down into the cell, high up on the outside wall, so that it let in very little daylight. I could just see a tiny patch of sky. Like an evil eye, a small Judas hole beckoned from the door.

My mind churned as I tried to think about the future. My face was swollen and painful from being banged repeatedly into the edge of the shelf, and my lips felt like bladders of lard. I was sore from being washed against the rocks, and totally exhausted, too drained to try to plan ahead or to think about what was going to happen to us. The prospect of more interrogations and more violence and then months of prison was unpleasant but, more importantly, there would be the constant risk that the Gestapo could find out what we had been doing. I could think of nothing to reassure myself.

Sometime later I heard someone calling. It was little more than a whisper. To begin with, I couldn't tell where the voice came from, but then I found a small hole which former prisoners had bored alongside the unused heating pipe that ran across the back wall of the cell. I can't remember who I talked to that first day. I am embarrassed now when I find I can no longer remember so many names and faces. Not that I saw too many for a while, except at a distance, because for much of the time before our trial they were just voices heard through distant windows or under the doors in the early hours, long after the guards had locked us in for the night.

I don't know where my clothes came from, but by that time I was covered and had some wooden-soled shoes. The clothes were too small and the shoes too tight.

The prisoner in the next cell told me through the hole that we weren't allowed to talk, and warned me that the guards sometimes took off their boots and sneaked up the corridor to try to catch us out. He told me to watch the Judas hole and that during the day we could sit but not lie on the bed.

The bed was three parallel planks. There was a raised wooden pillow at one end. At night, they gave those of us who were not on punishment, three thin horsehair biscuits to cover the bare boards and a small pillow of the same material. They were hard and uncomfortable even so and sleep didn't come easily. It was so cold after dark that most of us had to get up two or three times a night to pee. At times, rats or mice disturbed our rest.

Punishment was severe for anyone who broke the rules. There was no physical violence but they took away the biscuits and pillow and the old, thin blanket handed out at nightfall. If there was an empty cell, the culprit spent his punishment in solitary confinement but the real penalty was the cut in rations. The amount of food they gave us was pathetically small anyway. One night during a period of solitary, I stood in the middle of my freezing cell and cried with hunger. I am sure others did too.

For breakfast, we had a mug of ersatz coffee and a thin slice of bread or a small mug of watery porridge. At midday, thin soup. Sometimes, a few pig potatoes in a small zinc mug; they were often rotten. At night, there was a crust of bread, a tiny bit of grease, and more ersatz coffee. Those on *streng*, – strict punishment – only got the midday soup. The light went out a six o'clock

I hadn't been in the cell long when the Chef made his first call. He was a *feldwebel* – a sergeant major. A professional soldier, he wore brightly polished cavalry boots and told every new prisoner that he had met Anthony Eden before the war. He was strict but fair. Our first meeting was not auspicious. I didn't stand up when he came in, and received the full blast of his military wrath for my discourtesy; and then another salvo for having my hands in my pockets. I got the message. Knowing already about the cut in rations for those on *streng*, I quickly swallowed my pride.

He was not a bad German. When the remaining prisoners were released the day before formal Liberation of the Island in 1945, they were still nominally under his control. Although by then the war was officially over and they were outside the prison walls, they treated him with the kindness and respect he deserved.

Sinel's Diary tells us that the day after our capture the Germans published a warning notice that read: 'Desertion to the enemies of the German Forces is forbidden and will be severely punished as espionage. Furthermore, it is announced that in future these deserters can no longer count on being rescued as shipwrecked, by the Germans.'

For the first few weeks they kept us in solitary confinement, but we managed to communicate by transmitting messages through other prisoners, talking to them under the doors or from window to window. We had to be careful and were always concerned about the safety of keeping in touch by this method.

Several times, the naval police took us back to La Folie for more questioning. We always walked there and back under escort, sometimes separately, sometimes together, but we were never allowed to talk. It was usually during the day and, as we were marched through the town, friends and strangers shouted encouragement, or made surreptitious V-signs. It would have been easy to escape then. Several times there was only one soldier guarding us and we weren't handcuffed. It would have been simple to give him a quick shove and to disappear into the crowd. But we never even considered it that I can recall. There is something very threatening about the Schmeisser machine pistol but, more commonly, almost all prisoners miss easy opportunities to escape soon after capture.

The Germans questioned me several more times, possibly because of my previous record. I was still on probation from the deportation riots, but had also been involved in another incident with Mouse Le Brun, from which I was fortunate to escape with no more than a few days' acute anxiety, and without – as he did – having to go to Gestapo HQ at Silvertide for questioning. If he hadn't managed to keep my involvement in that episode from them, I might not be writing this book.

✳

Sometime in 1944, we lay in wait on a dark night for the traitor Durand. He was a nasty piece of work. His parents and sisters entertained German friends at their home in St. John's and Durand worked with the Gestapo. He was often seen with them and his OT mates on sweeps for escaped prisoners. He always carried a large stick, and several times shouted insults in our direction. We decided he needed a good lesson and took him in the road not far from Beauchamp as he cycled home after curfew. We gave him a good going over before taking his arms and legs and tossing him unconscious over a hedge into a field. His bike followed. We should have killed him there and then and buried his body – most suitably in the manure heap.

Somehow in the dark, he recognised Mouse and the next day, when we returned to Beauchamp with a load of hay, we found the Gestapo waiting in the yard. Le Brun was holding the reins and I was sitting on top of the load, ready to toss the bales into the hayloft. They arrested Mouse. I kept my mouth shut and made myself as small as possible on top of the hay, expecting to be told to get down at any minute, but they ignored me.

They took Le Brun to Silvertide where he survived a few intense hours of questioning with no more damage than a nasty fright. Eventually, the Gestapo let him go with a warning. He had strenuously denied any involvement. They must have suspected the truth though, because they sent me a message to say that they were still watching what I was doing, and warning me to be very careful. That incident and my involvement in the Deportation riots were probably the reason why I was interrogated more extensively, but the nature of those interrogations gave all three of us cause for concern. They had a good idea what we had been up to. They suspected us of espionage.

Twice they woke me after lights out. I jumped awake as a rifle butt banged against the cell door. Each time it seemed like the middle of the night but was probably earlier, though certainly after curfew because the streets were deserted as we drove to Havre des Pas. They took me to Silvertide instead of La Folie Inn and I was questioned each time by Gestapo agents, and not by the naval police. They asked time and time again about photographs and maps and what else had we with us in the canoe. I kept telling them a bugle and we'd taken it to use as a signal if we needed help. The bugle sank with everything else somewhere off Icho Tower, but with the vagaries of current, wind and tide which bedevil the seas around Jersey, I was frightened the canoe had washed up and that they had found incriminating documents. I learned 50 years later that the bugle did wash up and is now on display somewhere.

They frightened me with endless shouted questions and threats. It went on for what seemed hours and I became more and more confused and nervous as they continually accused me of being a spy. It was obvious they knew something, and suspected more, but I gave nothing away and both times returned to my cell unharmed.

It has never ceased to amaze me how one's concentration begins to go after prolonged questioning and how easy it then becomes to make a mistake. I am not ashamed to admit that I was very frightened. Even though there was no brutality, their threats and the bullying way they put the questions intimidated me and there was always an implication of violence to come. I am glad I didn't share Charles Gruchy's experience when they interrogated him in the prison and shoved him face-first into a corner with a clicking pistol jammed into each loin.

Just before they allowed us to join the other prisoners, I had a severe attack of dysentery. Most of us suffered intermittently from what John Lewis called Famine Diarrhoea, but this attack must have had a bacterial origin, probably salmonella. What followed was intensified because I have always been afraid of rats. When I was small, Father told us about a schoolmistress who cornered a rat in a schoolroom, and how it jumped up and bit her throat out and she died. I don't know if it was true, something he had seen, or just heard about, but ever after I carried a graphic picture of it and a horror of rats.

After a couple of days of increasing diarrhoea and constantly ringing the bell to be taken to the *abort*, they put me by myself in a cell in our own block for a couple of days. Then they took me to a cell in the military punishment block, where they kept some of their own prisoners and other unfortunate foreigners, and left me on my own with a bucket. It had no rim. The sharp edge dug in when I tried to sit on it, and I had lost so much weight it cut deeply into the backs of my thighs and buttocks. In the end I was too weak to lift myself on or off. If I did get on, I fell off again, and the bucket tipped over. Then I had no strength to try at all. I lay in my own mess. I thought I was going to die, but was too miserable to care. Water ran down damp, bare granite walls. It was intensely cold, but at times I burned with fever and knew I was delirious. A small high window let in just a little light. At night, mice and rats scampered round the cell and sometimes over me. I woke once with something on my head, yelled out and beat my arms around, but I wasn't bitten.

I can't remember what food or drink I had, or if I had any. Somewhere, someone was looking after me though because I survived. Knowing what I do now about dehydration, and fluid and electrolyte loss in surgical patients, I can only marvel and be grateful.

When I got back to my old cell, I experienced a minor miracle. Josie Mines, one of the Irish nurses literally flounced – I am told – into the German Guardroom on two occasions with plates of hospital food. How she heard about my condition, or how she managed to bulldoze her way past the guards, I can't imagine. It must have taken an awful lot of blarney. She was a formidable lady when roused, and a bit of a character.

Soon after, they put me in a temporary cell with several other prisoners. There were at least seven in that confined space. After the war, I read an article in one of the medical journals about prisoners-of-war having to pee a lot at night, and not just because of the cold. It claimed an inadequate diet and protein deficiency were at least partly responsible. There was an old jam tin in the corner near the door, and we slept transversely across the cell. Everyone rolled over one space towards the tin as the last man to pump ship lay down against the farthest wall.

With overcrowding and a need to keep prisoners separate, both before and during questioning, the few remaining cells soon filled to overflowing and for a couple of weeks it was like a giant game of musical chairs as we moved from one to another. For a few days I was with a man whose name I have forgotten. He smoked a pipe, when he could get anything to put in it, and taught me how to split a match in two with a razor blade. We hid spare blades somewhere in the cell or on ourselves. I kept one in the heel of my shoe.

One of the guards, Otto, acquired a cat to deal with the influx of rodents. It certainly dealt with the problem, but Otto had the cheek to ask us to give some of our rations to feed it! I remember him giving it a saucer of milk one day, and feeling that I would like to steal it to drink myself.

In time, the sudden gut-wrenching calls to go for questioning became less frequent and finally stopped altogether, as we waited with anxiety and some impatience for trial by military Court Martial. Once sentenced, we knew they would transfer us to the civilian side where conditions were said to be easier. We learned on the grapevine that prisoners were sometimes allowed visitors and even food parcels. The warders were Jerseymen. There were real criminals in the prison too. They were housed on the lower floor of the civilian side, where the cells looked small, dark and very uncomfortable. They kept us, the political prisoners, separate, mainly on the upper storey.

We began to think about escape long before the trial, but there seemed no easy way to break out of the German block and reach the outer wall without being shot. A bullet hit an escapee who got that far as he was getting over, and he was recaptured. It was also difficult to plan anything while they kept us separate, and we decided to wait until they transferred us.

Just before Christmas, I earned a week of *streng* for some unremembered crime and went back into solitary confinement. There were two Russians in the next cell. I learnt a few words of their language that I enjoyed trotting out from time to time after the war. One sentence was: 'I want to see my girlfriend out of the window.' If we propped the wooden bed against the outer wall when the guards weren't about, we could climb up it – with some difficulty – and peer out of the window and talk to female prisoners at exercise in the yard below. They had already been court-martialled for various offences and were supervised by a civilian wardress who was sympathetic. It was easy to whisper down to them and to pass on messages, provided we kept an eye on the Judas hole and listened for noises in the corridor. At times, we even lowered small articles or notes on a piece of string, and sometimes got something back.

The Germans had treated the Russians badly after capture, but I never found out why they were in the prison. They obviously thought themselves lucky to be there. It was better than being on a work gang. They survived the war, but in 1945 the British and American authorities forcibly repatriated them to the Soviet Union and to an unknown fate at the hands of Stalin's thugs. The way they and other Russians were forced back to Communist Russia by the Allies is one of the more disgraceful episodes of the post-war period. They well knew what awaited them.

One of the Russian prisoners had managed to keep a knife and carved a little puppet that he suspended on strings between two pencil-like pieces of wood. When he squeezed the sides, the figure did gymnastics. I must have done him a favour because he gave it to me for my sister; but I lost it in a search, or left it behind when we escaped the following year.

There was a North African soldier, Mohammed, who wore a red Fez. He had managed to hold on to a somewhat oversized army greatcoat that reached almost to his ankles. He was a quiet, cheerful man, with a wide white smile. His teeth became more obvious as he lost weight, so that they looked like gravestones. One day I got an apple and a crust of bread smuggled in by one of the Irish girls and gave the apple to Mohammed.

We were next to each other in the exercise yard, walking round and round in single file. We were not allowed to talk or to get too close to each other, but when something or someone diverted the guard's attention I managed to slip the apple to him. As we were going back into the cell block, I muttered, "Eat it quickly." I could see its bulge in the pocket of his greatcoat and knew the guards would spot it too. But he shook his head. Before they locked us in our cells, he whispered something that still makes me feel humble when I think about it today. I don't know if he really knew, or if he was guessing. Maybe he had kept a tally of the days. He said: "I can't eat it now. It's Ramadan."

I went to see him after Liberation. He was in a camp near Fort Regent with all the other African soldiers. He made a curry out of bully beef, and as people do on such occasions we talked about meeting again sometime in the future. We never did of course.

As we slipped into the final winter of the war, it got very cold and I developed sores at the corners of my mouth that wouldn't heal. They split and bled if I opened my mouth too widely. We still had no idea how long the war would last or when we would be free, but I can never remember feeling depressed or losing hope. We got snippets of news from various sources, mainly from new prisoners who had heard the BBC.

There was another miracle a couple of weeks before Christmas, just after I got out of solitary. I was so unwise as to complain of toothache and, before I really knew what he was up to, a German dental orderly pulled a tooth without anaesthetic. It was bloody painful! But not nearly as painful as when it went on bleeding and he sewed up the socket. It continued to bleed and they took me under guard to the hospital, where Mr Price put in another stitch, again without an anaesthetic!

I was still hawking and spitting into a kidney dish in Casualty, while my guard was waiting for the German doctor to give him permission to take me back to prison, when Dr Hanna surreptitiously pointed to a bottle of red ink on Sister's desk and mumbled, "Can't you do better than that?"

I took him at his word. When the guard wasn't looking, I tipped a little of the ink into my own offering. It didn't seem at all convincing to me, but it fooled the German doctor and I was admitted to the ward. I had several days of comfort, beautiful warmth, hot baths, and more food than I had seen for a long time. The nurses coddled and fussed over me and I enjoyed every minute. I even managed a short walk outside the Hospital after dark, but couldn't take advantage of the easy situation to escape. I'd given Dr Hanna a solemn promise not to. He didn't want to compromise the chances of other prisoners who might need hospital admission.

I put on a little weight and began to feel stronger and it soon became difficult to keep my promise not to make a break for freedom. My recovery was helped by another miracle. This time, a major one. Mrs Inverness-Bathe was one of my father's wealthier parishioners. She had been implicated in the tragedy that led to Clifford Cohu's death in a German camp. She sent me a roast duck. Such luxuries were unobtainable, even on the black market and where she got it I can't imagine. I took it to a quiet corner and ate the lot. I have remained partial to duck ever since.

The hunger I experienced in those days has left some permanent effects. Early in their lives, my family learnt that they should never try to take anything off my plate. I still hate to wait too long for a meal and am reluctant to leave anything, however small, on my plate. I dislike leaving things in serving dishes. If we have rice, I remove every last grain. I even scrape into the corners of the dish to make sure there is nothing left. It is stupid and I frequently tell myself so. But it is almost unconscious and I never stop. Michael Ginns told me that when he attends any reception in the Island, he can always tell who lived through the Occupation, because they always wet the tips of their forefingers and eat up all the crumbs on their plate. He added that when he had stayed at the homes of former German soldiers who were in the Islands, they were the same.

It was a rude shock to find myself back in a cell. It was colder, or seemed so after the comfort of the last few days, and the rations were getting smaller all the time. Almost all the potatoes they gave us were black or partly rotten, and there was no longer even a tiny scrap of horsemeat in the soup.

On Christmas Eve, the Germans sang *Stille Nacht* in beautiful harmony, but there were no presents, no extra rations. I had another burst of *streng*, and some enthusiasts up the corridor blocked the toilet when they tried to start a tunnel.

The Gestapo brought in two French ladies from St. Brelade's. They had caught them with a radio and found them guilty of passing the BBC News to German soldiers. John Lewis, who was their doctor, described how they typed several copies and slipped them, rolled up, into the pockets and knapsacks of the unsuspecting owners. The radio and typewriter were hidden in an ottoman and they never discussed their activities with anyone. They took care to cover their tracks, and frequently altered their appearances when making a delivery. It is a mystery how they were discovered. It is difficult to believe it was the work of an informer when they were so secretive and careful about what they did. They were certain they discussed their activities with no one. Perhaps they were spotted passing the bits of paper. It was a risky thing to do. Perhaps they were victims of a chance search. One of them tried to commit suicide. Fortunately she failed. The Germans sentenced them to death for espionage, but they survived the war and were lucky to do so. They were half Jewish, and the Germans knew it. They might not have survived if the Bailiff, Alexander Coutanche, hadn't intervened on their behalf, and had their sentences reduced to life imprisonment.

✳

In October and November 1944 there were several tragic, failed escape attempts. The survivors joined us in prison. In October, Doug Le Marchand, Michael Neil, Ken Collins and George Le Marquand got a boat from Eddie Langlois who had kept it hidden in a hayloft at his farm, Le Catillon. They left from Fauvic on the night of 10/11 October. The boat was unsuitable for heavy weather, and when the wind came up they were forced back after getting some way out to sea. They had to thread their way through extensive underwater tank traps which had mines fixed to the tops before beaching in Anne Port Bay.

Then their luck ran out. A sentry saw them and a flare lit the beach. They ducked behind the boat as bullets buzzed and whined around them and, when a second flare went up, three of them stood and raised their hands. Doug was killed by a round, which passed through the boat. The survivors stayed in gaol until the end of the war. Eddie Langlois served 5 months for giving them the boat.

Bernard Larbalestier and his brother John were pharmacists with a shop in St. Helier. They made an unsuccessful escape using a small boat, sometime in July/August 1944. When their outboard motor failed to start, they didn't feel strong enough to row to France and managed to get back to shore undetected.

They got another boat and engine and set off again from Fauvic on the night of 27/28 November, with an extra hand, Peter Noel. When the throttle cable parted some way out to sea and the weather deteriorated, the wind and tide drove them back into St. Catherine's Bay where they hit the breakwater. Peter managed to climb the rough granite wall and was lucky not to be killed by one of the mines festooned all over the breakwater when he tried to help the other two. He found a rope and pulled John along for some way, but lost him when he had to get round a barbed wire entanglement. Cold, exhausted and too weak to hang on, John was swept out to sea. Peter last saw Bernard sitting on top of their upturned boat as he too was carried out into rough water.

Peter almost made it to safety despite the mines and barbed wire, but a sentry spotted him just as he reached the main road. The Gestapo interrogated him for more than 10 hours before he reached prison. In *Lest We Forget*, Roy Thomas wrote that he was questioned at the Weighbridge, but it was probably at the Pomme D'Or Hotel. I recall someone whispering to me under a door in the prison to tell me about an escaper who had been taken into the hotel cellar and beaten with truncheons and prodded with an electric goad. It must have been

Peter.

They took John Larbalestier's body from the sea near St. Catherine's. His brother's body was never found. It lies with honour in that deep resting-place that is the home of all who lose their lives at sea.

Tragically, the sea claimed four more lives soon after. Madeleine Bisson died with three companions off the coast of Jersey. She drowned with husband, Ronald, with André Gorvel another Jerseyman, and with a young Frenchman, Roy Luciennes, when their boat broke up in heavy seas on rocks at the base of the cliff at La Saline on the north coast of the Island. The Germans were criticised for not going to their help but, in fairness, there was an extensive minefield as well as the obvious hazard of attempting a rescue in pounding seas.

In the second week of January 1945, the following NOTICE appeared in the *Evening Post*:

> On January 8th. 1945, the American prisoners-of-war Captain Clark and Lieutenant Haas escaped from the German prisoner-of-war camp. They will attempt to obtain shelter and help from the English civilian population. It is expressly announced that anyone who takes in or extends help in any way to Captain Clark or Lieutenant Haas will be punished by death according to paragraph 9 of the Order for the Protection of the Occupying Force.

A description of the wanted officers followed. The notice was signed by the *Feldkommandant* of *Festung Jersey* – Fortress Jersey.

Roy Thomas described their escape in detail, and told how it resulted from the successful bringing together of various links in a chain of events which involved, among others, Charles Gruchy. Ed Clark, a 6th Armoured Division Engineer, was captured near Dinan on 3 August 1944. He was taken to Saint Malo. George Haas was an artillery spotter. His Piper Cub was shot down on 2 August, and he broke his leg when fired on after he crashed near Dol. The two were evacuated by trawler to Jersey where Ed Clark went into the prisoner-of-war compound in the former British Garrison military prison on South Hill. It overlooked the harbour, and was unpleasantly close to targets suitable for aerial bombardment.

George was treated at the General Hospital. While he was still convalescent, he too was sent to South Hill. He was caught when he tried to bore a hole through the wall of a toilet and sentenced to 10 days solitary confinement in the prison. He took up residence in his 6 by 9 foot cell on Christmas Eve. By standing on a chair, he found he could talk to Charles Gruchy in the cell above. It was the start of a friendship that has lasted more than 50 years but, though they spoke to each other and later exchanged letters, it was several years before they met face to face.

Charles had stayed on at Victoria College. With Martin Le Cornu he made crystal sets for other people and also helped as a member of the launching party at Fauvic when Peter Crill – later the Bailiff of the Island – made a successful getaway with Roy Mourant and John Floyd.

While fixing up a crystal set for Mr Nobes, the owner of the Welcome Inn at Gorey, they saw a boat that they thought would do for an escape, but when they went back to the Inn to ask if they could buy it, Mr Nobes was out. They waited for him to come back in a shelter on the promenade and were arrested for no obvious reason. After separating them, the Germans took them to their respective homes. They kept Charles outside in the car while they told his father that he had drowned trying to escape. They searched the house and found radios, material for making crystal sets, a camera and a weapon. They imprisoned Charles' father and his sister, Yvette.

When Charles was satisfied that George Haas was who he said he was, he briefed him on possible safe houses and passed him a rough sketch map of the Island through a hole in the floorboards. Roy Thomas described what followed in *Lest We Forget*.

Using George's crutches to make a rough ladder, and a bent poker as a crude grappling iron, the American officers scaled a back wall just before dawn on January 7th. They got to the wall by separating the bars on a window. They packed their beds to fool any casual inspection and to cover their absence for as long as possible. By the time George was out of the window – his leg was still a problem – Ed had climbed the ladder and was dealing with the barbed wire on top of the wall. At any moment they expected shots, but they made very little noise and safely reached the street below. Silently, they disappeared into the snow which had fallen overnight and which continued into the day. They reached George Laurens' house at Samarès and were given shelter and a meal. Not wanting to put the family at risk, and seeing that their presence caused some alarm, they decided to sleep rough in a hedge near the house. They dug a small slit trench, camouflaged it with leaves and branches, and settled down to spend a cold, wet, miserable day and night. The Laurens gave them civilian hats, a compass, a large pocketknife and another map; and to maintain security, they didn't tell the family where they were going. The bad weather had returned and they walked through new snow to Bill Bertram's house at Fauvic where they were fed, given blankets and shown to a hayrick for the night. Once again they refused to jeopardise the safety of their helpers by staying in the house. They knew the penalty for those who harboured fugitives.

They managed to find a boat, but when the owner heard that the Germans were checking on all small craft, he changed his mind about selling it. Bill and his family were getting uneasy, and the Americans were then faced with the problem that all escapers have to deal with when they are on the run. How long do you stay when you are putting other people at risk of imprisonment or execution? They thought about giving themselves up, but decided to try to cut out one of the boats still in Gorey Harbour.

The harbour was surrounded by bunkers and disguised strongpoints. It was also heavily guarded. It would not be easy. Bill Bertram thought it too dangerous, but gave them oars and rowlocks and some canvas to muffle any noise.

They reached Gorey Harbour safely and hid in the shadow of the sea wall to watch for a while. They heard the German guards talking, but by keeping to the darker patches they made it safely over the wall onto the mud where they followed the ebb tide to some German coasters which had been laid up for lack of fuel. They were soon up to their waists in water and the cold was intensely painful. They couldn't find a rowing boat in the dark and eventually made their way back. They knew they wouldn't survive a night in the open and, once again, discussed giving themselves up. Fortunately they found a grounded cabin cruiser and managed to climb aboard by way of the anchor chain. They broke into the cabin and spent another cold miserable night, making plans to go back to Bill Bertram's house the next evening for food, and then to come back to the boat to lie low until a suitable opportunity appeared.

At 7.30 the next evening, they set off in the dark and again got past the sentries without being seen. Once again, the Bertrams gave them food and more warm clothes. Then they went back to the harbour, slipped past the sentries and boarded the boat, stowed the food and went to sleep. When daylight came, they saw a 12 foot-long rowing boat with a high freeboard. It was painted dark green and just what they needed. They also discovered that a building they had taken for an innocent bungalow was a camouflaged gun casement.

At 9.30 the next night they crept over to the rowing boat with all their gear and a bailing pump they had found in the cabin cruiser. Then they settled down to wait for the tide to float them off the mud. When it did, George cut the mooring line and Ed began to row. A rudder and a tiller they found on board proved life saving later on.

They had to row against the rising tide and it was heavy going. As they passed the end of the pier, the moon came out, but the sentries didn't see them. The sea was rough for a while and then the wind dropped and they saw Mont Orgueil fade into the distance.

Their relief was short lived. The weather deteriorated rapidly and they ran into a blizzard with gale force winds. In mountainous seas, snow and icy winds lashed them and their small craft. They thought their last moments had come. They pumped and bailed furiously, and just managed to keep afloat. When they saw the French coast, they began to worry about rocks, breakers and minefields. Just off the beach, a friendly wave washed them onto the shore and they ran to the shelter of a sand dune. They were fired at by an American patrol and had to put up their hands before they could convince them they were friendly.

⁂

New Year's Eve, 1944 was bitterly cold. There was a full moon and in my cell it was as bright as day. I was on my own again and lay on the freezing floor, my face close to the gap under the door as I yelled out Happy New Year in response to all the shouts that were going on up and down the corridor. The Russians were advancing on Berlin from the East. The British, Canadians, Free French and Americans were pushing into Germany from the West. We had every reason to hope that 1945 would be the last year of the war. But we couldn't be sure. We still had doubts and fears. We didn't know how much longer it would last. We didn't expect the Germans to cave in easily. They had surprised us already with their V1 and V2 weapons, and who could know what else they might have in store? Hitler continued to rant and rave about his secret weapons and boasted of ever more powerful ones that would turn the war in his favour. We could only wait.

⁂ ⁂ ⁂

Chapter Eleven

ESCAPE AND EVASION

There were no more excursions from the prison to La Folie Inn or to Silvertide. For a time the Gestapo lost interest in us. Not surprisingly, we hadn't seen the Naval Police again. There had been a spate of escapes for them to investigate and new prisoners arrived at the prison almost every day.

Making crystal sets became a cottage industry and, by July and August 1944, some of those who'd kept hidden radios became careless. They thought the Occupation was nearly over. It was easy to pick up the American Forces Network. More and more people hummed the popular tunes of the day and whistled Glen Miller favourites. 'Moonlight Serenade' replaced 'There'll Always be an England'.

The large number of radios in existence soon made it inevitable that more would be discovered. Frequent searches for illicit food stores, unregistered livestock and escaped prisoners made it even more likely. The Gestapo did not let up in their efforts to find and punish offenders. The *Feldgendarmes* were just as active. By late 1944, the prison was overflowing. There was a waiting list to go in! They let out minor offenders early to ease the crowding, but the number of prisoners in each cell rose to bursting point. By early 1945, new offenders took in their own beds or had to sleep on the floor.

At the end of November, a rifle butt crashed against my cell door and a shout of "Tribunal" raised me from my lethargy. With no more than a few minutes warning, an armed escort signed for the three of us and marched us to a house just off Queens Road. We enjoyed the walk. It was a grey day, but nowhere as grey as inside prison walls; the absence of the stagnant prison smell and the ever-present noise of clanging doors created an illusion of freedom. It more than compensated for any fear.

Friends had smuggled in messages to warn us that rumours of our espionage activities still circulated in the town, and uppermost in our minds for some weeks was the worry that they might have come to the ears of the Gestapo. We could not be sure how much they knew or suspected. We could not eliminate the possibility that they would bring up something unexpected at the court martial. A milkman spread some of the rumours on his daily rounds!

We hadn't given up looking for a way to escape. The warnings added a sense of urgency, but it was not the day to try. The MP40s slung across the guards' chests were deterrence enough and Rouge Bouillon, the main road to the Court, was empty of people. They had a clear field of fire.

The Court began at 10 o'clock, though we arrived much earlier. They kept us waiting in an unheated room that overlooked a back garden. To see green grass and a few winter plants almost made it worthwhile, but I felt the familiar lead weight of fear settle in the pit of my stomach and I could feel my fists opening and clenching as the tension rose. It was almost a relief when they marched us in.

Our worry that they could have found out more than we wanted them to was not unreasonable. Apart from nasty-minded informers who might betray us, the material we'd collected to take to France could have been washed up. It had happened before to Peter Hassall and his companions. Without our weight, the canoe could have floated just below the surface for some distance and then drifted into shore further along the coast. If that had happened, there was no way the Germans would consider us anything less than spies.

The prospect of a long sentence for trying to escape was unpleasant, but not catastrophic. With the sea route blocked and the neighbouring French ports now in Allied hands, the Island was cut off from Germany except by air. There was little risk of finishing up in a concentration camp. We were blissfully unaware of the plan Von Aufsess, a senior German officer, leaked to Charles Duret Aubin that the Germans intended to reopen the camp on Alderney. Even though the SS guards had gone back to the parent concentration camp in Germany, it would not have been pleasant. But our main worry was what the Gestapo might have found out. It could mean the death penalty.

While we waited for the Court the guards didn't stop us talking. They didn't seem to understand English but we couldn't be sure and were careful what we said; and like most expectant and nervous people in such situations we spoke in hushed tones or whispers anyway. Looking back now, it seems unlikely that given the late stage of the war and the local circumstances in the Island, they would have executed us, but we can't be sure, especially as by then the ardent Nazi, Admiral Hüffmeier, was about to replace Von Schmettow in overall command. They would have been within their rights to do so. We waited for the charges and cross-examination.

✳

The Court was made up of senior officers. They were impeccably uniformed. All wore brightly polished riding boots. They looked very Prussian. One even had a monocle. There was a lot of heel clicking and Heil Hitlering as witnesses and officials moved in and out and around the Court, but I can't remember if we had a defence counsel or not. Peter and Hugh are dead so I can't ask them. I think we did but, as at my previous court martial, he was a junior soldier who just clicked his heels, yelled the statutory Heil Hitler and sat down. If he did say more, it was in German, and not translated. I was tempted to add, and ineffectual too, but, given the light nature of our sentences, he could have been quite effective on our behalf without our knowing it.

The *Kriegsmarine* officer who saved me from a severe beating at La Folie Inn translated the indictment into English. The word sabotage was repeated several times, but there was no specific mention of espionage. He seemed fair in what he told the Court in German on our behalf, but we had no real way of knowing.

Our concerns were well founded. From the start of his opening address, the Judge Advocate claimed we had been carrying military information to the English and that we were deserters and spies. He said that those of our group who had not been caught, and who had presumably reached France, were also spies. We were guilty of espionage, as well as sabotage for trying to escape. We should be shot.

When he questioned us individually, he repeatedly accused each of us of being spies. Just as frequently, we denied it. Hearing his demand for the death penalty was not one of our better moments. He went on plugging away at each of us in turn, attacking our credibility for most of the morning, often rephrasing his accusations and trying to get us to contradict ourselves. But he always returned to the same questions: "What did you have in the boat? What maps did you have? What papers?" After a time we got fed up with his persistence and when he stupidly asked if we'd carried a radio, answered rudely, "and a kitchen sink and a grand piano too."

The President of the Court was not amused. It earned several shouted threats and a severe reprimand, but the interpreter had difficulty keeping a straight face and we decided we quite liked him.

When the Court broke for lunch, they didn't give us any and I don't think the guards got any either. When it reconvened, the questions went on again until the late afternoon. The light was fading and they closed the blackout curtains. Eventually they retired, and we nervously waited for the verdict. We were exhausted by all the verbal gymnastics and fear was never far away. They were not long. 'Guilty of sabotage by trying to escape.' But to our relief, there was no mention of espionage.

The prosecutor clearly thought differently, but our continued refusal to admit anything during interrogation by the Naval Police and Gestapo, and under questioning at the trial, together with the obvious lack of evidence, must have swayed the Court. We were given a year each. A very lenient sentence.

❋

We arrived back in Gloucester Street and were immediately returned to the cells that we had left that morning. It was several more days before there were vacancies in the Civilian Block and we didn't move over until after the New Year. The cells were even more crowded there, but conditions were better than on the German side. There were no extra rations but every so often they allowed visitors who could bring in small parcels of food and, occasionally, a small twist of tobacco. But our relatives had little to spare and, in retrospect, they must have sacrificed quite a bit to scrape together something for those they thought much worse off than themselves. It was, however, an opportunity to smuggle in anything we asked for, provided it wasn't too big.

When Red Cross parcels arrived at the start of 1945, I certainly got one before we escaped, and may have had a second. I would have thought that such an event would have been indelibly etched on my mind, but it has gone. I remember Nelson's Chocolate, Klim Milk Powder and breaking up some cigarettes to put in a pipe which father sent in. Klim was milk spelt backwards.

Our new cells were on the upper level of the civilian part of the prison. New is probably the wrong word. All the prison buildings were ancient and the whole edifice has since been demolished. The main block was built of bare granite and the smaller cells on the ground floor, which also housed common criminals, had thick wooden doors with small barred grilles. The grilles seemed the only source of light during the day and those cells looked thoroughly uninviting places to spend any time. The political prisoners were in bigger lighter cells, where the windows were relatively large and flush with the outer wall. Though they were heavily barred and the glass often opaque, there were places where we could see out easily.

Female political prisoners were detained in cells on the same level, but there was no direct contact. A thick door closed off the connecting corridor. Despite strict segregation, one or two sex-starved males did manage to infiltrate the women's quarters for short visits when their hormone levels rose too high. I have no idea how they did it. There must have been collusion with one of the warders.

Most warders were decent men, caught in an unenviable position. A few were right bastards. The Governor, Briard, was a cold unapproachable disciplinarian. Like the other unpleasant members of his staff, he seemed incapable of differentiating between political prisoners and common criminals. We seldom saw him. Some of his orders were restrictive and unnecessary. As far as we were concerned, he was a traitor.

One night, a man in the next cell to mine, a political prisoner, was rolling around in agony with severe abdominal pain. Briard and a warder came to see him. They knew I had worked in the hospital and had at least some medical knowledge, but they wouldn't let me out to have a look at him. It was probably severe colic, because he recovered soon after. I shouted at Briard through the door, but he refused to open up. I got more and more angry and frustrated by his attitude; recalling it today I can still feel anger and frustration. I was shivering with rage and yelling my head off. I would probably have killed him if I had got my hands on him just then.

We didn't expect Briard to open the gates and let us out. We knew he had an unpleasant job to do. Respect and courtesy would have been enough. When I see films today which show prisoners being treated with undue harshness and contempt by prison officers they remind me of Briard and, having experienced the pressure-cooker effect of imprisonment, I can readily understand the violence such behaviour provokes.

Perhaps Briard was afraid of us. There were several biggish fellows in our cell and, a week or so earlier, a warder had shoved and shouted at one of the politicals. I witnessed the event with Jock Macdonald, a policeman who was in prison for being rude and refusing to salute a German officer. I am not too proud of it now, but we grabbed the warder and gave him a thorough beating. The Governor hauled us up before the Prison Board on what amounted to a civilian charge of assault. We were furious and let the Board know it.

They were mostly dry, nondescript little men, though I felt sorry for the Rector of St. John who, as a member of the States in those days, was one of those sitting. We towered over them in a threatening manner and made it obvious by our body language that we considered they had no jurisdiction over us whatsoever. We told them in no uncertain terms that similar behaviour by prison staff would get the same reaction, if not from us, then from some of the other politicals. We also told them what we would do to them when we were liberated and after some ineffectual huffing and puffing they returned us to our cells.

Briard disappeared after Liberation. When we got over the wall in February, we left him a note on the barbed wire. It told him exactly what we thought of him and that he would not be comfortable when we met again. Fortunately, we never did. Sinel tells us that he was interrogated after our escape. I hope the Gestapo gave him a hard time.

Soon after I wrote the last few lines, I had a letter from Eddie Langlois with whom I shared a cell for a time. He reminded me how Briard stopped a Canadian prisoner, Belza Turner, from playing her guitar. Belza had escaped with a Dutchman, Sieba Koster, but unfavourable tides and weather washed them back to Jersey when they had almost made it to the French coast. Most of the time, however, they had no idea where they were and when they came ashore were just as surprised to see the German sentry as he was to see them.

Belza was very fond of 'Home on the Range' and played it a lot while the Dutchman sang back at her from a distance – 'Ome 'Ome on zee range. Belza played well, but Siebe didn't have a memorable voice. Taking her guitar was probably the only public-spirited thing the Governor ever did. It stopped Siebe's assault on our ears, but it was no doubt a great loss for Belza.

Eddie Langlois wrote that after we escaped, Briard tried to stop political prisoners having Red Cross parcels. The prisoners formed a committee and asked the Bailiff to come to see them. He did. Briard was put firmly in his place.

Most warders were helpful and courteous. They didn't hector or threaten and often addressed us *en masse* as gentlemen when locking us up at night. The Head Warder, Mr Parker and the Matron, Mrs Perkins, were particularly helpful and kind. They could not do enough for us. It has been said with truth that, throughout the war years, Mrs. Perkins' comforting shoulder was often the last kindness experienced by many of those on their way to abuse and death in Germany.

We didn't suffer the indignity of a tattooed arm, but we each had a prison number. Like my RAF number, I have never forgotten it: 12364. It was never used for any practical purpose that I can recall, except possibly when the guards signed for us to go for interrogation or to our court martial.

Peter and I stuck together. I have forgotten the reason now but we had fallen out with Hugh. Our first cell on the civil side was small and crowded. Jock Macdonald was a cellmate, and a man I will call Phil Bray. I think that was his name. Jock was a big man and took up a lot of room. Phil was small, and Irish. He'd been a waiter before the war and had worked at some of the best hotels in London. He amused us with endless, unrepeatable tales about the goings-on in such places, and particularly impressed us with the incredible amount of money he earned in tax-free tips.

The cell was bitterly cold and, hungry as we were, we tried to keep warm by wrestling and frequent bouts of mayhem. Jock had been Master-at-Arms on one of the Cunarders, the *Queen Mary* I think, and he told tales similar to Phil's to keep us entertained. He was a great source of knowledge about self-defence and taught us some of the methods policemen use to subdue recalcitrant offenders.

We were allowed books, but usually we could read only during the day. There was seldom any electricity at night. We talked endlessly, and we walked. We walked round ... and round ... and round ... and round the exercise area ... and then round again. There was little else to do.

Later they moved me to a larger cell at the front of the building. I can't remember why, but it may have been after Jock and I attacked the gaoler. They could have decided to separate us. It was lighter than the previous cell. It also had a fireplace, and for a while Eddie Langlois managed to get a small amount of wood brought in from his farm. We also burned some of the wooden slats from our bunks. It made sleeping on the lower level a bit risky when most of the slats from the upper bunk had been burnt: and the tiny fire made little impression on the cold.

My time in that cell saw another miracle. Eddie's wife, Iris, made a rabbit pie. It had a thick, brown crust made from potato flour. I can still see that crust. I can still taste that pie. Like the roast duck, it is indelibly printed on my mind. I shall never forget it. It is remarkable how the memory of hunger and such occasional treats evoke strong emotions after more than 50 years.

There was a security fence with peeling green bars around the exercise area and we spoke to any visitors through the gaps. I don't think I saw my parents or Stan more than once, but the whole period has become so contracted in my mind that it is difficult to be sure. They may have been allowed in more often, or I wasn't there long enough to see them again.

Those coming to see us could sometimes pass contraband through the fence as we talked, while other prisoners made endless circuits behind us or diverted the attention of any watchers. The exercise ground was more open than the high-walled internal exercise yard that we had been allowed in under guard on the German side. There, we had walked round and round in single file while the guards prevented any talking. One of the German jailers was a short tubby man called Otto. The weapon holstered on his belt looked like a cannon on his portly figure and when he was annoyed, he would pull it out and gesticulate in a threatening manner, shouting, *Streng, streng! Jedermann streng!* - strict, strict! Everybody on strict. It was rumoured unkindly that he had owned a fish and chip shop in Hamburg before the war and that his crooked nose was due to his breaking it when he fell off his bike trying to keep up with the advance into France in 1940. Somebody suggested its shape meant that he was Jewish and earned a good bout of solitary.

Otto and the other guards were always very nervous when the Gestapo visited the prison and they shouted and stamped about, trying to look stricter and more martial than usual. They always seemed as relieved as we were when the intruders left. On the civilian side, they allowed us out of our cells for most of the day and only locked us in again for the night at dusk. That usually meant soon to sleep. Even during the short time the electricity was supposed to be on there were frequent cuts.

During January the civilian police arrested a young man for stealing a Red Cross parcel and, while understanding the hunger that probably drove him to such an act, we had no sympathy for him and his fate. At that time, by Island Law, they still flogged criminals for certain offences. Youngsters got the birch. I have a horrible feeling they used something worse on adults. A warder showed us the birch and the horse they were going to strap him to. It was in a cell at the end of our corridor and reminiscent of Port Arthur in Tasmania in early penal times. It seemed barbaric to me even then. I have a vague recollection of some yells, but no clear memory of the sentence being carried out.

There was a carpenter's shop on the same floor. Rows of tools hung in racks above the workbenches, for use by criminal trusties under the supervision of one of the screws. We had found one of the means we needed for an escape.

By the middle of 1944, the prison was so overcrowded the authorities were forced to build a wooden hut between the main cellblock and the internal wall of the German side, to house the excess population of wrongdoers. It abutted against a square stone building with a flat roof which itself reached to the outer wall of the prison. Although it was festooned with barbed wire, a metal bar connected the two buildings about 8 feet above the ground and the distance from the flat roof to the top of the outer wall was only about 8 feet. Fragments of broken glass were firmly embedded in the cement that covered the top of the wall. They were a strong deterrent to anyone trying to climb over it to freedom, but not insurmountable.

One of the hut windows overlooked a narrow space between the buildings and was secured by strong thick, wooden bars firmly screwed into the mainframe of the building. They looked almost fragile in comparison with the iron bars everywhere else. We thought that if we could get through that window we could climb onto the roof and from there it was only a short distance to the outer wall, which let onto a side street away from the main prison gate. Fittingly, it was called Newgate Street. In the blackout and on a dark moonless night, the guards would be less likely to see us on the roof or going over the wall and we stood a good chance of getting clean away without being shot.

We wanted to speed up our plans but needed to be patient if we were to avoid disaster. With a little care and cunning, the tools would be easy enough to steal from the workshop and they would deal with the window bars. But we didn't have a rope or anything we could use as a rope. With careful timing, we knew we could get out of our cells and down to the wooden hut before they locked us in for the night. Prisoners from the hut could take our places upstairs. They could occupy our beds and cover their heads during the nightly check.

As well as a rope, we needed something to put over the barbed wire and broken glass. If we could get all the things we needed, it seemed a plan with a good chance of success. We decided to go ahead.

No one seemed to know what the Germans did in the flat-roofed building. We thought it might be an armoury or a storeroom. Later, I heard it was a cookhouse. I doubt that, since it seemed unoccupied most of the time and when we listened we heard no noises from there after dark.

A more serious consideration was the effect an escape would have on our families. We still got smuggled messages warning us that some stupid individuals were continuing to spread rumours about our activities; mainly a couple of misguided imbeciles who claimed they had been part of the group. The Gestapo still turned up at odd intervals to question prisoners, even some of those, like Charles Gruchy, who had already been sentenced: although they hadn't been back to interrogate us again since the trial, we felt insecure.

We thought it unlikely, but we had to accept the possibility of reprisals against our families if we did get out. The Germans might take hostages, to be released in return for our surrender. It would have happened before the siege, but the risk seemed low in 1945. To reduce the risk to them as much as possible, we smuggled out warning letters.

There were no bed sheets to knot together to make a rope, but red fire buckets and stirrup pumps with long hosepipes were kept in most buildings to deal with incendiary bombs. The prison was no exception. We would go on trying to get a rope but, if we weren't successful, the hosepipe would have to do. In the middle of winter, we couldn't ask our fellow prisoners to sacrifice their blankets to make a long enough substitute. The pipe in our corridor looked sound and we thought it would be strong enough to take our weight. We weren't very heavy just then!

Peter tried unsuccessfully to get a rope smuggled in, but it was too bulky a piece of contraband, even in sections, to get past the entrance search and then to pass to us through the bars. We decided to trust the hosepipe, but not to steal it until nearer the time. Our main concern was that someone else would think of using it first. There was no Escape Committee. We told as few people as possible.

Our disagreement with Hugh festered on. By then, we weren't even speaking. Our quarrel must have been more serious than I remember. We would not have left him behind otherwise. The risks were the same for him as they were for us. I am not proud of our decision now. Fortunately no harm was done, but I was told later that he was very angry and tried to follow us out when he discovered we had gone. He got as far as the outer wall, but without help and an intact pipe he had to turn back. He stayed in prison until Liberation.

In the previous September, Francis Le Sueur, Garnet Briard and George Whithy had tried to escape from the Island using the craziest type of craft imaginable. They tried to get to France on beach floats that were popular with summer holidaymakers before the war. The floats were designed to be paddled around close to the shore, but they planned to reach the Ecréhous – a reef roughly halfway to France – on the first night, and hide in the rocks and rest up for the day before going on to France the following night.

In spite of careful caulking, the floats were soon waterlogged and they were swept round the island. They nearly foundered on the Paternoster reef, but a friendly breeze and a favourable current took them in again and they landed near Ronez. Germans waiting on the shore arrested them.

Taken to Melbourne House in St. John's, they were interrogated by four reasonable officers. Francis, who was never one to suffer fools gladly, got very annoyed when a fifth officer arrived and accused them of having a radio on board. Fed up with persistent questioning, he admitted it was so, and when the interrogator demanded what else did he have on board. He gave the same reply we used at our court martial – only a grand piano.

Put in neighbouring cells, George and Francis cored a hole through the wall with spoons so that they could talk with less risk of being caught than if they shouted through the windows or under the doors. They put the scrapings in their piss pots – old jam tins – and emptied them each morning down the toilet. The blocked pipe flooded a German storeroom. The guards were not amused. Given a spell of *streng* they served it in the military punishment block the Germans used for their own deserters and other military criminals, and for slave labourers who had committed some offence – the block in which I had languished in solitary misery with a bout of dysentery.

Francis escaped when they let him out of prison under the care of a hungry German officer who wanted his fishing tackle and nets. He had stored it at his home, Beauvoir, in Samarès Lane and, as he helped the officer to load the nets onto the handlebars of his bike, he made sure they overflowed the front wheel. Then he nipped back through a gate, quickly latched it behind him and disappeared over a back wall.

While he was hiding at Joe Le Masurier's house, they were listening to the BBC news one night when the Breton maid dashed in shouting, *Les Boches son' là"* – the Boches are here. He jumped out of an upstairs window, but landed heavily on concrete and had to crawl painfully into a patch of cabbages, where he hid until the Germans had gone. He found another boat and escaped to France on 11 November 1944. He was the only escapee to make a home run after being caught once and then getting away from the prison.

George Whithy was older than most of us, somewhere between 45 and 50, positively ancient for an escapee, who as a group were predominantly of military age. He was one of the few who knew of our plan to break out and was keen to join us.

Late one afternoon, when daylight was fading and there were few others about, George helped me divert the attention of a warder who was guarding a criminal prisoner in the workshop. I sat on a bench with my back to a rack of tools, pretending to listen while they talked and the warder watched his charge at work on a similar bench opposite. It wasn't difficult to transfer a chisel and screwdriver into the waistband at the back of my trousers. At a suitable moment, I sidled out and hid them in my mattress. They would be reasonably safe there until needed, but were very uncomfortable to sleep on. All we had to do now was wait for a suitable opportunity and a dark night.

Once again, I began to wonder what I had got myself into. Waiting was always the hardest part. The tension seemed to build until the time to go. Finally, we decided to go on 6 February 1945, about half-an-hour before curfew. It would give us time to get out of the town, and once in the country we could take to the fields if necessary. Like other schemes 'o' mice and men', it nearly came undone.

We got into the wooden hut easily enough. Three other prisoners took our places in the upstairs cell. It was a dark moonless night, but there was enough starlight to see our way onto the roof and then to the wall. We unscrewed the wooden bars and pried them off while friends kept watch. They came away without too much difficulty, but we made some noise. Fortunately, other helpers in the hut covered this. They started a singsong and made a row loud enough to drown any sound we made, but not so loud as to bring warders to have a look. We got through the window quickly and roughly pushed the bars back so that they would pass a casual inspection.

Jumping up to grab the iron bar between the two buildings proved a lot more difficult than we thought it would be. The bar was higher than it looked from the hut window, and this time we made a lot of noise. But no one raised the alarm. We helped each other up as rapidly as we could, scrambling to avoid the barbed wire, and managed to reach the roof without alerting the German guards or the two or three civilian warders we couldn't trust.

We lay flat and rested for a few seconds to get our breath and to make sure there were no unforeseen obstacles in our way. There was a skylight in the middle of the roof but no chinks of light around the edge of any blackout, and no noises from below. We crept silently across to the outer wall, reached up and put two folded blankets over the broken glass. I was no longer as frightened as I had been during the waiting. Activity calms me. I seem better able to cope once things get under way.

Peter secured the hosepipe to a firm anchor on the skylight and the two of us helped George to the top of the wall where he lay precariously on the blankets, to our anxious minds his silhouette seeming to loom unnaturally large against the sky. Then he was gone. He had quickly lowered the free end of the pipe to the street below and just as quickly disappeared over the edge and out of view. He hadn't seemed to suffer any ill effects from glass cutting into the cloth. We worried that the fragments would cut through into the pipe as well as into us, and we were also afraid the pipe would not be long enough.

We waited silently until he gave it a gentle pull to let us know he was safely on the pavement. Then he crouched down and waited for us in the shadow at the bottom of the wall. The pipe almost reached the ground. We only had a short distance to drop. We watched and listened for a few more tense seconds, but there was no sign the Germans had seen or heard anything and I gave Peter a leg up. He too disappeared rapidly and soundlessly into the dark space beyond the wall.

Then it all went wrong. Prison walls are deliberately made smooth on the inside to make it difficult for prisoners to get out. The eight feet or so from the roof to the top of the wall was almost insurmountable without help, and the blanket's hold on the glass was surprisingly tenuous. I couldn't shout to Peter and George below to keep the pipe taut while I climbed up the short inside stretch and my heart began to thump wildly as I wondered what the hell I was going to do.

I thought about going back to get someone in the hut to help, but Peter and George wouldn't know what was happening and time was running out. It would soon be curfew. We didn't want to risk being picked up by a patrol or shot on the street. I tried repeatedly to clamber up but couldn't get a grip. Meanwhile, Peter and George became more and more anxious at my non-appearance and began to think the worst and to wonder if they should make off in the dark as quickly as possible.

Then a light came on in the building below me and a bell began to clang somewhere in the German Block. I thought it was the alarm. Then I heard noises coming from the building underneath and suddenly there was a lot of light escaping from the edges of the skylight. I felt naked and exposed. Light reflected off the inside of the outer prison wall and the roof was no longer in shadow.

I still thought the building below me was the German armoury and at any moment expected to hear the whine and ping of a bullet. There was only one thing to do. I moved back across the roof and took a running jump at the wall. I sounded like a herd of elephants in full charge, but made it at the second attempt.

Unfortunately, I pushed the blanket off as I made it to the top and for a time lay unprotected on the broken glass. I am no Indian mystic. The glass cut deeply into my arms and legs, and the palms of my hands were soon slippery with blood. I gripped the pipe as best I could and heaved myself over the edge. I had to jerk hard to free my clothes and felt the sharp edges cut in again, but I didn't dare let out more than a silent groan.

All might have been well if Peter hadn't started to climb back up to see what was wrong. Our combined weight would have been too much for the pipe even if it hadn't cut through on the now exposed glass. It was at least 30 feet to the pavement. How I missed Peter and George I don't know. I landed awkwardly. My right ankle went over and I felt a vicious pain in my lower back. Years later,

X-Rays showed an old fracture. Thankfully, the bell had stopped its clanging but we didn't know what it was and expected guards to come rushing round the corner at any moment. We had to move.

A little thought would have reassured us, but in the panic of the moment the last thing we were capable of was logical analysis. It couldn't have been an alarm bell. If it had been, the whole area would have been swarming with Germans already. They would have been there in seconds. It was probably some impatient soldier with his thumb firmly on the gate bell, demanding immediate admission, but we shall never know now.

We made our way as quickly as we could into Gloucester Street and hurried past the front gate of the prison, expecting it to fly open at any moment. But nothing happened. Blood dripped in a steady stream from my arms and legs. I told the others to leave me, but they refused and we staggered into the back entrance of the hospital where Ray Osmont and John Le Sueur let us into the medical officer's quarters. They bandaged my wounds as quickly and as tightly as they could. It slowed the bleeding, but there was no time for more. We stumbled off into the dark again as quickly as we could.

The prison was next door to the hospital. It would not be long before we were missed and the alarm raised. The trail of blood would have brought them to the hospital if it had been daylight, but the blackout covered our tracks. Nevertheless, we had to get as far away as we could before they threw a cordon around the area, and we had to be well out of the town before curfew. It was getting perilously close.

I have been told since that when they did throw a cordon, it included the Nurses' Home. To everyone's embarrassment, a young gentleman – who shall be nameless since he is now eminent in the Island – was discovered hiding behind a curtain in one of the nurse's bedrooms. The Home Sister and Matron who chaperoned the search were not amused. He was arrested and had to do a lot of fast talking to prove he wasn't one of us. Such are the perils of love and war!

I managed a limping staggering walk with Peter and George supporting me each side until we were out of the town. Then George went off by himself to a previously arranged safe house in St. Clement's. Sadly, I have never seen him since.

By now, it was long past curfew. We still had to be careful and kept to the shadows as much as we could, ready to throw ourselves at a moment's notice into any shelter available. Eventually, we made it safely to the Le Bruns' farm, Beauchamp, at Sion on La Grande Route de St. Jean. There was consternation when we staggered in. We hadn't been able to warn them in advance that we were coming. We didn't mean to stay anywhere so obvious, but I was in no state to go looking for somewhere safer.

We burrowed deep into hay in a loft above the cow stable, and Keith Le Brun and Harry Miller covered us with several more layers before leaving us for the night. I can't remember if we had anything to eat. It was a miserable freezing mid-winter night. I was in pain as well as cold and suffering from the shock of blood loss. I shivered and shook until morning. Since then, I have never believed anyone who claims that hay is warm in winter. Sometime during that first night, I remember wishing I were back in my cell.

At about 5 o'clock, and well before daylight, Keith and his father reconnoitered the road and got us safely across. Between them they carried me down a long avenue of trees to Mr Holmes' farm, where they put us in another loft above a cow stable and walled us in with bales of hay. We had a space of about three square metres to live in and blankets to lie on and cover ourselves with. When they walled us in, they put three layers of bails on the free side, which made it a bit more difficult to get in and out, but put a safe distance between us and any probing bayonets.

It had been too dangerous to stay at Beauchamp. The Gestapo knew I had lived there. Every household had to register living-in occupants and they would have checked their records. We worried that our present hiding place was too close, but I wasn't fit enough to move and Peter wouldn't leave me. We were only two hundred yards or so from Beauchamp. We needed to get further away as soon as we could.

I never got round to asking Peter what happened at his home after the Germans found we were missing. They woke my family in the middle of the night and searched the vicarage from the ground floor up to the attics. My mother woke to loud bangs on the front door and to what she later described as 'much shouting in typical Teutonic fashion.' It was about 11pm. The house was in complete darkness. There was no electricity. When Father opened the front door, several Gestapo agents and soldiers rushed in and manhandled him into his study, bellowing questions continuously and demanding to know where I was hiding. But the family didn't know we had escaped. My smuggled warning hadn't got through.

Mother sat on the edge of the bed and eventually father joined her as the search went on elsewhere. Other members of the family were kept apart until it was over. My brother, Stanley, woke up staring into the wrong end of a rifle. He was roughly hauled out of bed and when they asked for his identity card and he said that he didn't keep it in his pyjamas, they hit him across the head. My youngest brother David and I both had ginger hair. They started by feeling his feet through the bedclothes to see if he was wearing boots! He had some difficulty convincing them he wasn't me.

Stanley told me recently, "All this was conducted none too gently. We were continually pushed around, blinded by flashlights and frightened by shouting. How long it took, I can't remember, but certainly in the region of one and a half to two hours. When they'd gone, we all went downstairs. We were badly shaken, the more so because I'd just been told that they'd found my crystal set. Freddie (David) and I eventually went back to bed. Sleep didn't come easily and we lay awake until nearly morning discussing all the possibilities."

He went on to say that the absence of electric light saved them from much more serious trouble. With flashlights only, the Gestapo missed other things. In his bedroom under the floorboards he had another radio, a large box of photographic papers, some developing chemicals and, even worse, a weapon, some weapon parts and ammunition. The searchers eventually went away, but left a watcher in the garden. Soon after daylight, the family found cigarette butts on the lawn. They watched the house for a couple of weeks and Stanley believes that he and the others were followed for a time.

Father had kept a diary which was written in rather forceful language, but they didn't find it; when they left he lit a small spirit lamp kept for emergencies and, with Mother's help, spent the rest of the night burning it page by page. He reported next day to the *Feldkommandantur* as ordered and was given a one-year prison sentence for allowing a radio in the house: 'To be served after the end of hostilities!' Some Nazis still thought they could win the war!

Mother never lost her resentment at the way one of the searchers made off with the last tin of jam from a Red Cross parcel. She got quite irate when she told me about it again just before she died in 1995.

When I was fit to move, Peter and I went our separate ways. Peter hid for some weeks with Captain Yates in his house at the top of Queens Road before he did something I would not have even contemplated. He moved into the family home and hid in the attic until the end of the war.

Although I saw Peter many times in later years, we only chatted briefly about that period of our lives. Unfortunately, we never sat down for a good long talk. We never discussed in detail what happened after we separated. Now it is too late.

During our time in the hayloft, the Holmes gave us food and milk twice a day and I began to get some strength back. When I was ready to move, Keith took me to another farm about a mile away and we met the owner in a field after dark. I will not give his name because when Keith asked him to hide me he got all tremulous and nervously offered me some Red Cross cigarettes instead. He wouldn't give me shelter even for one night. The poor fellow was hopping from foot to foot and was obviously too frightened. He kept repeating that a nearby anti-aircraft battery made it too dangerous. It was a good half-mile away! People react to fear in different ways. We all feel frightened at times unless we are stupid. Most of us can control it, but he could not, poor man. We can only feel sympathy.

By then it was well after curfew. It was too dangerous to go to Beauchamp or back to Mr Holmes' loft for the night, so I slept in a field and Keith brought me some food and something to drink before daylight. Then Bill and Gwenda Sarre at Millbrook agreed to take me in. They hid me for several weeks, despite having two small children. Gwenda is a Scot, a very forthright kindly lady. I became her cousin and took the name of Cameron. They shared their food with me on an equal basis and eventually Dr McKinstry got me a false identity card and a ration book to make things easier. Mac risked his life helping many escaped prisoners of all nationalities; for that and his medical work during the Occupation he received an OBE after the war.

The luxury of sleeping in a proper bed was unbelievable, but it took some time to adjust to the soft comfort. After the hard wooden prison beds and sleeping rough I had grown accustomed to stiff painful hips and shoulders and to waking with cramp several times a night.

There was enough wood on the property so that the house was always warm, but food was still a problem. The Germans kept a strict watch on what farmers and growers like Bill produced, and the Sarres had two growing children to feed as well. There was not a lot to go round.

Time passed incredibly slowly. For several days, I worked in an outhouse making sugar beet syrup in a big cauldron, and later I worked for a while in one of the fields until my back was too painful to continue. I may have been wrong, but I think Bill thought I was a bit of a bludger and wasn't doing as much as I could. It made me feel uneasy in the midst of so much kindness.

As part of my disguise, Gwenda dyed my hair black. It was bright ginger at that stage of my life. Of all things, she tried coffee first. I have no idea where she got it and for all the good it did we would have done better just to drink it. Maybe we did. I can't remember. Eventually, she got some black hair dye from a hairdresser in St. Helier. It did the trick, but my eyebrows stayed stubbornly and obviously ginger. Then she dug up some mascara and a tiny brush from somewhere and I applied it religiously for a time. I felt a right nonker putting it on and had to renew it fairly frequently, but the hairs were now a satisfactory black. Later, I got fed up with the whole palaver and reverted to my normal colour. Turning black didn't do much good anyway. I was recognised by several people. One day, on the road to Sion, I passed a lady I knew. We didn't acknowledge each other, but later she told me that she had known who I was by my walk.

Dr Mortimer-Evans, the Sarre family GP, gave me the once over and lent me some medical textbooks to pass the time when I had to stay indoors and out of sight. There was nothing he could do about my back and ankle except advise rest. I was beginning to get plenty of that and boredom was never far away.

I was not the only visitor to the Sarres' home. From time to time an escaped Russian officer dropped in for something to eat and a bit of warmth. I think he lived rough most of the time. Like so many Russians, he was a chess player and we played a few games. He was much too good and always won in about ten moves. When I returned to the Island for the 50th Anniversary of Liberation in 1995, he was staying with Gwenda Sarre and I had the pleasure of talking to him briefly on the telephone. He is deafer now than I am though and, even if his English is adequate it was not a great conversation and we barely understood each other. I wasn't sure that he remembered me at all.

He was one of the lucky ones. He managed to escape again, this time from the British or Americans before they could send him back to Stalin's Russia. The Soviet Government recognised Bill Sarre after the war for helping escaped Russian prisoners, but not until Stalin was dead and others somewhat less evil were in power.

The lower edge of the Sarres' property overlooked Waterworks Valley and there was a path down a slope through the trees. Bill arranged for my parents to walk out from town to see me and we met in the valley. That meeting is fixed firmly in my memory. It was a dull grey day, dry, with high cloud, but very cold. The trees were bare and crows wheeled above them and cawed from the upper branches, disturbed by our invasion of their territory. I was shocked to see how thin and haggard my parents looked. Their threadbare clothes hung like cast-offs on a scarecrow and Father supported himself with a stick. I can't remember what we talked about. I think we all felt a bit awkward.

Living on the run is a constant strain. It puts other people in danger and for me there was often an almost irresistible desire to be in the open and to keep moving. The longer I stayed in one place, the more anxious I became that I would be discovered and that the people hiding me would be in trouble. Each time I moved there was a brief feeling of relief.

I hadn't given up hope of getting to France and, when I began to feel stronger and the pain in my ankle and back lessened, I contacted Gordon Stuart who lived at Bonne Nuit Bay. His parents owned and ran Les Chalets Hotel. It was close to the beach and well within the forbidden coastal zone. Sentries manned boom gates on the two hills leading into the bay and the surrounding cliffs were heavily mined. To keep the hotel the Stuarts had been forced to billet German soldiers.

I walked into St. John's village to meet Gordon. It was already late and near to curfew, so he fixed one of the sentries he knew and I slept at the hotel for the night. As we ducked under the boom gate in the black-out and walked down the hill, the back of my neck prickled and I felt distinctly nervous. I found it difficult to trust the soldier who let us through, despite his cheerful *Guten Abend*, and Gordon's reassurance that he was a rabid anti-Nazi. It was good to be warm and dry again, but I found it impossible to sleep in a building surrounded by the enemy.

I had slept rough for the previous two nights near Handois reservoir, and had had no food for about 36 hours. One of those nights in the open was the third time, the last time that I cried with hunger. Soon after dawn I discovered a bit of swede in the field. It was just the upper leaves and a disc of flesh sliced away from the body, but I grabbed it and wolfed it down. Before I knew what I was doing I ate a large amount of soil too, but by some miracle it didn't make me sick.

Gordon took me to meet Olga and her father, Frank Le Calvez, who farmed Les Fougères, in St. John. They agreed to take me in and I had a meal with them before walking back to the Sarres to tell them I was moving on and to thank them for all they had done. They must have been relieved to see me go, and not just because of the danger. It was one less mouth to feed.

The next day, I moved into an upstairs bedroom at Les Fougères. To begin with I spent most of the day there, coming out only for meals and after dark. The farmhouse was on the road and we needed to be careful, but at least I could spend some of the time looking at what went past from behind the bedroom curtains. I spent a lot of time reading.

Mr Le Calvez introduced me to the cutthroat razor. He was a *Vrai Jerriais* – a real Jersey person – as was his wife. Olga, their daughter, helped to run the farm. Their son was away in the British Army. They shared everything and I was fed so well that I soon began to fatten up and to feel much stronger.

From time to time there were other visitors at Les Fougères because, like the Sarres, Mrs Le Calvez never turned escaped slave labourers or anyone else away without at least a little something to eat. It is hard to express enough gratitude to people like the Sarres and the Le Calvez family. They helped so many and at so much risk to themselves.

A young Russian we called Michael came to the farm quite often. I think he was hiding at Frank Dorey's farm next door for part of the time, but for the rest he had no fixed abode and usually slept rough. He spoke a fair amount of English and always called Olga, Wolya. He had been badly beaten and starved, and hated the Germans with an intensity we could never match.

Gordon Stuart had a Calvados still in the loft of a barn. His brew didn't taste too good by itself, but mixed with a little sugar beet syrup it was drinkable. One night he and Olga took me to a house at Les Platons where I met a man who brewed his own grog in the bath!

As my confidence grew, I went out more and more for short walks, but not often in daylight. One night Olga took me to an amateur concert at a Nonconformist Chapel in St. John's village and a lady started talking about me and repeating some of the rumours that had made the rounds. We'd never met before and she didn't know who I was. I can't recall that she said anything derogatory.

The Germans made several sweeps of the area, but didn't come to the farm; one day, one of the civilian prison warders turned up to ask for food. I saw him first and quickly ducked out of sight. I didn't think he had seen me and thought he was probably trustworthy anyway but, to be safe, I moved on again. Just before I left, I was in the front bedroom getting my few things together when two German motorcycles came down the road towards the farm. They each had a rider and a sidecar passenger. They were *Feldgendarmes* with menacing MP40s slung across their chests and they drove past slowly, looking at the house.

I wasn't taking any chances. My only weapon was a blackjack, a very professional rubber cosh, which Olga got from somewhere in case I needed it on one of my walks after dark, but it wouldn't have been much use against submachine guns. As soon as the patrol was out of sight, I jumped from the window. It was quite a drop, but I landed without doing any more damage to myself than had been done already, and then bolted across the garden and into a field where I hid behind a haystack. My heart was pounding and I felt like vomiting. But they weren't after me that day. They rode on past the main farm entrance and on towards St. John's Church.

The Rector of St. John's had been one of the Prison Board when Jock Macdonald and I were paraded before them for beating up the bullying warder. I bore the Rector no ill will. He was a pleasant kindly man, but being young and foolish, we thought it would be a good idea to give him a bit of a shock by attending his Sunday morning service. We didn't hang around to shake hands afterwards though and in retrospect it was pure bravado, a stupid thing to do in broad daylight. It put Olga and her parents at risk. But it felt good at the time.

I hid for a few weeks in a house near the top of the Mourier Valley with a Canadian lady, Mrs Mitchell, and her son, Peter. They had very little food, but willingly shared what little they did have. Olga called when she could with a basket of something from the farm. Even so, I was very hungry the whole time I was there and boredom was still a constant problem. At times, the pressure to get into the open or to move on again was almost intolerable, and I think it was that need which was at least partly responsible for our ill-advised visit to St. John's Church.

Peter was a musician. We used to sneak out after dark to visit a lady down the lane who had a piano. I think she was a retired actress. I have no idea why, but she and Peter decided to give me singing lessons. I suppose it was a challenge. Peter, who was the main force, probably fancied himself as an alchemist and wanted to turn base metal into gold. I can still remember most of the words to the 'Prologue to Pagliacci'.

One evening we decided to go for a walk down the valley towards the sea in a direction we hadn't taken before. An unpleasant surprise greeted us when we walked round a bend and saw a roadblock and a sentry about 50 metres further on. He had obviously seen us, so there was nothing for it but to go on and bluff it out. Fortunately, as we got nearer, he seemed unconcerned and we strolled up to him as nonchalantly as we could and politely asked the time in our best pidgin German, and then, *Ist es verboten hier?* – or something like that. He told us that indeed it was a forbidden zone, and we strolled slowly back to the corner, forcing ourselves to look equally unconcerned, but expecting to be called back at any moment. I had that prickling sensation at the back of my neck again and, as soon as we were out of view, we ducked off the road and took off up the side of the valley and walked along the railway track the Germans had built with slave labour, until it was safe to get back onto the road again.

With no radio, no television and, at that stage of the Occupation no light to read by, we passed the evenings in conversation and usually went to bed very early. It was warm in bed. Peter and his mother were heavily into Couéism and hypnotism, and one evening Peter put me under. We didn't have time to repeat the exercise because the next day Olga called to say that it was safe to go back to Les Fougères. We were anxious to get on with our new escape plans. We had no idea the war was nearly over.

Olga collected me after dark but we nearly didn't make it. For some unknown and unexpected reason, the Germans had put extra guards around Melbourne House in St. John's village. Fortunately, we saw them just in time and managed to get into a field and crawl safely past in the dark.

Meanwhile, Gordon had found a boat. It was moored in a reservoir in Waterworks Valley and, since it was afloat and obviously used by reservoir staff we thought it safe to presume it seaworthy. The plan, as I remember it, was that we would steal it one night just before curfew and hide it at the top of Bonne Nuit Bay. From there, when moon and tide were right, we would take it to a spot near La Saline. Gordon had found an engine and a supply of petrol. All we needed was a lorry to hijack the boat and to find a way to get down to the beach through a minefield in the dark without blowing ourselves up or getting shot.

To hijack the boat needed careful timing. If someone raised the alarm as soon as we got it onto the lorry, we would have to run the gauntlet of German positions dug into each side of the valley. The evenings were getting lighter, but we thought that in the semi-darkness just before curfew, we could get away with it.

It is here that my memory and Olga's divide. As I recall it, she and I spent some hours in the gorse at the top of the cliff near La Saline, carefully watching the path the Germans took through the mines and fixing landmarks in our minds. We thought it should be possible to take the same course at night, though it would obviously be more difficult in the dark carrying the boat and engine, and without alerting the sentries. It seemed highly dangerous.

I have described the plan as I remember it, but at the 50th Anniversary of Liberation, I caught up with Olga again for the first time in more than forty years. She couldn't remember any plan to leave from La Saline and said that we went to see Bill Bertram so that we could leave from Fauvic. I still think I am right, but 53 years is a long time and my memory is not what it used to be. But I do remember clearly that yet again I began to wonder what I had talked myself into, and again that I lost my fear as we waited at the top of Bonne Nuit Bay for the lorry to pick us up. It never came.

The driver changed his mind. His courage deserted him at the last moment. I don't know how the others felt, but looking back from the safety of time and distance I can't say I blamed him. Getting that boat would have been hair-raising. Before we could make new plans, it was obvious to everybody that the war was nearly over.

Chapter Twelve

WAITING FOR THE END

L iberation was an anticlimax. The war had lasted so long. For most of it we had been occupied. We were conditioned to defeat and to disappointment. Our daily lives were taken up with finding food and keeping warm. With surviving.

We were never sure until the end that we would be free, and when freedom came it was hard to accept as real, even though the emotion was intense. Sinel was right when he said and wrote nearly half a century later that we can still feel that emotion today. It was like recovering from a fatal illness. Gradually it dawned on us. It was true. We were FREE.

Excitement and anticipation filled the final days. Hitler was dead. Germany was reeling in the face of assaults from both East and West. Berlin was in flames. As the centre of the Nazi Empire crumbled, we knew it would soon be in Russian hands.

※

The final year of the Occupation was the worst. By Christmas 1944, we were starving. Nothing had come into the island from France since before D-Day. Before that, supplies were poor and intermittent. There were frequent rumours that the Red Cross was coming to our aid, but nothing happened. There was no gas, no electricity and no coal; for three weeks, there was no bread.

The Island was stripped of trees. People could be seen, doubled over, thin and weak, looking like bent old witches in a fairy story as they searched for a few twigs to try to cook or to keep warm. The winter of 1944-45 was harsh. The cold was bitter.

The few OT workers left in the island dug up the railway tracks. They used the sleepers for firewood. Earlier in the war, while supplies lasted, people could get buckets of tar mixed with sawdust to use as fuel. The pavements to and from the gas works were stained with black trails. Now intruders gutted empty houses. They plundered doors, floorboards, rafters, gates, anything that would burn. Friends of Dr Lewis cut down their back staircase for firewood.

In November, the Department of Education announced they would no longer prosecute parents who kept their children at home during bad weather. So many children had ragged, inadequate clothing. Some no longer had proper shoes. Church services were held in the afternoon; there was no electric light, no power for the organ. Farmers stopped planting seed potatoes. If they planted them, starving Islanders or Germans dug them up again as soon as it was dark.

Every night, thieves broke into houses, shops and stores. They were often violent. It was a battle to survive. You needed food to live, but if you were weak or careless you could be killed defending the larder. Farmers took poultry and other livestock into the farmhouse at night. When I was hiding at Les Fougères, our last job as darkness fell was to catch all the hens and lock them away for the night in one of the barns.

Until late in the Occupation, the Germans took a reasonable share of the milk and potatoes which local farms produced. They never took food the Island authorities imported from France, nor did they take the corn we grew for ourselves. Now, the States had to fight to stop them taking anything they wanted.

Just before the Invasion, the Germans changed their command structure. Like us, they expected the Island to become a battleground. They replaced the *Feldkommandantur*, which dealt mainly with civil affairs, with a more military *Platzkommandantur*. In January 1944, Hitler ordered twelve areas along the western coast of Europe – mainly major ports between Holland and the Gironde estuary in southwest France – to be *Festungen* – Fortresses. In February he added the Channel Islands. The *Festungen* were the most heavily fortified positions and he ordered that they be defended to the last man and to the last bullet.

Vizeadmiral Friedrich Hüffmeier had commanded *Scharnhorst* on its daring dash up the Channel with her sister ship, the *Gneisanau*, in February 1942. A fervent Nazi, he was appointed Naval Commander in the Islands in June 1944. Through Admiral Doenitz, he had Hitler's ear, and by constantly intriguing against him he eventually replaced Von Schmettow as *Befehlshaber*; the Count was removed on health grounds, even though he hadn't seen a doctor during the previous fifteen months! After the 20 July plot to assassinate him, Hitler became more and more suspicious of the Army and depended increasingly on the Navy for support.

Whatever else may be said about Hüffmeier, he did not lack courage or tenacity. He became a significant threat to the civilian population of the Islands in the final months of the war. Although Von Schmettow planned it first, he carried out a daring commando raid on Granville. In late 1944, a German Naval Assault Troop cadet and four paratroopers escaped from a work party on the docks at Granville. When it was dark, they hijacked an American landing craft and slipped out of port on the evening tide. They only had a rough sketch map and a small pocket compass, but they reached the Maîtresse Ile on the Minquiers reef where the German garrison fired on them before they could establish their identity. When they reached Jersey, the Germans treated them as heroes, and as a reward Hüffmeier arranged to send them back to Germany by air. Unfortunately, except for one of them, their glory was short lived; he had been wounded by friendly fire on the Minquiers and was still in the Jersey General Hospital when a night fighter shot down the plane taking the others to Germany. There were no survivors. Fate was not entirely on his side though. He was an instructor at the Palace Hotel, where the raiding force planned and trained for the Granville raid. When the hotel was blown up, he lost his left leg below the knee.

Their debriefing in Jersey before that ill-fated flight showed that Granville was an operational port and that there were usually at least five vessels in harbour, many of which carried coal. Hüffmeier intended to cut out one or more of the colliers and then to destroy the harbour. Though they did some damage to the port and captured some prisoners, and caused undoubted embarrassment to the Americans, the plan misfired.

The assault took place on the night of 8/9 March. Two minesweepers and a tug carried the raiding force. They flashed the same Morse letter back when challenged and got into Granville without incident. They severely damaged the port and some shipping, but were less lucky with the coal boats. Most were aground. The German planners had misjudged the tide.

They towed one British collier, the *Eskwood*, to Jersey, but she was almost empty. They captured an American Colonel, four other American officers, an UNRRA official and twenty enlisted men. Most of the officers were caught in bed at the Hotel des Bains. Von Schmettow said later: "They left the girls behind," but his claim was probably untrue.

During the raid, three artillery carriers took up a blocking position between St. Malo and Chausey, and two minesweepers stationed themselves between Jersey and the French coast. The American vessel PC564 was guard boat that night. When ordered to investigate the radar echoes of the approaching raider force, her skipper didn't hesitate. He attacked immediately. Unfortunately, his one small gun jammed after the first shot and with casualties and severe damage, the captain slipped away and beached his vessel near Cancale. She was soon repaired and back in service. She finished her days with the South Korean Navy.

On their way back to Jersey, the raiders attacked the American lighthouse and signal station on Grande Ile de Chausey and put them out of action. The German Command was delighted. Fifty-five German prisoners freed during the raid probably thought otherwise when they were suddenly transformed from warm, well-fed, safely-out-of-the-war prisoners, to active combat status in a cold, starving, besieged island. It must have been a terrible shock.

The new American prisoners had no idea how bad conditions in the Islands were, and caused some embarrassment to their own people as well as to a few Islanders. American servicemen who had been in the bag longer knew how desperate things were, but the new arrivals were less than appreciative of the meagre offerings thrown to them over the wire. They soon learned. The hard way.

Cruickshank mentions another raid on the Cherbourg peninsula launched from Alderney. He presumed its intention was to establish a beachhead which could be enlarged by reinforcements from the Channel Islands, and seriously embarrass the Allies. Von Schmettow briefly mentioned the planned raid in a statement he made when a prisoner, but the only other detail is that it failed and that only one of the raiders returned.

By late August 1944, the Bailiff was painfully aware just how serious the situation in the Island had become. He knew it would soon be much worse. He wrote to the *Platzkommandantur*:

> Sooner or later the clash of arms will cease, and the Powers will meet not only to consider the means to an enduring peace, but also to pass judgment on the authorities, be they civil or military, upon whose conceptions of the principles of honour, justice and humanity, the fate of people and places, and not least of occupied peoples and places, has temporarily been determined.
>
> The Insular Government believes that, at that day, it or such of its members as survive will stand with a clear conscience born of the conviction that it has failed neither in its duty to the people of Jersey, nor in its interpretation and observance of the rules of International Law. May the Insular Government be spared the duty of adding to the problems which will face the Powers an allegation that, by an unjustified prolongation of the siege of Jersey, the military representatives endangered the health, and indeed the lives, of the people of Jersey.

The Bailiff asked that his note be sent to both the German and British Governments, but had no means of knowing if it was delivered. He was so worried that he suggested to Von Aufsess that he be allowed to give his parole and go by yacht to England to tell the British authorities how serious things were and then return to the island. He was not surprised when the *Kommandant* refused.

The Island was by now totally isolated. Most of the German ships that had sailed between Jersey and France before D-Day had been sunk or damaged at the time of the Invasion. Those still serviceable had little or no fuel. As Cruickshank pointed out, when the German High Command realised the Allies were going to starve out the garrison to make them surrender, they first cut down the number of mouths to feed. They sent slave labourers and other workers back to France. They closed the concentration camp on Alderney. Those maltreated, starved prisoners would hardly have affected the overall level of food consumption, but their guards were entitled to military rations.

By July 1944, the German High Command was talking about evacuating the civilian population too. The only exceptions would be those working on the land to produce food. A quaint but sinister order survives. It reads: 'Their removal by sea seems possible if the enemy is informed that English civilians are on vessels leaving the Channel Islands. We should also make sure that during the evacuation period Englishmen, preferably of the ruling class, are on board ships both coming and going.'

But Hitler left it too late. As soon as the Allied Forces took the French ports opposite the Islands, evacuation was impossible. At one time, the Germans contemplated the rather bizarre idea of evacuating the garrison from one of the islands and putting all the civilians from the other islands there and leaving them for the British to feed.

In August, the German commander on each island was told that to guarantee his garrison's survival as long as possible, he should rigidly control their food supplies and ruthlessly cut down civilian rations. Both the British and German Commands knew that once the shipping routes were blockaded, food and other necessary supplies wouldn't last forever. Eventually, the garrison would have to surrender. One German official suggested they ask Britain to take off all civilians not of military age, and not needed for the war effort.

On 19 September 1944, the German Government asked the Protecting Power, Switzerland, to tell the British that, 'on the former British Channel Islands supplies for the civilian population are exhausted.' They added that they would allow the evacuation of all except men of military age, or allow food to be sent in.

The British Chiefs of Staff did not object. The Islands were no longer of any military importance to the Allies, and sending food would take fewer ships than evacuating the population. At that time, they needed all the shipping space they could find to supply and maintain the momentum of their advance into Germany.

A note scribbled by Churchill said: 'Let 'em starve. No fighting. They can rot at their leisure.' It is claimed by some that Churchill only meant the Germans and not the civilian population. Like others, I am not convinced. He would not have liked it, but he might well have agreed to sacrifice the people of the Islands for a military need.I for one would not have criticised him for making such a decision in order to keep the momentum of the push into Germany going at full bore.

In a minute of 27 September, he added:

I am entirely opposed to our sending any rations to the Channel Islands, ostensibly for the civil population but in fact enabling the German garrison to prolong their resistance. I therefore prefer to evacuate the women and children at once, and I would offer that men capable of bearing arms should be bound not to take any further part in the war. It is possible that the Germans would accept this, as with the reduction of the population their existing food supplies would last them longer. I would rather face this than go on feeding them. It is no part of out job to feed armed Germans and enable them to prolong their hold on British territory. Moreover our aircraft have many other tasks to perform.

At the next meeting of the War Cabinet, he said that any reply to the German Government should make it clear that, as long as their troops remained in occupation, they were responsible for feeding the population. If they couldn't, they should surrender immediately. If the Germans were unable to feed the Islanders, he suggested the Red Cross be asked to do so.

The German policy was still one of no surrender, and despite information on the perilous state of the Islands taken out by escapees, Churchill persisted with his hard line. On 6 November, he told the Foreign Secretary, "I am entirely opposed to our feeding the German garrison in the Channel Islands and thus prolonging its resistance."

Fortunately for the Islanders, he changed his mind the next day. He gave permission for the Red Cross to send in food parcels and medical supplies. The garrison was now in a position to prolong the siege, but our lives were saved. Before the parcels arrived, the weekly rations were minimal. Many potatoes were poor quality or rotten. A few swedes and turnips added little to the diet.

During all the political and diplomatic activity, we still went hungry. It was not until after Christmas 1944 that the first parcels arrived in Guernsey. In Jersey, we had to wait until the New Year, and even then the *Vega*, which had arrived on 30 December, wasn't unloaded until 2 January. They began off-loading on the 31st, but stopped again for the New Year's Day public holiday!

During the months after D-Day, the Bailiff was in some personal danger. In his memoirs, he records how Baron Von Aufsess told him: "There are four people in the fortress who are under suspicion. One is Von Schmettow, one is von Helldorf, one is myself and the other is you. The end is on the way. I have an idea that we are going to be eliminated. I should not like you to be under the impression that there is nowhere they can send you because they are preparing a concentration camp on Alderney for you, and a few others like you."

He warned Coutanche: "I will keep you posted. One day I will telephone and say we are now only three. Later, I will say that we are now only two. When

I telephone and say we are now only one, that will be the time for you to look out."

While I don't doubt the validity of this account by Lord Coutanche, or that there was a definite menace, it seems an odd story. Von Aufsess could not expect that any arrests would not to be made at the same time, or expect them to be carried out in a particular order, so that he was the last but one and the Bailiff last of all.

✳

As the war drew to its end, I lived quietly at Les Fougères. The false ration book Dr McKinstry had provided allowed Mrs Le Calvez to get a Red Cross parcel for me. With a bit more food available on the farm and the contents of the parcels, we lived reasonably well. We were much better off than my family in town, but there was no way I could help them. Every so often, I sent a message to let them know I was well. I spent a lot of time reading and there was enough tobacco in the Red Cross supplies to have an occasional smoke.

The joy when the first parcels arrived was unforgettable. Before they were distributed, everything available was being made into stew at the communal kitchen. In reality, it was little more than thin soup. Miss Fraser's staff kept the kitchen going with the last fuel available, and handed out stew in milk bottles.

Norman Le Brocq described how Christmas Dinner in 1944 was a roast potato each for himself, his fiancée and her parents. He described it as 'a memorable treat.'

There were only two Red Cross parcels a month. It wasn't much, but it was enough to keep people alive. Volunteer members of St. John Ambulance supervised the unloading and distribution of the parcels. St. John acted as representative for the Red Cross. When broken parcels needed sorting and repacking, St. John was put in charge. It is strange now to look at film and photographs of thin but happy people collecting their parcels, while members of St. John, in their distinctive black and white uniforms, stand guard alongside German sentries.

Ron Skinner, a 17 year-old St. John Ambulance volunteer, was on duty on the Albert Pier when the Red Cross ship *Vega* was being unloaded. He saw the first batch brought ashore by German naval personnel. They touched nothing. French North African POWs unloaded the second batch. Several crates were damaged and the Germans spotted the prisoners filling their pockets. Who could blame them? They were starving too. The guards lined them up and made them turn out their pockets. The German officer in charge collected all the stolen tins and packets into a hamper and delivered them, in person, to the Red Cross store in Patriotic Street.

There were frequent robberies from homes, from farms, from shops and stores.

They were all blamed on starving soldiers, but, in general, German discipline was good. Others were guilty too. Many of the culprits were hungry locals, as hungry as the French North African POWs. Those Germans who unloaded parcels and helped store and distribute them behaved impeccably. It must have been hard to bear at a time when they would shortly be seen scavenging in dustbins for anything left behind in the corner of a Red Cross tin. In February 1945, when things were at their worst for the troops, a notice appeared in the *Evening Post*. It read: 'If any member of the public has mislaid a Red Cross parcel, they may claim it at this office where it has been handed in by a German soldier who found it lying in the road.'

Less than a year before we had seen living skeletons: Jews, Russians, and other nationalities. Now the Germans too were reduced to eating cats and dogs. They collected nettles for soup and ate the stalks of potato plants. They collected limpets from the rocks. They begged for food at the back doors of farms. There was enough humanity for some local people to see they didn't all go away empty-handed, but most of us hadn't reached that stage of forgiveness. The garrison had a good reserve of food, but Hüffmeier wouldn't let them use it. Many soldiers spent the day in bed to conserve what little energy they had.

Though everyone else could see that Germany's days were numbered, the *Vizeadmiral* refused to accept that Germany would be defeated. He remained bellicose and hostile to any suggestion of surrender. In March, he harangued his troops in the Forum Cinema. He told them he intended to hold out until the Fatherland had won back its lost territory and final victory was won.

When even Hüffmeier eventually realised that Germany couldn't win, he decided he would hold on to the Islands after the war ended. He would use the population as bargaining counters at any Peace Conference. He was a rabid Nazi. He would have carried out his threat if Admiral Doenitz hadn't given him a direct order to surrender. His threat would have been lethal for most Islanders and for the garrison as well.

In April, Von Helldorf and Von Aufsess agreed they might have to kill him, but the Admiral became suspicious of their loyalty, and banished Von Helldorf to Herm. On that tiny islet he had only a fisherman and the fisherman's wife for company.

'Free Germany' elements in the army planned a mutiny and to kill all Nazi sympathisers. The late Norman Le Brocq, who later became Deputy Le Brocq, was then a staunch communist. He described how he and Les Huelin were contacted by one of the plotters, and how his fiancée, later his wife, helped print leaflets for distribution among the troops. He used to rendezvous with the Germans in a secondhand bookshop. When one of the coup leaders deserted, they fed and clothed him. Communists also helped Russian escapees throughout the Occupation. We may not have agreed with their political ideas, but they did not lack courage. They did not sit on their backsides and see out the war in complete safety.

One of their leaflets read: 'Comrades! In Germany today the breaking up of the Hitler regime is nearly completed. The German people have seen through the swindle, and now the Nazi clique must defend their own lives after sending millions to their deaths for the obstinate ideas of the man called Hitler. When the signal is given for rebellion, tie a white towel or handkerchief round your left arm.' Another leaflets exhorted: 'Death to the Nazis! Long live a free Germany!'

They planned their mutiny for May Day. To signal the start of the uprising, they would fire a gun from Elizabeth Castle. They would then kill all officers known to be Nazis.

Les Huelin was a rabid communist. Sometime before the war, he emigrated to Australia and worked on the docks, where he was probably indoctrinated further. He took part in strikes. He was a known agitator. He returned to Europe to fight in Spain, but arrived too late. He returned to Jersey. Bob Le Sueur, who at that time was a member of the communist-inspired JDM, the Jersey Democratic Movement, knew all the players well. Though he had no hard evidence, he thinks Huelin was sent back to the Island from Australia to stir things up. Le Sueur also believes he was the power behind the throne. Though recognising that Le Brocq was very vociferous and active, he considered he was only the front man.

With Red Spaniards, the JDM helped escaped slave workers and took great risks. But their activities against the Germans were otherwise minimal. They directed much of their energy to undermining the Bailiff and the States. Dr Caspar admitted to a friend of Michael Ginns, in about 1973: "Yes, we knew all about Norman Le Brocq and his merry men and what they got up to; but as long as they didn't do anything stupid, we let them get on with it. If we had rounded them all up, we would have been inviting the SS and the real *Gestapo* to descend upon Jersey, and we at the *Feldkommandantur* didn't want that any more than the civilian population would"

Bob Le Sueur no longer has a circular he was given at the time of the planned mutiny, but maintains that it was Huelin's intention to eliminate the Bailiff and Crown Officers as traitors. As no help could have been expected from Britain for a few days after any uprising, the JDM intended to declare itself as the only organisation capable of keeping law and order, and to set up an interim Socialist Government, as happened over most of Eastern Europe, and was attempted in parts of France. This may sound far-fetched, but if the Communist Resistance in neighbouring France, which was very strong, had succeeded in seizing power, events might have been different in the Island.

The German soldier who deserted was Paul Mulbach. He always claimed he was responsible for blowing up the Palace Hotel as well as for setting fire to an

OT dump at Georgetown. In the past, his version was always accepted as fact. However, a former German military engineer, Hans Kegelmann, told Michael Ginns that he had no doubt at all who blew it up. He did. By accident.

A fire broke out during the planning stage for the Granville raid. Mulbach may have lit it. Kegelmann was ordered to blow a firebreak to contain the fire, which had taken hold with some ferocity, but was too enthusiastic with his charges and triggered a sympathetic explosion in the ammunition store. It blew the hotel sky high. Even if Mulbach deliberately set the fire, Kegelmann seems to have finished the job off for him.

The mutiny never took place. Catholic officers involved didn't want it to take place on socialist May Day. Then, with Hitler dead, everyone knew the war was almost over.

Michael Ginns raises an intriguing issue. The senior German officer involved in the proposed mutiny was a Colonel Lindner. He was posted to Guernsey on 28 April, two days before the proposed uprising. This brings up the possibility of an informer in the JDM ranks and that Lindner was deliberately moved. In view of Dr Casper's remarks, Ginns thinks there was an informer, and asks the additional question: 'Why otherwise would Hüffmeier have started to move officers around – Von Helldorf, Von Aufsess, and others?'

Among the senior German officers, Baron Von Aufsess' position was now precarious. The Gestapo had arrested his wife in Germany for making anti-Hitler remarks. He didn't know what had happened to her. Fortunately, she survived.

Before he left Jersey for banishment on Herm, Von Helldorf asked Duret Aubin to see him at a German Officers' club. They sat in deck chairs on a lawn to avoid being overheard and he told the Attorney-General that his life too was in danger. The *Platzkommandantur* had made a list of a hundred civilians they considered dangerous, with a view to deporting them to a punishment camp on Alderney. Those still in prison would no doubt have been included.

Even after Hitler's death, Hüffmeier remained truculent and abrasive. He ordered the Captain of the Red Cross ship, *Vega*, to fly his flag at half-mast. The captain refused. When an Allied vessel signalled the garrison on Alderney with a proposal for surrender of the Islands, he signalled back: *Ihr Angebot ist überflüssig* – Your offer is superfluous. Other senior German officers in the Islands were relieved when Admiral Doenitz and not Heinrich Himmler succeeded Hitler. Himmler and Hüffmeier together might very well have carried out the threat to use Channel Islanders as bargaining chips in any negotiations and Churchill would have been faced with the choice of a complete blockade, with all its consequences for the civilian population, or an invasion which, in the absence of a mutiny would be terribly costly in lives on both sides.

Evidence suggests, however, that by that time, Hüffmeier's hold on his troops' loyalty was weakening fast. Most Germans wanted the war to end as quickly as possible and to go back home to their families. It seems likely that there would have been a mutiny and that any resistance, except from a few hardliners, would have been minimal. There is also evidence that Hüffmeier knew this, and that he realised just how dangerous his own position was. He knew he could no longer trust his own staff and took precautions against being assassinated.

Sinel wrote: 'May 1st was cold. The temperature was just above freezing point. Light snow fell over night. In the town, shops openly sold Union Jacks, and a portrait of Churchill by a Russian fetched 400 Marks at a Red Cross auction.'

The Military Police arrested a man for spreading anti-Nazi propaganda! Many Germans looked glum. Most looked cheerful. Some proclaimed they were conscripted Poles, or Czechs. Not Germans. None had ever been Nazis!

On 6 May, the Admiral left his headquarters in Guernsey to talk to the Bailiff and Attorney-General in Jersey. He went back to Guernsey the same day. The Secret Police, 'the Gestapo of the Army', as they were entitled to do, put on ordinary uniforms and mixed with the troops. Bolder spirits baited individual Germans and other enthusiasts put out the Union Flag too soon. A German soldier looking for food attacked and badly wounded a local woman. The BBC forecast the end of the war in a day or two.

The town was full of rumours and we could barely keep a hold on our excitement. On the 7th, a German official called the Department of Agriculture. He said the German authorities were not happy about the milk situation!

Some of the political prisoners were let out of prison. Four ounces of dried peas were issued. The States told us the potato ration would be increased to 6 lbs a week, as there was no bread.

Even when the BBC announced that tomorrow would be VE-Day, some of the garrison still huffed and puffed and postured. Sentries stood guard outside important buildings. Soldiers dug and manned new gun positions. That night searchlights swept the sea.

Tomorrow was another day. It was the one thousand, seven hundred and seventy-second day of the Occupation. We still didn't know what was happening. Nothing official had been said. There was still doubt. There was still anxiety.

❋   ❋   ❋

Chapter Thirteen

EPILOGUE: RESISTANCE
OR COLLABORATION?

I decided to go home. I got up early and said *au revoir* and thank you to the Le Calvez family. I shall always be in their debt, as I am to all those others who hid or helped me. Even if the risk that it would be carried out had decreased by then, the Germans had made it abundantly clear that helping escaped prisoners was sabotage. The penalty was death.

It was early morning, just after dawn, when I walked up the road to Hautes Croix and caught the milk lorry into town. The weather had fined up but it was still chilly. The sun was out but it hadn't warmed the air. The ride home amid the rattle and bang of churns could not have been a happier one. The cold wind on my face was itself a taste of freedom. I can't describe how I felt. I can only say it was a day of repeated emotion, the memory of which can only be shared with those who belong, with those who were there.

I was reunited with my family. I saw my friends again. Though I still felt uneasy, I walked in the streets openly and without fear of being arrested. I listened to Churchill's speech relayed over loudspeakers in the Royal Square. I was there when he said, "And our dear Channel Islands are also to be freed today." I saw the Union Flag raised and joined in singing the National Anthem. Tears streamed down my cheeks. I was not ashamed then, nor am I now to tell of it.

I heard the Bailiff speak. Then he came down into the crowd to shake hands with us. I saw *HMS Beagle* steam into St. Aubin's Bay. I saw British uniforms for the first time in five years. It was over. But despite all the emotion, Liberation seemed unreal, almost like a dream. Slowly, reality took hold. We had food. We were warm. The electricity stopped going off. We no longer talked in whispers. We stopped looking over our shoulders. Suddenly, we became aware of normal sounds again. After curfew, except when the wind blew or the guns broke the stillness, there had been little noise. Empty roads, devoid of vehicles and people, had projected an almost cathedral-like quiet, so that ordinary sounds – a banging door, or the clatter of approaching jackboots – were magnified.

Evacuees who had gone to England in 1940 and deportees who had been carted off to Germany came back. And some of those who had gone to concentration camps returned. For relatives of those who died in Germany, there were months of uncertainty. They suffered agonies of alternating hope and despair before they knew the awful truth. Some waited years for another prisoner who had survived to tell them of a loved one's last moments.

The Germans went away. They were taken away. Landing craft appeared at the water's edge in St. Aubin's Bay, and long columns of disconsolate men trudged across the sand into captivity; as we had seen in news-reels our men doing after Dunkirk and Dieppe and after early defeats by Rommel in North Africa. But now the uniforms were field grey, not khaki. I can't remember feeling any triumph. Only happiness. Later there was sadness for those who hadn't made it.

Soldiers came home to children they had last seen as infants, or who had been born after they left. It was a time of joy and sadness. Some came home to tragedy to find a loved one had died, or a wife had been a Jerrybag. Relatives of the missing and killed in action, whose deaths had not come through in Red Cross messages, grieved at their new found loss among so much happiness and wondered how they were going to rebuild their lives alone. Nan Le Ruez, whose *Jersey Occupation Diary* is a simple and moving account of how ordinary people fared, would soon be reunited with her fiancé whom she had last seen in September 1938, when he sailed for Nigeria to work as a missionary.

I put on weight, though not much to begin with. Our stomachs had shrunk and at first we couldn't eat big meals. We felt sick and risked diarrhoea. I heard a lady say on the BBC how she missed much of Liberation Day because she had diarrhoea. She blamed 'laxative chewing gum given to her by a Taffy soldier.' I doubt it. It was far more likely that her stomach had forgotten how to deal with sweets and chocolate.

Soldiers handed out such luxuries and cigarettes as soon as they landed. I went aboard a small naval vessel moored in the harbour and the sailors gave me a meal of fried Spam. I shall never forget it. It is engraved on my cerebral cortex alongside Iris Langlois' rabbit pie and Mrs Bathe's roast duck. My young sister, Margaret, saw, or at least recognised an orange for the first time. There may have been two issues of an orange on ration to children only, early in the war, but she would have been too young to remember. For her, it was, and has remained, the first orange.

I didn't join those who it was said shaved the heads of Jerrybags, but I remember feeling at least some pleasure when I heard what had been done to them. I regret it now. From the safety of time and distance, such brutality is best forgotten, but I can't entirely condemn those who sought revenge. There was so much pent-up anger. Recently, Michael Ginns eased my conscience when he asked: "Did you personally see any Jerrybag have her head shaved? Or know anyone who took part in such an act?" I did not.

Ginns wrote: 'Tarring and feathering was another myth. By 1945 there wasn't any tar.' There was, however, a nasty scene at the Weighbridge on May 9th or 10th, reported by the *Evening Post*. Some Jerrybags unwisely joined the crowds and if a couple of men, and then British troops, hadn't intervened, those girls might well have been killed, or at least have finished up in the harbour. Joe Mière saw a girl run screaming up the town with hardly any clothes on, but no shaved heads. He put his coat round her and sent her home. Eric Walker, later Jersey's Bomb Disposal Officer and his mate (both Royal Engineers) rescued a girl from the doorway of the Opera House. Cornered by a gang of youths, she was down in a corner, sobbing and screaming, but the youths didn't seem to know what to do about her: apart from kicking out at her without actually making contact. Eric and his mate unslung their rifles and drove them off. They took the girl home and told her to stay out of sight until the excitement died down. Within a couple of weeks, those same girls were going out with the Liberation soldiers and giving them the same favours they had been giving to the Germans a few weeks earlier.

I must be honest. I looked for Durand. He had disappeared. We 'liberated' some souvenirs from his house and gave them to the *Connétable* for safe-keeping. They lay in the safe in St. John's Parish Hall for years, until someone else 'liberated' them in turn. I learned recently that the Durand family were chased from their home after Liberation and found sanctuary in the little Roman Catholic chapel at Ville à l'Eveque in Trinity.

John Hanna, our family doctor, was looking at some X-Rays when I told him that a well-known traitor and her daughter had been roughed up a bit and were now in prison for their own protection. He said, quietly: "It's a pity to spoil such a wonderful time with acts of revenge." I shall always remember his words. They were said without contempt. I felt very small.

They were a Mrs Robbins and her daughter. Joe Mière saw them cornered in Midvale Road. A crowd was putting a rope on a lamp-post to hang them, when they too were rescued by British soldiers. They left the Island soon after.

Two other traitors joined them in the prison: Mother Baudains and her son. One day during the Occupation, two youths caught the son in the Minden Street toilets and shoved his head down a bowl and pulled the flush. Those youths too became important in the Island later, so must remain nameless.

The Baudains were still in prison the following March. The *Sunday Pictorial* discovered them and published their details. There was an outcry. Why should such treacherous creatures be kept at public expense? They were booted out of prison, and given a few days shelter by The Little Sisters of the Poor before being taken to the harbour and given a one-way ticket. They were told never to set foot in Jersey again. Sometime later, someone reported seeing Mrs Baudains working in a shoe shop in Bristol. She and her son have since died.

✻

I have tried to keep emotion out of this account. It has slipped in at times. I have tried to be fair. Not all Germans were bad. Fifty years on, I have come to believe that there were more good ones than we thought at the time. Most of them were like us – survivors. But I can never forget the attitude of normal-looking soldiers to the plight of slave labourers. Nor can I fail to remember the hypocrisy of Von Schmettow in the speech he made to his troops just before the Invasion.

A few Germans showed me kindness when least expected: the elderly marine at La Folie Inn; a prison guard called Heinrich, who was a farmer in Schleswig-Holstein before the army got him. There were others too. Most of our guards were reasonable men. They were as much prisoners as we were: prisoners of the system, prisoners of military law and discipline and, as the Bailiff once told Hüffmeier, to the Admiral's great annoyance, prisoners of the Royal Navy.

I am told that in Sark, there is a 'Traitor's Tree'. Some evil-minded informer pinned to its trunk a list of people who had kept secret radios. Someone told the German *Kommandant*. He said, "This was the work of a traitor," and ignored it.

I was perhaps a little too scathing in what I wrote earlier about Graf Von Schmettow. When the SS and their concentration camp prisoners were en route from Alderney to France, they spent a couple of nights in Guernsey, and then in Jersey. While in Guernsey, they were housed in the former OT punishment camp at Les Vauxbelets. A soldier who did sentry duty at the camp told Michael Ginns that Von Schmettow ordered the SS guards to push off for 48 hours, and while they were away he made sure the prisoners had full Army rations.

Just before the transfer of power, the Bailiff issued a statement appealing to us to maintain our calm and dignity in the days ahead. I think most did. But it was more by luck than good judgment that I didn't find Durand. I am glad now.

✻

When I started writing, I intended to talk about collaboration in some detail. Now, I find that I don't want to. However, a book by Madeleine Bunting (*The Model Occupation*, 1994) and hasty judgements by others makes it necessary to answer some of the criticism. And, since initially writing this chapter, the United Kingdom Public Records Office has opened more secret files to scrutiny. Once again the British Press has latched on to all the negative aspects and has emphasised collaboration, while hardly mentioning those who resisted. Once again they have distorted the true picture and stimulated a barrage of angry letters. They have caused enormous hurt.

Of course there were collaborators as there were in every other occupied country; but in Jersey at least the number was small – a very tiny proportion of the total population. They did not include the Island authorities. Things said, written and done by the hierarchy in Sark and Guernsey still offend me today, but anything I write can only cause pain to a new generation and, since I wasn't there, I will confine my remarks to Jersey and comment no further on events in those two islands.

It is a sad reflection on the British media that without exception, every time I listened to a radio programme or looked at television during the 50th Anniversary of Liberation, the reporters all asked as their primary question: "What about collaboration?" Not one newspaper articles I saw, in Britain or Australia, failed to mention the subject.

More recently, David Cesarani wrote in the *Guardian* that in the Islands 'cooperation and fraternisation with the Germans was the rule. There were,' he claimed, 'almost no protests against the application of Nazi race laws.' I am told that Professor Cesarani has since retracted his statement and apologised. I hope so.

There were traitors in Jersey, just as there were in France and in every other occupied country. The only relevant question about collaboration and treachery is: was it more or less in the Island than in other occupied territories? It is true there was no fighting *Résistance* in Jersey, but there was resistance enough for us to hold our heads high.

I read somewhere that those who have never been occupied should not criticise those who have. It may be true. It is a remarkably sad thing to lose one's freedom. Freedom is not just a word to those who have lost it. It is a complex emotional experience which even years later can make the voice husky and bring a tear to the eye. Those who have lost their liberty in the past empathise with those who in recent times have thrown off the yoke of communism, apartheid, or some other evil.

For many Jersey people, especially in the first year or two, German rule was benign and fair, surprisingly and comfortingly so after the Nazis' barbarous behaviour elsewhere. It proved seductive to some, and they became collaborators or outright traitors: but it was not a crime for ordinary, loyal people to think or even say in most of 1940 and 1941 – before the iron fist contracted – "Well things are not as bad as we thought they were going to be. They have behaved pretty well up to now." They had.

It did not remain a benign occupation for long. Bunting claims the authorities in Jersey and Guernsey did nothing to protect the Jews caught in the Island. She has since been proved wrong in almost everything she wrote. One Guernsey official resigned in protest at anti-Jewish legislation to which the States of that Island put its name. In Jersey, the Bailiff, Alexander Coutanche, objected strongly and had the order that Jews should wear a yellow Star of David cancelled. The Jews had to register. But so did we all. Their businesses had to display notices saying *Juedisches Geschaeft* - Jewish Undertaking. But those were German orders, not civilian ones.

Mr Freddie Cohen, President of Jersey's Jewish Congregation has researched the matter in detail. A Memorial Service was held in the Synagogue on 2 September 1998 to honour those Jews who suffered during the Occupation, and those who helped them. Lord Jakobovits, Emeritus Chief Rabbi, missed a special sitting of the House of Lords to attend; he also turned down an invitation to be principal guest at the opening of the new central synagogue in Moscow. Lady Jaobovits unveiled a memorial plaque. Island dignitaries made speeches, and among others who lived through the Occupation, my friend Basil Le Brun was there. Joe Mière, who as Freddie Cohen wrote in the introduction to his book, 'has steadfastly endeavoured to record for posterity the details of all those who suffered during the Occupation, for whatever reason, regardless of their nationality or religion,' was given special mention and thanks.

Cruickshank's opinion was that in historical terms the Island Jews suffered little more than anyone else. He wrote that they had the indignity of an earlier curfew and reduced shopping hours, and the threat of worse hanging over them, but no British Jews went to concentration camps. Cohen corrects this erroneous impression. He wrote that the Orders and measures imposed on the Jews had a substantial effect on their lives. Some had their businesses closed and were deprived of the ability to find a job or earn their living in any way. They had an earlier curfew and were repeatedly interviewed by the Germans. There was the constant fear and threat of deportation. On a more personal level, Elizabeth Duquemin, who was deported from Guernsey with her husband and baby daughter, but fortunately survived, said: "Every day, for a year and a half until I was deported, I lived in fear and terror. Every day I was frightened and did not know if they would take me away, or my baby daughter, or my husband." Non-Jewish deportees found the fear bad enough, even though they didn't have a long period of anxiety before being transported into the unknown.

When the Jews in Jersey were ordered to register, the Aliens Officer, Clifford Orange, invited them into his office. He told them they could register, or not. It was up to them. If they didn't want to, 'then he wouldn't shop them.' Most chose to register. They feared what might happen if they disobeyed the German order and were found out.

The only Jew who went to a concentration camp was Max Finkelstein, a Romanian. He survived Buchenwald and returned after the war. Various Jewish women were deported to Biberach with other Channel Islanders in February 1943. They all returned safely. Mrs Lloyd, who was half Jewish, was deported to Biberach but made such a fuss that the Germans sent her back to Jersey in April 1944.

The wife of Jersey artist, Edmund Blampied, was left undisturbed in the Island throughout the Occupation. Mrs Mary Richardson was warned for deportation in 1942, but Albert Bedane, a masseur in Roseville Street, hid her for 30 months. She reappeared in 1944, when the Islands were cut off, to look after her invalid husband. One Jew committed suicide, a not uncommon event in wartime among all sections of the community. Another went insane; a few others died of natural causes. Some did not register, and went undetected.

Bunting blames the Guernsey authorities for the deaths of three foreign women in Auschwitz. It has been suggested that a fellow worker denounced one of them, Marianne Grunfeld. Cohen found no evidence that she was betrayed. All foreigners in the Islands at the outbreak of war had to register. Many were deemed 'enemy aliens' and were interned. They were released before the Germans arrived, but were not allowed to enter Britain. Lists of these unfortunates were later available to the Germans. It was rumoured that two of the women gave themselves away by asking the Germans for help to trace their families in Vienna. I have seen no evidence to support such a contention. Cohen does not blame the Guernsey officials in any way for these deaths.

In judging the Island authorities remiss for not having done anything more active to protect Jews, Bunting and others would do well to remember that like the Jews themselves, the Bailiff and his officers knew nothing in 1940 of the Holocaust to come. If the Jews had known the full horror awaiting them, they would not have gone to their deaths so passively. Those who registered did so out of fear, but if they could have foreseen the future they would probably not have registered, and would most certainly have tried to hide; if not in the Islands, then when they got to France, where some of them lived in relative freedom for a time before being transported to Auschwitz-Birkenau. They too were ignorant of the danger. I do not believe the Island Government or the Islanders would have failed to help if they too had known in advance the degree of risk to which the Jews were exposed. Ordinary Jersey men and women did not fail to help escaped Russians. They would have done the same for Jews if they had been aware of the peril. The Islanders described in these pages that were caught and punished for helping escapees, were not the only ones who assisted such unfortunates. Many more, whose names go unrecorded, did so.

✳

When the Germans deported specific categories in January 1943, five were included because they were Jews. Finklestein was not British. They interned the remaining four with the other Channel Islanders.

In his own address at the Memorial Service, Freddie Cohen said: "There were a number of non-Jewish Islanders who during the Occupation showed great compassion to persecuted Jews and who in doing so took great personal risks." He added: "Today we remember and honour Albert Bedane who hid Mary Richardson for two and a half years. We remember Dorothea Weber and Bozena Kotyzova who hid Hedwig Bercu for one and a half years. All risked a death sentence had they been uncovered. We remember the action of Sir Abraham Laine the Guernsey Jurat who refused to give his assent to the promulgation of the first Order against the Jews in 1940. We remember the action of Lord Coutanche, the Bailiff of Jersey, in engineering that the order requiring Jews to wear a yellow star was not registered in Jersey. We also remember Lord Coutanche's action in successfully pleading for mercy against the death sentence imposed on two women who the Germans regarded as Jews. We remember Edward Ogier who appealed to the Germans against the deportation of Marianne Grunfeld. His appeal was tragically unsuccessful and she perished at Auschwitz. We remember Dr Lewis who aided a Jewish patient ordered for deportation. We remember the Belgium resistance and the residents of Dixmunde who saved and cared for the ex-Alderney slave workers. Finally we remember all those who endeavoured to protect the assets of their Jewish clients and employers."

Cohen also pointed out that the persecution of the Island Jews was unique, in that it was the German garrison and its officers that carried it out: not, as elsewhere in Europe, the SS or special anti-Jewish units. He also wrote that the civilian authorities in Jersey and Guernsey faced complex decisions in relation to the German orders. Though it was sad that they helped to implement those orders by registering administrative measures, the primary blame was German, and German alone. While the Nazis received encouragement and many times active help in their cruelty to Jews in other occupied countries, it was "a great credit to the Islanders that despite German efforts to stimulate anti-semitism, there was no general denunciation of Jewish residents."

When the Germans first arrived, they believed they would soon be in London. They could afford to be well behaved and benevolent. They no doubt wanted news of their benign rule to reach Britain in the hope that it would lessen resistance to them there. They acted accordingly. Hitler's personal interference changed that. If his minions had carried out his orders, the result for many, if not for most of us, would have been very different. Even ignoring the harsh winter climate there, the Pripet Marshes of Byelorussia in the middle of the fighting on the Russian Front would not have been a pleasant destination, especially if Himmler had in reality taken charge as he was supposed to do. We were fortunate that German efficiency, at least in administrative affairs, was not all it was said to be.

Those who have not been occupied tend to interpret resistance as being the same as The *Résistance*, particularly as it became in France. But even in that country, they imagine it was something heroic and continuous, involving many people, which started after defeat in 1940, and went on until Liberation. The reality was different.

Only a small proportion of the French population resisted actively: so few in fact that early resisters were given the honourable title 'Vintage'. Even at the end, when the ranks swelled dramatically, they were not all that numerous in terms of total population, although afterwards, of course, everybody claimed they had been involved.

As in France, most Islanders went about their daily lives in as normal a way as possible. They got up in the morning, opened their bowels, washed, ate breakfast if they were lucky, and went to work. They returned in the evening. They obeyed the curfew and went to sleep when it was dark in preparation for another day. They followed the pattern set in France. As H.R. Kedward wrote in his study, *Occupied France: Collaboration and Resistance, 1940-1944*, people spent their time trying to outwit what the Bretons call *La chienne du monde* - the malevolent beast of poverty, hunger and personal or family disaster.

The lives of the majority consisted of queuing for food and looking for the necessities of life far more than would have been the case in normal times. In general, they kept their heads down. They kept out of trouble, and survived. It is how the majority of people in Britain would have behaved if they too had been occupied. Those people should not be criticised unless the critic is willing to be specific in saying what they should have done, and then, more importantly, after examining his or her own conscience, to say what he or she personally would have been willing to do. As Dan Van der Vat wrote in *The Good Nazi*: '... those never subjected to dictatorship or foreign occupation have been over eager to demand moral courage, a rare quality, of such people, sometimes retrospectively.' He further wrote, when discussing the Germans' own resistance to Hitler: 'If there is one overriding trend in the historiography of the Second World War, it is that anti-Nazi resistance is generally exaggerated (a form of inflation surpassed only by pilots reporting bomb damage and the like). This tendency is as pronounced in Germany as it is in France and other erstwhile occupied countries.'

Madeleine Bunting was right in discussing what collaboration there was in the Islands when she wrote that the the myth of the distinctiveness of the British character from that of Continental Europeans is slowly weakening its hold. Though she badly overestimated the degree of collaboration, she was also right when she added that the truth about the Islands' war record should not be an opportunity for Britain to indulge in moral indignation, but a chance to gain an understanding of an experience shared with Continental Europe.

That she missed the essential truth about our behaviour is unfortunate, but her statement does contain the nub of a profound truth. In the long run the British, like every other involved nationality, became the most important victims of their own propaganda. When the war was over, they could not allow the myth to be broken. Exaggeration of *résistance* was the way in which France and other defeated nations salvaged their pride. We could not match their tales of derring-do. We could not tell stories of sabotage and ambushes, and were a poor comparison. We had no dramatic exploits to bolster British pride, and at least in some minds we were probably seen as failing to show that the population of the only British territory to be occupied could do what others could do, and our reputation suffered as a consequence.

Rollo Sherwill, son of the Guernsey Procureur, a boy during the Occupation, was wrong when he said to Bunting that we didn't behave as British people should. His added comparison of our feelings since the war as being akin to how a woman must feel in a rape trial is utter nonsense.

Bunting is also correct when she says that Islanders are resentful because they believe they have been misunderstood and misjudged. They have good reason to be resentful. The majority have been misjudged and vilified on the basis of inflated and distorted descriptions of the number who did behave badly, but she is totally wrong when she claims that they feel guilty, that they judge themselves. People in Jersey did behave as people would have behaved in Britain. There is no collective, or even singular guilt for the majority. It is easy to collect and collate individual acts of treachery or simple bad behaviour and list them over many pages. It distorts what really happened. That is journalism. It is not history.

✳

Jersey is small, 11 miles by 6 at the most, about 45 square miles in total area. The other islands are smaller. There is no *maquis*, few places to hide. There is no distant place to escape to after killing a German, or blowing something up. In France, the perpetrator could be miles away from the scene of his crime in no time at all. There were no suitable targets. Public utilities were as necessary to our own survival as they were to the enemy. You do not find the Senior British Officer in a POW camp being asked to destroy the cookhouse or power supply. Burgomaster Max of Brussels in the Great War was praised for his resistance with the pen. Why should the officials and administrators of our Island in the Second World War have been expected to behave differently?

After the war, Resistance was glorified. Endless books and films did credit and honour to those brave souls who did something useful, but in many accounts there are stark examples of the stupidity of some whose thoughtlessness brought unacceptable tragedy to others, as well as the death penalty for themselves.

For most of the time, the garrison on Jersey approached 12,000 men. That is roughly 266 soldiers for every square mile. In France the ratio of German soldiers to Frenchmen was one to a hundred. In Jersey, it was one to three. Since the island was then mainly made up of farms and open fields, the figure gives some idea of the concentration of troops. It would have taken more cunning than even the SAS could muster to blow up fortifications and get away with it. The defences around the coast were equal to those in the *Pas de Calais*, and just as heavily guarded. By the spring of 1944, German fortifications in the Channel Islands boasted 11 heavy batteries with 37 strongpoints on its 92 miles of coastline, while the whole of the French coast from St. Nazaire to Dieppe, some 620 miles, had the same number of batteries and only 38 strongpoints. There was nowhere in the island where one could be more than a few hundred yards from major defensive positions. It is unreasonable to expect people to commit suicide by direct attacks on such installations, especially when there is no prospect of achieving anything worthwhile, and they have nothing but carving knives to do it with.

There were no large open areas to receive parachute drops of agents or supplies, no explosives to blow things up, even if we had known how to use them. There were no forests or swamps to hide men or arms, nowhere to run to for those conscripted to work for the Germans. Much of the resistance that did occur in France came from those hiding in the *maquis* to avoid forced labour. Resistance had to take other forms in the Island, and of that there was plenty. It is reassuring to know that at last the true history of the Occupation is being taken out of the hands of journalists. In his recent book, *The Ultimate Sacrifice*, historian Paul Sanders showed that during the five years of occupation the Germans arrested more than 4,000 Channel Islanders: 5% of the population. Many of course were detained for relatively simple offences against curfew laws and the like, but from Jersey's tiny population alone, 172 men and women were deported to penal prisons and concentration camps on the Continent. Twenty died in the camps, some the victims of the infamous *Nacht und Nebel* – Night and Fog – decree. As Sanders emphasised, the penal prisons in France and Germany were often stepping stones to the better known camps, and were frequently as bad and just as lethal as the camps themselves. Some prisoners who had finished their sentences in those prisons were sent on to the camps for work and 're-education'.

From that same small population in Jersey, approximately 125 men and 11 women attempted to escape or succeeded in doing so. Nine drowned. One was shot on the beach. At least one died in a concentration camp. 26 were recaptured and imprisoned. Of those, at least seven escaped from prison. One was shot during the attempt and recaptured. Five evaded until Liberation, and one made a further escape from the Island and achieved a home run. All prisoners with a sentence of more than two months were liable to serve it on the Continent, where they risked being sucked into the German concentration camp system. All prisoners were in peril of being shot as hostages. The British authorities, and Special Operations Executive (SOE) in particular, did nothing to encourage resistance of any kind in the islands. They did nothing in the way of infiltrating training officers, weapons, or supplies of explosives.

Most prisoners who offended against German rule served their sentences in the Island, but if Patton's tanks hadn't swept into Brittany and cut off the French ports, many more would have died in Germany. While it is true there was no organised *Résistance*, as in France, it is offensive and grossly unfair to claim that in the Channel Islands there was no resistance. It dishonours those who perished. That only 20 died from Jersey is fortunate. It is no measure of the suffering that afflicted Peter Hassall, Stan Green and Harold Le Druillenec until they died, and similarly affected others who did come back.

In a language that seems to have more slang words than English for prostitutes, homosexuals and various delicate parts of the human anatomy, one of the most insulting words for French people of our generation is *Collabo*, or *Collaborateur*. But what constitutes collaboration with an occupying power, with the enemy? Before labelling anyone, it is only fair to define what activities amount to collaboration of a traitorous nature, as opposed to essential daily cooperation which cannot be avoided if the community is to survive.

It is all very well for Bunting to spend several pages describing the antics and opinions of Jerrybags and their German friends, and to quote from the diary of an obvious collaborator, but all she achieves is a false impression that we all behaved like that, and that all the women of the Island took German lovers. The expressed opinions of those who did collaborate, or the opinions of their Germans friends, will obviously attempt to show themselves in the best possible light and to exaggerate the number of those they claim acted as they did. Some accounts by escapees talk of seven women out of ten. Nothing could be further from the truth. If there were a hundred of them, which I doubt, their profile was greater than their concentration. We hated and despised them, but they were not on every corner, and the vast majority of women was intensely loyal and would not have been seen dead in the company of an enemy soldier.

Critics frequently quote the increased rate of illegitimate births during the Occupation, as if it proves something about such behaviour. If anything, it suggests the contrary. Local men and women continued with normal sexual activity, and as there was little else to do in the dark, probably did it more often than usual: and since the Germans were the only ones who could still get condoms, such sexual activity was more risky for civilians, both in terms of pregnancy and venereal disease. It is often forgotten that OT workers were sexually active too. Irish citizens, Spaniards and others who voluntarily worked for the Germans often had a lot of money to throw around. At the time of the 50th anniversary of Liberation, Michael Ginns had several phone calls asking if there was any list of OT workers held anywhere, as they were 'trying to trace their fathers who the Germans had brought to Jersey to work on the bunkers.'

There were farmers who sold their produce at inflated prices, sometimes directly to the enemy, but there weren't many of them, and most did all they could to provide something extra for the townspeople who begged at their doors. There were many that profited by selling on the black market, as there were in Britain and elsewhere. They were often caught in a state of double jeopardy and punished by both the civil authority and by the Germans. Some of those caught by the Occupying Authority finished up in Germany.

Starvation and fear provoke strong emotions. In any small, closed community, spite and internecine strife is common; the Channel Islands are no different. Criticism of other people during the Occupation was common, for reasons which included jealousy and anger against those who were better off, or who were presumed to be so. Immediately after the war, there were many only too ready to point the finger against individual members of the States or at certain farmers or businessmen, as they had done during the war, and usually with as little or no real evidence. Unfortunately, it is a too familiar human failing to believe such things at the time, and for some people to perpetuate them indefinitely. Critics, however, would do better to concentrate on the positive aspects, on people like the Le Calvez family, on Mrs Gould and Mrs Forster, on the Le Bruns and the Sarres, on Norman Le Brocq and his wife, on Les Huelin, Bob Le Sueur and their helpers, and on all the many others who always tried to do something for those less fortunate than themselves, and who took tremendous risks hiding escaped Russians and other prisoners. The Communists and those I have mentioned were not the only people who took such risks.

Recent articles in the press, written in late 1996, since the Public Record Office released more secret papers, talk about 'information from agents in the islands.' There may have been a real British agent or two; I have already mentioned the mystery man Holmes. However, most of the reports quoted by British Intelligence were based on information provided by prisoners freed in France, or escapees. Roger Le Rouilly, who got away with Basil Le Brun in September 1944, deliberately took a job with the Naval Harbour Construction Section and, once established, made friends with all the Germans on the staff. He was so trusted, they used to send him to Granville to bring back spare parts and other material. He sketched and noted everything he saw around the harbour. He sewed much of the material into the lining of his coat, to hand over to his *Résistance* contacts in France for onward transmission to London.

In those emotion-charged times, angry feelings about collaborators and Jerrybags filled our minds. Nearly everybody criticised members of the States and those we thought might be better off than ourselves. We often formed such opinions without hard evidence, often scurrilously, because that is the way people behave under occupation or in prison camps. Some escapees passed on those false beliefs to British Intelligence, and I believe they were passed on and sometimes received in a grossly exaggerated form despite a footnote to one file which warned: 'When assessing these reports from escapees, care should be taken regarding accusations of collaboration etc., as in many cases the informants may not be in possession of the full facts.' I believe some of these debriefings were an important reason for the inaccurate picture which emerged then, and which has, unfortunately, persisted.

✳

The more florid examples of collaboration by Quisling in Norway and Laval in France are obvious and easy to categorise, as are those of lesser-known names in the Vichy government and in such organisations as the pro-Nazi, paramilitary *Milice*. Apart from a few individuals like Durand, there were none of those in Jersey. A Jersey schoolmistress was indicted after the war for broadcasting on Radio Bremen. But there was no Lord Haw Haw, and the one broadcast by a Guernsey official, Sherwill, which can be criticised, was made by a man from Devon, not by an indigenous Islander.

There were British POWs in Germany who joined the *Waffen SS*. French, Poles, Dutch, Danes, Norwegians and other nationalities joined as well. There were no Channel Islanders!

There was no Nazi Party in the Islands. There were such organisations in Norway, Denmark, Holland, Belgium and France. There were no public rallies, no public meetings in support of the Germans. No island politician set himself up as a Laval or a Quisling.

When fear is a daily experience, and there are shortages of almost every commodity that we accept as part of normal life, it is not difficult for people to become bitter and resentful. They take out their anger and frustration wherever they can. In all the Islands the most common targets were the Bailiffs, the States and the farmers. The King ordered the former to stay at their posts. They were not given the choice. The most they could do was to try to emulate Burgomaster Max of Brussels. They had to protect the King's subjects. That was their primary duty. Like the Senior British Officer in a prisoner-of-war camp, they had to make sure that people were fed and clothed, and provided with medical and other welfare services. They could not do that without daily contact with the Germans. However unpleasant it was for them, they had to pass on German orders to the population. They also had to try local people for certain crimes to save them from court martial.

When a Senior British Officer met the German *Kommandant* of a POW camp, they usually exchanged military courtesies. Some German *kommandants* were accorded respect and gratitude for their fairness and cooperation, yet similar civilised behaviour by Island authorities and Germans in the Islands is unfairly considered a form of collaboration. It is necessary cooperation. It is not collaboration.

In times of acute shortage, when starvation is staring people in the face, when they faint from hunger in the street, and there is no means of cooking or keeping warm and fear is to some degree a daily experience, people become selfish as well as emotional. It is human to look for someone to blame. It was easy and comforting to blame the Island authorities for the way they handled the Germans. I must confess there were times when I thought like that too. But it was unreasonable and historical analysis as opposed to journalism shows it was wrong.

I was pleased to hear the former Communist Deputy Norman Le Brocq – one of the most vociferous critics of the Island authorities after the war and as late as ten years ago – say on a BBC television program before he died that he too had mellowed and changed his mind. He too could no longer see that the Bailiff and his officers could have behaved any differently.

As Cruickshank pointed out, the Island governments were in an invidious position throughout the Occupation. There was no precedent. There were no guidelines on how they should behave towards the enemy. What was surprising, he emphasised, was that in the end it was not that they did some things that were wrong, but that they did so much that was right. There were notices and orders that could have been better worded, but the States did not cooperate to the degree of collaboration.

It was only too easy for contact with Germans to be interpreted as collaboration. My brother, Stanley, was once refused service in a shop. When he asked why, the owner said, "because your father is a collaborator. Germans have been seen entering the vicarage." He was lucky not to be flattened. He was told in no uncertain terms that all sorts of people visit vicarages, including German padres who want to arrange a time to hold their own church services. Such an episode illustrates how easy it is for innocent people to be condemned. It also shows how a shopkeeper, one of the ordinary people, was willing to openly and dangerously exhibit disapproval.

There were men and women forced to work for the Germans. In Jersey, few worked on military installations. Of those who did, many were neutral Irishmen. Some worked for them to get military information. It is unfair to consider those employed in public utilities and on similar tasks needed by both the occupiers and the civilian population as working for the enemy. In France, only 15 miles away, there are memorials to those forced to work for the Germans in the *Service du Travail Obligatoire*. In this Island, the same men have been vilified, though they had as little choice – probably less – as their neighbours in France to refuse, and certainly no place like the *maquis* to hide. Their simple choice was to work, or to go to prison and see their wives and children starve.

The most evil of all traitorous activities was without doubt informing on neighbours, workmates, or even family. It was spiteful. It was dangerous. And almost always done in cowardly fashion by anonymous letters addressed to the *Feldkommandantur*, or to the *Gestapo* at Silvertide. This vicious form of mischief or revenge went on in all occupied territories. In Jersey, as elsewhere, the instigators were not always pro-German. Sometimes they were just nasty people working off old scores. Neighbour betrayed neighbour. A sister betrayed her brother. A father beat his daughter for going out with a German officer. She reported him and he was imprisoned.

Fortunately, Post Office staff managed to divert or delay many letters addressed to such dangerous destinations. Some got through with tragic results. Post Office sorters prevented over four hundred reaching their destination, not two hundred a week as reported by one Fleet Street writer. Sometimes the sorters steamed them open and warned whoever was involved. Those men were truly brave. The risk of being discovered was enormous, the consequences lethal. Pat Tatam, the Headmaster of Victoria College took the same risks with letters that were incorrectly addressed to the school and not to the *Feldkommanantur* at College House. Must the critics denigrate such courageous individuals by claiming that they did not resist?

It is fair to say that, as in other countries, the majority of the population carried on with their daily lives as best they could, as the majority would have done in Britain if it too had been occupied. Some – not many – resented those who got into trouble. They criticised us for putting them and their safety at risk. However, few were like the well-fed lady who, when I begged some food while on the run said, "If it wasn't for people like you, we would have much less trouble with the Germans."

She was no doubt frightened. I feel more charitable towards her now than I did then. However, her attitude raises an important issue. Do any people in any occupied territory, and I include the Channel Islands, have the right to put their heads down and just survive when others are fighting and dying for their liberty? I do not believe anyone can claim that right, but the number who will resist actively will always be small.

If it had come to an Allied invasion, there were those prepared to help. Those who escaped or fell foul of the Germans in other ways did so with their eyes open, not for some 'Boy's Own' reason, as has been suggested by a few detractors. Charles Cruickshank wrote that some escapers got away 'as they simply wanted to escape from the harsh life in the occupied islands on the assumption that life in Britain was less disagreeable.' Paul Sanders made a similar error in *The Ultimate*

Sacrifice when he ascribed some acts of resistance as akin to adolescent defiance of authority. I can think of no less likely reasons to risk life and limb.

It is wrong to think that the only form of resistance is sabotage and assassination. Even Sinel made that mistake when he wrote: 'There was no resistance.' He too confused resistance with the *Résistance*. There were many minor acts of sabotage soon after we were occupied. They were futile and, as a rule, not particularly dangerous. The Germans reacted swiftly and effectively, and in a manner out of all proportion to any damage done. Hostages were taken. Men of military age were conscripted to patrol their neighbourhood after curfew, with their own well-being at stake if they failed to do their 'duty'. The curfew was extended. It was made clear that even minor acts of defiance constituted sabotage and would be punished by imprisonment, or death.

In 1942, the *Feldkommandant* issued a proclamation which pointed out that since 1941, all inhabitants of the Channel Islands held in custody were liable to the death penalty in the event of sabotage against the occupying power. It added:

In addition I declare that henceforth I reserve to myself the right to nominate certain members of any parish who will be liable to the death penalty in the event of any attack against communications as for instance harbours, cranes, bridges, cables and wires, if these are made with the assistance or the knowledge of the inhabitants of the parish concerned.

As Cruickshank wrote: 'Punitive action could have been directed individually against almost the whole population at any time, and every man, woman and child could have been gassed and incinerated in a single day in one of the larger and more efficient German concentration camps.'

In his study of occupied France, Kedward discusses resistance under several headings. He includes escape, intelligence gathering and armed resistance. He points out that many of the multitude of individual resistance groups which sprung up after 1940, unknown to each other, often began as escape routes, intelligence gathering operations, or as publishing outlets for the spread of news from Allied sources. Embryonic though they sometimes were, other intelligence gathering groups similar to ours existed in Jersey. In several cases, that information was taken out. Listening to radios and disseminating the BBC news was almost a cottage industry. I suspect the proportion of escapes per head of population was higher than in other occupied territories. The percentage of the population sentenced by German court martial was certainly higher. We have ample evidence of all these activities. I wonder why it is that they are considered acts of resistance elsewhere, but not in the Channel Islands!

✳

I have written about the Occupation as I saw it. Others saw it differently. I still believe the British Government and Island authorities were wrong not to search out and punish traitors after the war, especially those who caused misery and death. But it is too late now.

There are some that claim there was so much collaboration that the arrest and trial of such people would have embarrassed Churchill's Government. The British plans to resume control of the Island, Operation Nestegg, included investigation and punishment of the worst cases. After Liberation, the Civil Affairs Unit found that 'a number of people acted in an unseemly, undesirable, or even disgraceful way.' They believed about 20 cases of collaboration warranted prosecution. Twelve briefs were sent to the Director of Public Prosecutions. The DPP rejected them, but he never gave a satisfactory reason. If these matters had been dealt with properly at the time, much of today's unfair criticism of the Islanders would have been prevented.

It is probable our liberators were brainwashed before they left Britain and that Churchill's mind too was prejudiced against us. Major Pantchef, who investigated atrocities on Alderney, wrote privately after the war that Churchill had been adversely impressed by how families had been split over allegations of collaboration. He added: 'It was rightly decided to go canny. I thought at the time this was very unfair, because it seemed to me that a chap who had put his life on the line for King and Country, was being equated with a chap who had been comforting the enemy.'

With the benefit of hindsight as well as personal experience, and in Jersey at least, I believe the balance was so one-sided in favour of loyalty and what resistance was possible, that there would have been no embarrassment: but Churchill's mind may have been poisoned, and he may have been influenced by such reports as followed the commando raid, which said that there was no resistance and that the population was not hostile to the Germans. He never visited the Islands after the war.

Jerrybags were small fry. They were the scum which is evident in any population in similar circumstances. They were not important if they stuck to sexual and social favours. Those of the Island population who helped the Germans deliberately and actively, and who betrayed fellow Islanders, should have been hunted down and punished at the time, and not, as has been suggested, sent to Australia, or somewhere similar, with new identities!

There are still those who, unlike Norman Le Brocq, are unable to forget the emotions that led to unjust criticism of the Island authorities in 1945. The Jersey authorities could no more protect Jews than they could protect non-Jewish Islanders deported to Germany. They did not arrest Jews. They did not help the Germans in any unreasonable or culpable way with their departure. They did assist the deportees with food to ease their going. They did allow the Parish

Constables to help deliver the deportation notices, but only so that the victims would have more time to prepare. No civilian policemen hunted Jews in Jersey, as they did in France and Holland and elsewhere. No civilian clerk supervised them to make sure they filled in the forms correctly.

Hitler's intentions for those Channel Islanders of English birth were just as dangerous as those for the Island Jews. That it ended happily is a reason for joy. Sadness and outrage at what happened to Jews from other occupied territories must not be translated into blaming innocent people for their fate.

Perhaps the most difficult part of the Occupation was the sense of isolation, a feeling that we had been forgotten. Most RAF leaflets, which landed on the island, were intended for France. They only reached us by mistake when the wind was in the right direction. For some obscure reason, the British Government ordered that there should be no specific broadcasts to the Islands from the BBC, though, according to Cruickshank, the Corporation was encouraged to mention us in other programmes, particularly those which concerned Channel Islanders then in Britain, or fighting overseas. It was almost impossible to get the BBC to send *messages personnels*, such as those sent to the *Résistance* in France, so that relatives in the Islands would know that escapees had made it safely. This was largely on security grounds, and understandable, but it gave Ed Le Corre's family almost a year of agony after his coat was washed up and they thought he had drowned.

From time to time since the war, when I tell people that I was brought up in the Channel Islands, they ask me about the Occupation. I have seldom replied in any detail until recently, especially when they have made some such remark as: "You were occupied, weren't you? Wasn't there something about a cow – called Venus – or something?"

I have tried to show a different picture, to give some idea of how ordinary people saw those five years of Occupation. It was not a vicious occupation like those of Russia and Poland, but there were hardships and tragedies too.

I could not have written this account without help from books that I have mentioned. I have listened to tapes, to many personal accounts by Islanders who recalled their experiences in a series of BBC programmes in 1985. Some told of dreadful things, and of adventures barely survived. Others told of the little things, sometimes blown up to seem dangerous or brave, though nothing of the kind, but very real and important to those ordinary people who spoke about them. All brought back memories and emotions.

Growing up during those years left its mark. My generation of Islanders lost many things associated with the formative years. We missed out on much, but we gained something as well. We learned the value of simple pleasures, and how to do without. We learned the worth of true friendship.

There is no doubt that I still think of my life with total mathematical inexactitude as having two equal parts. The five years of the Occupation, and the rest. To this day, the Islanders are divided into those who were there, and those who were not, into those who belong, and those who do not.

By all the rules, I should be dead. I hit a German officer. With my friends, I was guilty of espionage. In France, we would have been tortured and shot. Perhaps those of us who survived feel a little guilty at our good fortune. There are no medals for what we did, but I feel vaguely proud of what must be a rare distinction: of having been court-martialled twice by the German Army; and I was both proud and sad to be present when the Prince of Wales shook our hands and unveiled a plaque to those of our friends who died trying to escape.

I recognise now that growing up during the Occupation has left a few scars. They are perhaps summed up best by some words my brother, Stanley, wrote: 'I heard the silence of friends departed as we buried our youth and grew to manly ways.'

There is much left out. Some things are still forgotten. A few, better forgotten. But there is pride too. And most certainly, there is no guilt.

BIBLIOGRAPHY

Balleine, G R.: *The Bailiwick of Jersey*, 1970.

Bunting, M.: *The Model Occupation*, 1995.

Channel Islands Occupation Society: *Archives Book No. 8* 1994, and *Review Book No. 25* 1997.

Cohen, Frederick: *The Jews in the Channel Islands during the German Occupation*. Published by the Institute of Contemporary History and Wiener Library Limited, in association with the Jersey Jewish Congregation., 1998.

Coles, Joan: *Three Years Behind Barbed Wire*, 1985.

Cruickshank, Charles: *The German Occupation Of The Channel Islands*, 1975.

Doyle, Robert C.: Voices From Captivity, 1994.

Dalmau, John: *Slave Worker*.

Gilbert, Martin: *The Holocaust*, 1986.

Kedward, H R.: *Occupied France. Collaboration and Resistance 1940-1944*, 1985.

King, Peter: *The Channel Islands War*, 1991.

Le Ruez, Nan: *Jersey Occupation Diary*, 1994.

Le Sauteur, P.: *Jersey Under The Swastika*, 1968.

Lewis, John: *A Doctor's Occupation*, 1982.

Maugham, R C F.: *Jersey Under The Jackboot*, 1946.

Pocock, H.R.S.: *The Memoirs of Lord Coutanche*, 1975.

Sanders, Paul: *The Ultimate Sacrifice*, 1998.

Sinel, Leslie: *The German Occupation of Jersey*, 1945.

Syvret, M and Stevens, J.: *Balleine's History of Jersey*, 1981.

Thomas, Roy: *Lest We Forget*, 1992.

Toland, John: *Adolf Hitler*, 1976.

Tuchmann, Barbara: *A Distant Mirror*, 1978.

Van der Vat, Dan: *The Good Nazi*, 1997.

Woods, Alan and Mary: *Islands In Danger*, 1955.

Reference is also made to:

(1) BBC Radio Jersey. 1985. 'Occupation': The Story of the German Occupation of Jersey during World War 2, told by the people who lived through it.

(2) 'Jackboots Buckets and Spades'. Television programme. Presenter Hugh Scully, BBC South West.

A fter service in UK and Far East, fished and played up with Basil Le Brun for a year. Lived in a fisherman's hut on Bonne Nuit pier. 1948, medical student Bristol University. Qualified 1954. After hospital appointments and a year in general practice, rejoined Royal Air Force. Polio cut short plans to fly and specialize in aviation medicine. Duncan Sandys had just decided that rockets would replace manned aircraft so, on recovery, trained in surgery in RAF hospitals and in Edinburgh. Served in Aden, Cyprus and West Africa. Short spell in North Africa when Colonel Nasser was stirring things up a bit. MBE in Aden for up-country activities with Aden Protectorate Levies and Hadhrami Bedouin Legion. Retired early from RAF as Wing Commander and migrated to Australia 1972. Surgical specialist Latrobe Valley, Victoria for some years. Moved to Canberra as a medico-legal specialist just over ten years ago. Married WAAF, Enid Glew, in 1948. Both blown out of bed in *coup d'état* that toppled Kwame Nkrumah. Two children. Jenny is a nurse in Canberra. Andrew helps to look after Rupert Murdoch's electronics in Melbourne. He was a boarder at Victoria College. Four grandchildren, Sarah, Kate, James and Patrick. Dog called Rumpole. Love them all. Now retired, but like Enid, still involved with St. John Ambulance. Promoted to Officer Brother in the Most Venerable Order of the Hospital of St. John of Jerusalem 1998.

More books from SEAFLOWER on the German Occupation of the Channel Islands:

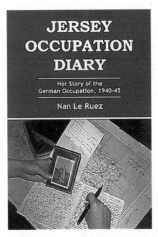

JERSEY OCCUPATION DIARY
by Nan Le Ruez
First published 1994
New edition 2003
240 pages; £9.95

NO CAUSE FOR PANIC
by Brian Ahier Read
The story of the evacuees,
not previously told
160 pages; £6.95

JERSEY OCCUPATION REMEMBERED
in the voices of the Islanders themselves
Compiled by Sonia Hillsdon
160 pages; £5.95

JERSEY IN LONDON
by Brian Ahier Read
The story of the Jersey Society in
London which played such a vital role
during the Second World War
192 pages; £6.95

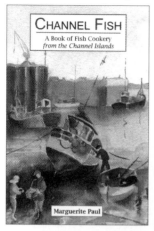
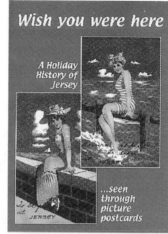

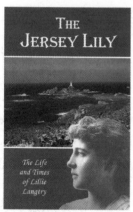
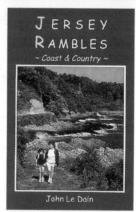
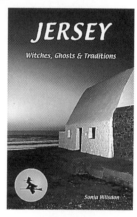

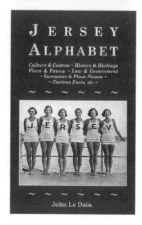